HOUSING POLICY
AND HOUSING NEEDS

Paul N. Balchin

M

First published 1981 by
THE MACMILLAN PRESS LTD
London and Basingstoke
Associated companies in Delhi Dublin
Hong Kong Johannesburg Lagos Melbourne
New York Singapore and Tokyo

ISBN 0 333 30701 1 (hard cover)
ISBN 0 333 23695 5 (paper cover)

Typeset in 10/12 Times
and printed in Hong Kong

CONTENTS

The voluntary movement. Public policy towards the voluntary housing movement. The weaknesses of co-ownership. The 1970s. The advantages and disadvantages of housing associations and the Housing Corporation. Tenant co-operatives. Equity sharing.

The housebuilding cycle. The contractors' response to the housebuilding cycle. Housebuilding, house prices and land costs. Material, labour and finance costs. Conclusion.

History of housing rehabilitation policy to 1969. The Housing Act of 1969. Some effects of the Housing Act of 1969. Proposals for reform 1972–4. Rehabilitation policy since 1974. Conclusion.

LIST OF FIGURES

LIST OF TABLES

PREFACE

This book is intended as a text for students on degree and diploma courses in Economics, Public Adminstration and Sociology in which a consideration of housing policy is an important component, and it is especially relevant to courses geared to the examination syllabuses of the Institute of Housing Management. It is envisaged that the book will in addition serve as an essential reader for students preparing for the examinations of the Royal Institute of British Architects, the Royal Institution of Chartered Surveyors (General Practice, and Planning and Development Divisions) and the Royal Town Planning Institute. The book may also be of interest to the general reader, and although some basic knowledge of micro- and macro-economics may be useful, most of the subject matter should be fully comprehensible to anyone who is aware that there are serious housing problems in Britain, and is concerned enough to seek an explanation and to ponder possible solutions.

I began lecturing on housing economics not long after the Milner–Holland Report (1965) highlighted the abysmal condition of housing in parts of Greater London, and during the past decade and a half I have been impressed by the continual flow of publications on housing policy and the complexities of the housing market—often the product of intensive research and highly quantitative. But housing too frequently has become a mere vehicle for the testing of esoteric polemical hypotheses, most of which are unintelligible to housing policy-makers and managers, and largely ignored by students, at least at undergraduate level. The problem of source material is further exacerbated by the inevitability of textbooks becoming out-dated or worse out of print, or by authors confining their attention to limited aspects of the subject. One book which did bring together the economics of housing and policy was Lionel Needleman's, *The Economics of Housing* (Needleman, 1965), and more recently Ray Robinson attempted the same task in *Housing Economics and Public Policy* (Robinson, 1979), but the latter book, as its author admits, concentrates on applying micro-economic theory to housing, and is less concerned with individual markets and policies. At the time of writing, however, there is a deficiency of books which concentrate sectorially on the housing system, the underlying economic influences, and on policies. This book is intended to fill the gap in the literature.

The book is divided into nine chapters. Chapter 1 provides an introductory background to housing policy. Chapter 2 deals with the growth and problems of the owner-occupied sector. Chapter 3 seeks to explain why private rented housing has been in decline since the turn of the century. Chapter 4 considers social ownership. Chapter 5 deals with the history and problems of local authority housing. Chapter 6 reviews the progress of the voluntary housing movement. Chapter 7 sets out to explore the cyclical activity of the housebuilding industry. Chapter 8 considers housing rehabilitation in an economic and social context, and Chapter 9 concludes by itemising proposals for reform.

In writing this book, I was continually conscious of being overtaken by events. Housing policy, perhaps more than most other policy, is subject to sudden and sometimes unexpected change. At the half-way stage in the production of this book, this problem was compounded by a General Election and change of government. However, every effort has been made to ensure that statistical and legislative detail is accurate at the time of writing.

I must acknowledge a debt I owe to my colleagues and to numerous other people who have stimulated and advised me in the preparation of this book. My thanks are particularly due to my wife, Maria, who has given me endless encouragement and understanding, and to my children Richard and Elizabeth who have learnt that the sound of a typewriter is a prelude to being taken-off on countless picnics or to the zoo.

London,   PAUL N. BALCHIN
Summer 1980

1 Introduction

Among constituency party activists, within the trade unions, and at Conference, members of the Labour Party after the General Election of 3 May 1979 were asking the question 'where did we go wrong?'. Labour had attracted only 36.9 per cent of the votes—its lowest share of the poll since the 1931 election. A plethora of factors were cited to explain why Labour had lost, but few if any of the party's leading members made any reference to its housing policy. It was as though man's most important material need next to nourishment—housing—was of no interest to the electorate. It is highly probable, however, that one of the principal reasons for Labour's electoral defeat in 1979 was its housing record. Indeed, the apparent success or failure of housing policy has been a major influence over voting behaviour in every General Election since at least the Second World War. Although Labour lost the 1951 election it gained its largest-ever share of the poll, 48.8 per cent, and received more votes than the Conservative victors, after undertaking a massive housebuilding programme and re-establishing council housing as a 'general need' tenure. The Conservative wins in the 1955 and 1959 elections followed periods in which by contrast the number of owner-occupied houses had increased dramatically. It was the new 'class' of homeowners who had 'never had it so good'. In the 1964 and 1974 elections attention was focused on the abuses of private landlordism; and in 1974 there was concern about property speculation and the way in which house prices had recently rocketted, and resentment among council tenants as they were being brought into the so-called 'fair rent' system. In promising to tackle these grievances, the Labour Party helped to ensure its electoral success. Without doubt, one of the principal reasons why the Conservative Party won in 1979 was its pledge to enforce the selling-off of council houses to local authority tenants.

To achieve a greater understanding of the housing policies of the previous and present governments, and ideally to predict or even influence the future, it is necessary to analyse and comprehend policies historically. This book therefore refers back (where appropriate) to the inter-war years or earlier,

1

but most of the emphasis is placed on the 1970s when the debate on the respective roles of the housing sectors was particularly heated. Yet despite (or because of) a succession of housing White Papers and Acts, and a consultative Green Paper, the debate continues, and is likely to become more vociferous before equitable remedies are applied to Britain's housing problems.

Housing Need

In very crude terms, housing need in Britain is largely satisfied. The housing situation has been transformed since the Second World War. There has been a substantial growth in owner-occupation and council housing, a decline in private rented accommodation, and the physical condition of most of the housing stock has greatly improved. By the late 1960s a crude surplus of dwellings over households was achieved for the first time, and by 1976 it reached half a million (table 1.1).

Table 1.1 The Number of Dwellings and Households, England and Wales, 1951–76 (millions)

	1951	1956	1961	1966	1971	1976
Dwellings	12.5	13.7	14.6	15.8	17.0	18.1
Households	13.3	14.0	14.7	15.9	16.8	17.6
Balance	−0.8	−0.3	−0.1	−0.1	+0.2	+0.5

Source: Housing Policy: a Consultative Document.

The crude surpluses in 1971 and 1976 did not however indicate the true relationship between supply and need. Of the 18.1 million dwellings in 1976, there were still 3 million dwellings unfit, lacking in amenities, or in a bad state of repair. There were some 200 000 second homes included in the number of dwellings, while about 360 000 'concealed households' (such as married couples sharing with their parents) were omitted from the above data. There were great spatial variations in supply and demand, most notably a surplus of expensive houses in the countryside or on the edge of towns, and a shortage of cheaper houses in the inner urban areas. Although many dwellings need to be temporarily empty to facilitate population movement, movement means that dwellings of the right kind or price are not always where they are needed. An ageing population also produces a mis-match between housing occupied and the size and type of dwellings required.

Clearly the crude housing surplus provides no clue to the severity of Britain's housing problems. There are major causes for concern in the three housing sectors (owner-occupied, private rented and public), and in housebuilding and rehabilitation; and there are very worrying trends in council waiting lists, homelessness, and unemployment in the construction industry.

Despite the growth in owner-occupation over the years, it is very difficult for prospective first-time buyers to acquire property. The average price of a house in the United Kingdom in the last quarter of 1979 was £21 807, and allowing for a 10 per cent deposit and assuming that mortgages are allotted at two and a half times an applicant's income, a housebuyer would have required earnings of at least £7850 in order to have bought an ordinary three bedroom house. In Greater London, where the average price was £29 059, houses would have been out of reach to all except those with earnings of at least £10 460, or with sizeable funds of their own. Anyone on average earnings of only £7123 with little or no savings would have found it virtually impossible to have become an owner-occupier—except perhaps in the case of the cheapest houses in the lowest price regions. The problem of disqualification was compounded by 'redlining'—the reluctance of building societies to lend on housing in the inner cities, often the only housing accessible to those with low incomes. Building societies were clearly not giving due weight to social factors when deciding how to apportion their mortgage funds.

The supply of private rented housing has decreased continuously since the First World War. In London in the late 1970s, for example, a landlord would have needed on average a rent of £40 to have provided a satisfactory two-room self-contained flat. With rents of less than this, the dwelling normally would have been very small, lacking in amenities and in a very poor condition. It has been frequently argued that the Rent Acts of 1965 and 1974 have been mainly responsible for the recent decline of this sector. But there is little evidence of this. Security of tenure and regulated rents have not caused the rate of decline to increase—indeed the rate has been slower than during the period of relatively free market conditions, 1957–65. With or without constraints on private landlordism, there has been a diversion of supply (and to some extent demand) to owner-occupation. There has also been little incentive to develop new private rented housing. With the prevailing cost of construction, rents would be much higher than most people could afford or be willing to pay.

In a modern complex society, people normally desire a choice of goods and services. In housing, given perfect market conditions, the fundamental choice would be between buying and renting. But market imperfections and the demise of the private landlord have removed this choice in the private sector. Only the public provision of rented accommodation can ensure that households who cannot or do not prefer to buy are supplied with housing at a rent within their means. In performing this role, local authority housing is now the second most important sector, but waiting lists are growing rapidly.

In July 1978, there were 1 075 520 households registered on council waiting lists in England and Wales, yet in many areas—because of the need to re-house people displaced by clearance schemes and to house families who may have been homeless for several years—only a small proportion of households on waiting lists received council dwellings (in Greater London, for example, only 19 500 out of 209 551 registered households were offered council houses in 1978). It is certain that the proportion will get even lower as local authorities embark upon large scale selling campaigns. Families in need will consequently have to wait even longer for a decent home.

In some areas, particularly where local authorities are ideologically opposed to council housing, housing associations provide an alternative choice to owner-occupation. But the rapid expansion of the voluntary housing movement in recent years has been problematic in respect of management and purpose, and it is unlikely that it will continue to grow and provide an effective substitute to private or council letting.

Housing need will remain far from satisfied while housebuilding is at a low level. The total number of house starts in Britain in 1979 was only 220 200, the lowest for 28 years, and the number of council houses started was only 80 100, the lowest since the Second World War. This abysmally low level of council house building should be a major cause of concern of all local authorities with long waiting lists and large numbers of registered homeless.

In the late 1960s and early 1970s it was thought that a shift of emphasis from housebuilding to rehabilitation would offset the shortfall in the supply of new houses. But since 1973 there has been a substantial decline in the amount of housing improvement—at least on a par with the slump in housebuilding. By the late 1970s, moreover, the rate of obsolescence exceeded the pace of rehabiltation. There was also a very large number of empty houses—650 000 in England and Wales in 1978 (excluding second homes). Many were local authority dwellings awaiting eventual improvement or demolition.

A major result of all these deficiencies was that there were 26 083 housholds registered as homeless in England in the second half of 1976, and countless others did not register. Nearly a third of the registered number (8036) were homeless in London. Following the Housing (Homeless Persons) Act of 1977, housing authorities have a statutory duty to provide accommodation for families with children, pensioners, the disabled and other priority groups if they have not become homeless intentionally. Because of the provision of the Act, the number of homeless households registering increased to over 53 000 in 1979.

It is tragically ironic that at the same time as council waiting lists and the number of registered homeless reach record levels, there are over 250 000 building workers unemployed—a result of the worst ever slump in the construction industry in peacetime since before 1914.

Fiscal Assistance

From a peak of £7141 million in 1974/75 public expenditure on housing fell by 19 per cent to £5375 million in 1979/80, while total public spending remained broadly unchanged. Investment in new and rehabilitated housing was thus severely cut, but mortgage tax relief and housing subsidies actually increased—families in need, in effect, being penalised to the benefit of those reasonably housed. But since the housing market is dominated by the existing stock of buildings (the net addition to the stock each year being very small), competition for resources does not so much involve households seeking either newly completed accommodation or existing housing, but people competing for assistance either to help them acquire existing housing or to supplement the cost of retaining their homes.

In each of the three housing sectors, householders feel that they are penalised to the advantage of others. Owner-occupiers believe that as ratepayers and taxpayers they are subsidising council tenants. Private tenants again as taxpayers (and possibly as ratepayers), similarly believe that they are subsidising council housing and find this irreconcilable with the fact that most council units are superior to their own dwellings. Council tenants may think that they are being helped less than homebuyers, and some will be aware that assistance to the owner-occupier increases with income and size of mortgage. Within each sector too, there may be resentment and jealousy. First-time housebuyers, and even those who bought in the early 1970s, incur substantially greater mortgage outgoings often on inferior houses, than owner-occupiers of long standing. The latter owners either incur very low repayments or have been able to 'trade-up' over the years at comparatively little extra expense. In the private rented sector (until the Rent Act of 1974), furnished tenants were normally charged much higher rents than controlled or regulated unfurnished tenants, but often had the worst accommodation, and private landlords (because of rent regulation) are convinced that they are subsidising their tenants. Tenants of older council housing believe that they are subsidising the tenants of new estates. Why else should rents be broadly similar when it is obvious that the cost of developing new properties must be much higher than the historic cost of old dwellings?

Inter- and intra-sector rivalry is not usually manifested by households taking direct action such as rent or mortgage repayment strikes. The anomalies and distortions within and between sectors are not products of the market place, but are consequences of government intervention dating back to the nineteenth century. No tenure is left 'free' to face market forces. Intervention affects owner-occupation just as much as, if not more than, other sectors.

From time to time, governments attempt to ameliorate some of the apparent unfairness in the housing system, strive to ensure that housing costs and benefits are more equitably distributed, and as far as possible try to eliminate circumstances which clearly discriminate against the less privileged. But at the time of writing it was clear that the newly elected Conservative government did not intend doing any of these things. Whereas in the past, successive housing policies, in the view of Robinson (1979), have—

> often . . . lacked direction and consistency . . . have resulted from a lack of knowledge about the housing situation . . . [and] have been attributable to a lack of understanding of the way in which the housing market functions—

the policy of the Conservative government is in addition marred by a philosophy of inequality manifested by a regressive approach to taxation and public expenditure of a sort not seen since the 1930s. In analysing each of the housing sectors and the construction industry, this book is an attempt to examine policies both historically and in their current political context, and with regard to the proposed 48 per cent cut in public expenditure on housing (to £2790 million), 1979/80 to 1983/84.

2 Owner-Occupation

In 1914, owner-occupation accounted for only 10.6 per cent of the housing stock of the United Kingdom, but largely due to extensive housebuilding in the 1930s the proportion reached 28.6 per cent in 1953 (little private development taking place in the period 1939–52). Table 2.1 shows that the proportion then increased to 44.6 per cent in 1963 and reached 54.5 per cent in 1979—comparing very favourably with other European countries, although in the United States and Australia some 65–70 per cent of dwellings were owner-occupied.

Table 2.1   Housing Tenure, United Kingdom, 1963–79

	Owner-occupied (per cent)	Rented from Local Authorities (per cent)	Private rented and other tenures (per cent)
1963	44.6	28.0	27.4
1964	45.6	28.1	26.3
1965	46.5	28.2	25.3
1966	47.1	28.7	24.2
1967	47.8	29.2	23.0
1968	48.7	29.6	21.7
1969	49.3	30.0	20.7
1970	49.8	30.6	19.6
1971	50.4	30.7	18.9
1972	51.4	30.6	18.0
1973	52.2	30.6	17.2
1974	52.6	31.0	16.4
1975	52.9	31.4	15.7
1976	53.2	31.8	15.0
1977	53.5	32.2	14.3
1978	53.9	32.3	13.8
1979	54.5	32.2	13.3

Source: Central Statistical Office, *Social Trends*. Department of the Environment, *Housing and Construction Statistics*

The post-war period in Britain has seen the consolidation of owner-occupation as the most important numerical and therefore most politically sensitive sector of the housing market. Owner-occupation has been encouraged by favourable government policy; the expansion of specialist financial institutions; an investment climate generally favourable to property development, and the difficulty of households finding alternative accommodation. But although 16.0 million houses in all sectors were built in the period 1919–79 only a very small number are added annually, for example 132 900 owner-occupied houses were completed in 1979 equal to 1.2 per cent of the total owner-occupied stock and 0.6 per cent of the total stock—not taking into account demolitions.

New housing sets off a series of 'housing chains'. Newly formed households move into new dwellings; existing households displaced from demolished housing move into replacement dwellings (new or old), and existing owner-occupiers move into alternative owner-occupied properties. In the 1970s two-thirds of new dwellings were bought by households who were already owner-occupiers. Housing chains may also be set off by households who decide to sell up and share accommodation; owners who emigrate or die; owners who move into local authority or housing association dwellings, and owners who move into private rented accommodation. But the latter two links in the chain were hypothetical rather than real in the 1960s and 1970s. Although the proportion of local authority housing increased slightly in the period 1966–77, virtually none of the increase became available to reluctant owner-occupiers, and there was a substantial reduction in private rented housing with consequent scarcity. The extent of the reduction was however greatest in the period 1957–62 when 1.8 million rented dwellings were sold for owner-occupation. The diversion of supply from the local authorities and new town development corporations also added to the stock of owner-occupied houses. The housing chain thus increasingly involves the mobility of households either entering the owner-occupied sector or within it. With less available alternative accommodation there is little outward mobility.

Very few houses are bought outright—except some cheap or old properties (prior to renovation) and retirement dwellings often on the coast or in the country. The rapid increase in owner-occupation has been facilitated by the availability of finance, and it has produced a major redistribution of wealth away from tenants (and landlords) to owner-occupiers. In theory, households would prefer to rent rather than buy property if the rental is less than the interest on a loan, and prefer to buy if the reverse relationship applies. But this is only true if there is no inherent preference by individuals to rent or buy; everyone is prepared to engage in a transaction which would yield a gain, however small; there is a perfect market; there are no taxes or tax allowances on property or interest; households can always obtain capital at current long term rates of interest—subject to size of income; there is no government intervention; there is a stable population; there are no additions to the housing stock, and there is a homogeneous housing stock and an equal distribution of incomes. Of course, these underlying conditions are very hypothetical as households are not faced with perfect market conditions.

Owner-occupation has become the most sought-after form of tenure regardless of any comparison which might be made between rents and interest payments. Home ownership provides households with a sense of independence; security; a shelter or 'hedge' against inflation, and a means of accumulating a capital asset—perhaps the only means available to the majority of families—advantages acknowledged in the White Paper, *Fair Deal for Housing* (1971). But rented property still houses almost 50 per cent of the households of Britain. Many tenants prefer not to have their capital tied up in their accommodation—they may wish to invest or save it elsewhere, or they may prefer to rent cheaply and indulge in consuming goods and services other than housing. Many 'traditional' tenants may regard owner-occupation as too risky, especially if they are employed in occupations where there is a high incidence of redundancy; many tenants may be ignorant of housebuying finance, interest payments, subsidies or tax relief; and there is a tendency for the children of tenants to in turn become tenants—believing that renting is the 'normal' form of tenure. But in the case of young people, newly-married couples, transients, short-stay visitors, and new immigrants, renting is probably a more appropriate form of tenure than owner-occupation—almost regardless of rent and loan interest comparability.

The market for owner-occupied housing is very imperfect. Buyers and sellers have a very imperfect knowledge of the market—a weakness which estate agents attempt to exploit; buildings though very durable cannot last for ever and this has an important influence on the valuation of freehold and leasehold rights; there may be an unwillingness of an owner to sell even when a would-be buyer offers a market price based on comparable valuation; the valuation of properties is no simple task as each building and each site is unique and there are difficulties of comparison; there is the legal complexity of transferring property; a part of a house may be occupied by a sitting tenant (or even a squatter); planning permission may not be forthcoming, deterring a would-be buyer intent on modifying the building; and the construction industry is very slow to respond to changes in demand. These and other factors result in a disequilibrium of supply and demand. At some price levels and in some areas, there may be a glut of properties on the market. At other price levels or in other areas there may be scarcity. Even when there is an apparent equilibrium (with market prices being offered) sales may not proceed because owners may decide to withdraw their properties from the market in anticipation of a higher price being realised in the future, or because they may decide to place a high non-monetary value on their home.

The Ideology of Owner-Occupation

During the nineteenth century employers were able to keep wages to a minimum, and landlords attempted to maximise rents. The inevitable result of this dichotomy of interest was appalling housing in our industrial towns and cities. By the middle of the century it became recognised that the improvement of housing was necessary for health reasons; to indirectly raise productivity at work; and to alleviate political agitation. The only practicable way of ending the employer–landlord conflict, other than by employers (benevolent or otherwise) and charities providing housing, was by means of an extension of owner-occupation and the introduction of local authority housing. It was not until 'the period 1945–51 that the latter alternative became the dominant solution. The growth of owner-occupation in the nineteenth century was made possible by the setting up of building societies—'self help'organisations for the higher paid workers.

But in the first three decades of the twentieth century owner-occupation was by no means considered by most households to be the 'ideal' or 'natural' form of tenure. During the 1920s, except for the council houses produced under the Housing Act of 1923 (the Chamberlain Act), local authority dwellings were:

> in every sense the ideal, being better produced at high standard for the better-off members of the working class.
>
> (Clarke and Ginsburg, 1975)

Owner-occupation only began to be popularly attractive when local authority housing became generally restricted to the displaced families of slum clearance schemes in the 1930s. The desire for home ownership was more of a response to a lack of choice, than a reaction against renting. The housing policy of the 1930s was, according to Clarke and Ginsburg:

> directly associated with the drive to make the better-off members of the working class into owner occupiers.

During the inter-war period, the increase in owner-occupation was a combined result of the Chamberlain Act (which provided subsidies for private construction); local authority guarantee of mortgages; falling building costs 1929–35; and the lengthening of mortgage repayments from 15 to 20–25 years. Increased car-ownership and the lack of effective planning controls over suburban development meant that cheap land could be used for extensive speculative housebuilding.

After the Second World War, the building licensing system (introduced in 1939) was continued—severely restricting private development. But resources concentrated in the public housing sector became available for private housebuilding when building licences were abolished in 1952—one year after the Conservative government had replaced Labour, and the

Conservatives have pledged their support for owner-occupation to the present day. Between 1954 and 1957 the Conservative government guaranteed loans to mortgagors in excess of the percentage of valuation that the societies would normally advance; the party fought the 1955 General Election with a pledge that it would create a 'property owning democracy'; between 1959 and 1962 the government lent £100 million to building societies to fund the purchase of pre-1919 dwellings; in 1963 it abolished tax on imputed income (Schedule A) from owner-occupied property; in 1971 its White Paper, *Fair Deal for Housing* and in 1972 the Housing Finance Act both continued the system of tax relief on mortgage interest, and in the period 1971-4, and from 1977 (at first at a local government level) sales of council housing have been encouraged.

In recent years Labour governments have also attempted to extend home ownership. The *Housing Programme 1965-70* (1965) outlined Labour's aims for the late 1960s, one of which was, 'the stimulation of the planned growth of owner-occupation'. This aim was achieved by encouraging lease-holders to buy their freehold under the Leasehold Reform Act of 1967, the introduction of the Option Mortgage Scheme in 1968 which made low income housebuyers eligible for subsidies (equivalent to tax relief on mortgage interest payments), and by the continuation of tax relief to other mortgagors. There was little change of policy during 1974-9 although interest relief was withdrawn in 1974 on mortgages in excess of £25 000. In the same year mortgagors were protected from rising interest rates by government loans of £500 million to building societies to offset a shortfall in funds. Until March 1979 (two months before Labour was defeated in the General Election), the Labour government permitted the sale of council houses—although it did not encourage the practice.

The bulk of the Labour movement has never been opposed in principal to owner-occupation. Socialism draws a distinction between property owned for the purpose of realising a profit, and property which does not carry an income with it. The former consists of stocks and shares, rented buildings and land acquired for speculative reasons—all forms of capital; and the latter includes the personal ownership of for example motor cars, washing machines, and owner-occupied houses—all of which could be defined as consumption. If 'profits' are made on the resale of these goods they are usually incidental, and if an owner-occupier sells his house at a price higher than he paid for it he may be unable to realise the profit, as he might have to pay the same high price for a comparable alternative property. Also by 1973, one-third of housebuyers were manual workers (and 40 per cent by 1979), a fact not escaping the Labour Party in formulating its policy towards home ownership. Miliband (1972) and Coates (1975) suggested that the growing electoral influence of owner-occupiers (who owned over half of the nation's housing stock by the 1970s) went someway to explaining why the Labour Party seemed to be increasingly embracing the Conservatives' idea of a property owning democracy. Both political parties clearly have a commitment to extend owner-occupation, but both have had to rely upon making adjustments to the principal source of housing finance—building society mortgage funds. Both recognise that there is a conflict between the need to promote a growing private sector and the possibility that if left to itself the results might be socially and politically unacceptable.

Britain's third largest party, the Liberals, have also supported the owner-occupied sector—believing in a property owning democracy. In the 1970s, the party was concerned with the problems of first-time housebuyers and called for measures to make it easier for young married couples to buy their own homes.

Owner-occupation is perhaps the most appropriate form of tenure in a mainly private enterprise or capitalist economy. It emphasises the philosophy of personal 'self help', and it has generated in Britain a substantial vested interest in maintaining or expanding this sector. Generally owner-occupiers attempt to keep their properties in good order, in contrast to council tenants who have to rely upon their public landlords for repairs and maintenance. Owner-occupiers usually tolerate increased mortgage interest rates far more readily than tenants face rent increases. Whereas there have been rent strikes against private landlords (Glasgow 1915 and Stepney 1939) and against local authorities (St Pancras 1959 and in effect Clay Cross 1972), there has never been an organised mortgage strike. Within the rented sector there is greater solidarity than in owner-occupation. Tenants' associations have a common cause—the minimisation of rents and security of tenure. But residential associations of owner-occupiers are usually concerned with amenity and maintaining property values. Mortgage interest payments are far more anonymous than rents and vary from one mortgagor to another. Whereas local authority housing solidifies the working class, owner-occupation divides it and converts a part of it into the bourgeoisie.

But it would be a mistake to assume that the dominance of owner-occupation in Britain is a result of unimpeded market forces, of *laissez faire* conditions. The situation has arisen due to very substantial tax allowances being given on mortgage interest, amounts which in most years have exceeded Exchequer subsidies and rate contributions to local authority housing. The cost of owner-occupation has also been reduced by the absence of the need to pay current market prices (on houses already owned) but only historic costs; the realisation of capital gains on the sale of a house (involving the transfer of wealth from buyers to sellers), and the payment of what are usually modest interest rates on mortgages (involving the transfer of wealth from creditors to debtors—the former normally receiving interest at less than the rate of inflation). Had there been an absence of government intervention in the owner-occupied sector, advantages to the housebuyer would have been considerably less, and a very different pattern of tenure may have emerged.

House Prices

The price of owner-occupied housing has increased substantially in recent years (table 2.2). In the 1960s and early 1970s the rate of increase in house prices was usually greater than the rate of inflation (as measured by the General Index of Retail Prices), and in 1971–3 house prices increased at a faster rate than average earnings, resulting in the House Prices/Earnings Ratio rising from 3.38 to 4.65. This unprecedented increase in prices was associated with an accumulated demand for property as the investment aspects of house purchase were emphasised. Mr. Anthony Crosland, Shadow Minister for the Environment (1971a) drew attention to the advantages of owner-occupation in this situation;

> Unlike the tenant, the owner-occupier gains from inflation; he repays his mortgage in depreciated pounds. Since, moreover, house prices rise faster than prices generally, he has a profitable investment on which he makes a real capital gain; and, unlike the private landlord, he pays no tax on that gain.

But whilst existing owner-occupiers benefitted, would-be purchasers were increasingly being priced out of the market. Apart from rapidly rising house prices, mortgage interest rates had increased from 8.5 to 11 per cent (October 1972–October 1973). It was ironic that in 1970 when house prices averaged only £5180 and mortgage interest was only 8.5 per cent the Conservative Party's Manifesto stated:

> The increase in the cost of new houses and the highest mortgage rates in our history have prevented thousands of young people from becoming owners of their own homes. Our policies will help to keep down house prices.

But Conservative policies, or the lack of them, raised house prices by 31.5 and 36.2 per cent in 1972 and 1973 respectively. By 1973 house prices on average had doubled since 1970, but in the period 1974–7 they increased at a slower rate than retail prices and average earnings. The decrease in real earnings in these years (largely a result of a punitive Incomes Policy) stabilised demand for owner-occupied houses and helped to lower the House Prices/Earnings Ratio from 4.65 to 3.41 (1973–7). In 1978–9, earnings again increased at a faster rate than retail prices, pushing up the demand for houses, and increasing their price—the House Prices/Earnings Ratio rising to 4.06 by the second quarter of 1979. The house price boom of 1971–3 was recurring.

The price of new houses is largely determined by the price of secondhand properties. Because of the durability of houses, the supply of properties is dominated by the existing stock. Housebuilding only increased the housing stock by a net average of 1.3 per cent per annum 1911–79, and in the 1970s

Table 2.2 House Prices, Retail Prices and Average Earnings, 1966–79

Period	Average prices of new houses at mortgage approval stage			General Index of Retail Prices		Average earnings			House prices/ earnings ratio
	Price £	Index 1970 =100	Annual change %	Index 1970 =100	Annual change %	Earnings p.a. £	Index 1970 =100	Annual change %	
1966	4 100	79.2	5.9	81.9	3.8	1 147	71.1	4.3	3.57
1967	4 340	83.8	5.9	83.6	2.1	1 212	75.1	5.7	3.58
1968	4 640	89.6	7.1	88.3	5.6	1 309	81.1	8.0	3.54
1969	4 880	94.2	5.2	92.8	5.1	1 417	87.8	8.3	3.44
1970	5 180	100.0	6.1	100.0	7.7	1 613	100.0	13.8	3.21
1971	5 970	115.3	15.3	109.2	9.2	1 765	109.5	9.5	3.38
1972	7 850	151.5	31.5	117.6	7.7	2 042	126.6	15.6	3.84
1973	10 690	206.4	36.2	129.7	10.3	2 294	142.3	12.4	4.65
1974	11 340	218.9	6.1	153.3	18.2	2 876	178.3	25.4	3.94
1975	12 406	239.5	9.4	192.1	25.3	3 498	216.9	21.6	3.55
1976	13 442	259.5	8.4	220.8	14.9	3 928	243.6	12.3	3.42
1977	14 768	285.1	9.9	249.6	13.0	4 329	268.4	10.2	3.41
1978	17 685	341.4	19.8	272.0	9.0	4 952	307.0	14.4	3.57
1979									
Q.1	20 613	397.9	27.4	278.0	9.5	5 129	318.0	14.5	4.02
Q.2	22 105	426.7	29.2	287.0	6.5	5 435	337.0	6.0	4.06

Source: The Building Societies Association, *BSA Bulletin*; Department of Employment, *Gazette*
Note: Increases are over previous year or same period of previous year.

there was a drastic reduction in the number of housing starts in the private sector from 227 400 in 1972 to 140 100 in 1979. Since the supply of houses is relatively inelastic, price changes are therefore caused mainly by changes in demand. Rising construction costs can only be passed on to the consumer if the market is buoyant. Table 2.3 shows that there was a close correlation between the increase in price of new and secondhand properties (1973–9). Increases in the value of secondhand properties enabled developers to ask higher prices for new. But housebuilding costs increased at a greater rate than house prices during this period with adverse effects on profitability and output. This was in contrast to 1971–2 when house prices rose faster than building costs and resulted in frenzied activity as developers made super-normal profits, and private sector housing starts increased from 165 100 in 1970 to 227 400 in 1972. But because of the nature of housebuilding there is usually a time-lag of 12–18 months between changing demand conditions and the rate of construction. Supply may thus be excessive during the downturn of demand causing house prices to lag behind the increase in the general level of prices (as in 1974–7), or it may be inadequate when demand begins to increase causing house prices to increase ahead of the general level of prices (as in 1971–3 and 1978–9).

Table 2.3   **Indices of New and Existing House Price and Housebuilding Costs, United Kingdom, 1973–9**

Quarter	*New properties*	*Secondhand properties*		*Housebuilding (wages and materials) cost*
		Modern	*Older*	
1973 4th Qtr	100	100	100	100
1974 4th Qtr	105	104	106	121
1975 4th Qtr	119	114	116	149
1976 4th Qtr	131	123	125	177
1977 4th Qtr	145	132	134	193
1978 4th Qtr	181	170	169	209
1979 3rd Qtr	221	204	211	236

Source: Nationwide Building Society, *Housing Trends*

There have been substantial regional differences in house prices. Table 2.4 shows that of the English regions, the Outer Metropolitan Area, Greater London and the Outer South East had the highest house prices in 1979, reflecting higher earnings, higher activity rates (the proportion of the insured population aged 16 and over) and relatively low unemployment. The South West had the fourth highest level of prices in England—the area attracting a large in-migration of retired households, and benefitted from newly completed motorway communications. In all regions new properties were more expensive than modern and older secondhand houses. In the year ending 30 September 1979, the greatest rates of increase in house prices (in

Table 2.4   Average Regional House Prices in 3rd Quarter 1979, and House Price Increases during Year Ended 30 September 1979

Economic planning region	Modern secondhand properties		Older secondhand properties		New properties		All properties	
	£	% inc.	£	% inc.	£	% inc.	£	% inc.
Outer Met. Area	27 500	29	24 720	32	29 600	30	26 940	29
Greater London	27 450	31	25 420	35	32 190	33	25 950	33
Outer South East	22 420	35	19 570	34	24 900	36	22 420	34
South West	21 480	28	18 830	32	21 080	30	20 480	29
West Midlands	19 400	27	16 520	27	22 990	33	18 980	28
East Anglia	19 660	31	16 100	36	21 240	35	18 900	33
North West	19 270	31	14 220	28	21 620	33	17 360	30
Northern	18 140	23	12 530	23	19 610	25	16 100	23
East Midlands	17 210	26	12 360	28	19 060	33	15 870	27
Yorks and Humber	17 750	27	12 060	26	18 630	25	15 720	26
Wales	18 710	25	15 150	35	20 110	33	17 480	30
Scotland	21 190	19	17 170	22	20 620	16	19 530	19
Northern Ireland	21 770	20	19 210	12	23 380	15	21 930	17
United Kingdom	21 260	28	18 420	31	22 220	29	20 250	29

Source: Nationwide Building Society, *Housing Trends*

descending order) were found in Outer South East, Greater London and East Anglia—regions in which demand was outstripping supply by an increasing extent. The price of secondhand properties—both modern and older—increased more rapidly than the more expensive new properties, prospective housebuyers being able to raise finance more easily for the former than the latter. Over the long term, regional disparities have been gradually narrowing. In the period 1969–78, the average price of houses in the United Kingdom increased by 246 per cent, but the rates of increase in Northern Ireland, Yorkshire and Humberside, the North West, the Northern region and Scotland were 401, 265, 264, 259 and 258 per cent respectively, whereas the increase in Greater London was only 221 per cent.

The increase in demand, the main cause of rising house prices, is a result of a combination of many factors, namely: the growth in population and the number of households; the increased supply of funds for house purchase; the increase in incomes; and the provision of tax relief on mortgage interest. These will be examined in turn, and it will be shown that house prices, far from being determined by *laissez-faire* market forces, are influenced very greatly by government policy.

Population and Household Trends

Changes in population and the number of households are important determinants of housing demand. The total population of Great Britain increased by 11 per cent from 48.9 to 54.3 million 1951–71, and the total stock of dwellings also increased by 11 per cent—from 13.8 to 19.3 million in the same period, But although the number of households increased by about the same amount (11.4 per cent), the virtual equilibrium between dwellings and households concealed many serious deficiencies. In some parts of Britain— particularly in the major cities—there is a high proportion of dwellings which are statutorily unfit or lacking basic amenities, similarly there are severe local shortages. Houses available for sale may either be too expensive or in the wrong localities for households wishing to buy. There is little accommodation for single persons (only 0.5 per cent of dwellings built privately in England and Wales in the 1970s had one bedroom), one-parent families, the disabled, and discharged prisoners and council waiting lists and the numbers of registered homeless are growing. There is also a need to allow for a vacancy rate to promote mobility—especially if governments, faced with technological and economic change, pursue policies aimed at reducing regional imbalance.

Although Britain—like most industrial countries—has an ageing population due to a reduction in birth and death rates, during certain periods the birth rate might rise and have a long term effect on housing demand. The sharp increase in the birth rate after 1945 resulted in a large increase in single person households during 1961–71 with consequent increases in the demand for single person or shared housing. The number of marriages also increased in this period, rising from 346 000 in 1961 to 410 000 in 1971. On the assumption that in the former year 42.7 per cent of newly-weds (the same percentage of total households which were owner-occupied) wished to buy their homes, this would have necessitated a supply of 147 000 dwellings. In the latter year (and calculated on the same basis), 50 per cent would have wished to have become owner-occupiers, requiring a supply of 205 000 dwellings—an increase of 42 per cent on 1961. But only 7 per cent more owner-occupied houses were built in 1971. Increased amounts of mortgage loans were thus being used by an increasing number of households to acquire a less than proportionate increase in the supply of new houses. This stimulated the provision of housing for sale from the private rented sector.

By 1978, approximately 19 per cent of all mortgages were granted to purchasers under 25 years of age and a further 27 per cent to the 25–9 age group. More than 46 per cent of first-time buyers were under 30 (Nationwide Building Society, 1978). Much of this demand had to be satisfied by the supply of new houses because life expectancy was increasing—slowing down the recycling of houses, although retirement led to the mobility of a small proportion of households away from the cities releasing houses for younger age groups.

Households which are the most significant in considering housing demand are therefore not those which stay where they are, but those which are recently formed often in localities away from their places of origin—such as single person households, newly-weds and the mobile retired. Other groups which have an influence on demand include migrants, the divorced, and elderly households going to live as part of another household, for example living with their children. The number of households formed is therefore the result of a very complex pattern of flows and relationships.

Finance for House Purchase

The availability of long-term finance is essential to an expanding owner-occupied sector. In the United Kingdom the principal lending institutions are the building societies, local authorities and insurance companies (and to a much lesser extent the commercial banks). The loans market is dominated by the building societies whose main function is the provision of long term finance for owner-occupation. In recent years building societies provided more than 90 per cent of the long term finance for house purchase (table 2.5), particularly in respect of new dwellings. By 1977 building societies had £31 696 million of mortgage loans outstanding, compared with £2935

Table 2.5   **Mortgage Lending—Amount Advanced (Gross) by Main United Kingdom Institutional Sources, 1967–1978**

Year	Building societies Amount (£ million)	%	Local authorities Amount (£ million)	%	Insurance companies Amount (£ million)	%	Total Amount (£ million)
1967	1477	83	168	9	124	8	1769
1970	2021	87	157	7	154	6	2332
1971	2758	88	232	7	149	5	3139
1972	3649	88	337	8	149	4	4135
1973	3540	82	519	12	259	6	4318
1974	2950	76	699	18	249	6	3898
1975	4965	82	852	14	240	4	6057
1976	6117	91	438	6	202	3	6757
1977	6889	91	462	6	221	3	7572
1978	8734	93	343	4	297	3	9374

Source: Bristol and West Building Society, *Factual Background*; and Building Societies Association, *BSA Bulletin*

million by local authorities, and £1640 million by insurance companies. In 1978 building societies made 801 900 advances (a peak year), 133 700 on new houses.

Because of their dominance, building societies exert a very great influence over the housing stock, favouring traditionally built modern houses of two to four bedrooms. It may be difficult for prospective buyers to obtain a mortgage on unorthodox dwellings or conversions. Partly as a result of the conservative attitude of building societies, there have been few changes in the type or method of constructing houses built for occupation. Although building societies are not profit-making by law, they cannot afford to make a loss. They try to minimise risk, and usually succeed in doing this, for example in 1974 they were lending £16 039 million but their mortgage losses were only £48 000. When considering whether to allocate a mortgage they take into account two fundamental considerations. First: that a borrower should be able to maintain the flow of capital and interest payments appropriate to the required mortgage, thus the mortgage is geared to the likely length of the working life and job security of the prospective borrower. Usually, older borrowers have to accept smaller loans and shorter repayment periods and therefore need higher incomes or higher deposits to buy property; and skilled manual and 'white collared' applicants may be better favoured than semi- or unskilled manual workers. Second: that in the event of the borrower failing to repay, the market price of the property at this future date will be sufficient to recoup the outstanding debt plus the cost of foreclosure; therefore the age, quality and type of property and its location are of utmost concern to the building society. Generally, freehold properties are expected to have thirty years of life after the expiry of the loan, but with older properties this deficiency may be offset by larger deposits and monthly repayments, and shorter repayment periods which normally necessitate a higher financial status of the borrower. Table 2.6 shows which categories of

Table 2.6   Distribution of Mortgages, 2nd Quarter 1979

Borrower, finance and property	*% mortgages*
Borrowers aged 45 and over	12
Previous tenure of borrowers:	
Privately renting, renting from local authorities, in other accommodation	23
[New householders and former owner-occupiers	77]
Income of borrower under £5000	29
Mortgages of under £8000	21
Deposits of less than £2000	29
Pre-1919 dwellings	24
Converted and purpose built flats	8

Source: The Building Societies Association and Department of the Environment: Five per cent sample survey of building society mortgage completions

applicant and which types of property are regarded as 'bad risks' by building societies, and indicates that societies are not particularly involved in financing the purchase of down-market property.

Local authorities have powers to grant mortgages under the Housing (Financial Provisions) Act of 1958. They tend to limit their lending to borrowers unable to obtain a mortgage from a building society. Generally local authorities lend to a higher proportion of low income, young and first time buyers; they lend on generally cheaper and older properties and provide smaller advances, although these can often exceed 90 per cent of the price of the property. They also prefer to limit their lending to borrowers within their physical boundaries. They tend to act as lenders of the last resort, and generally charge higher rates of interest than building societies— fixed over the whole period of the loan. Changes in economic policy have resulted in considerable variation in the assistance given by local authorities to would-be buyers, for example there was a large reduction in lending in 1975–8.

Insurance companies have tended to lend mainly on commercial rather than residential property. Loans are generally linked to an endowment policy, therefore repayments are normally higher than with a conventional building society mortgage. Insurance companies have been important in providing finance above the special advance limit of building societies— £13 000 (1973–5), £20 000 (1975–9) and £25 000 subsequently, although their relative significance has declined since the 1960s (table 2.5).

Until recently, the commercial banks have not been interested in providing long-term finance for house purchase—concentrating mainly on the provision of bridging finance. Nevertheless during the 'price boom' years of 1972–3 they advanced £345 and £290 million, amounts greater than those provided by the insurance companies (and local authorities in 1972), and in 1978 there were £1715 millions of outstanding bank loans for house purchase (equal to 4.5 per cent of the total). In 1979 Lloyds Bank provided £40 million of home loans (January–June)—the minimum mortgage being £20 000 (with the average being around £32 000)—the bank clearly specialising in 'up-market' purchases; the Midland Bank began to offer home loans ranging from £20 000 to £150 000 for periods of up to 25 years; and the Trustee Savings Bank launched its mortgage lending scheme with £100 million of funds available for the first year of its operation. Although these facilities did not pose a serious threat to the building societies they heralded increased competition in the home loans market.

Building Society Funds

Building societies date back to the eighteenth century, the first one being formed in Birmingham in 1775. Originally, societies were actually concerned with financing housebuilding for their members and were temporary,

Table 2.7 Building Societies: Progress 1890–1978

Year	Number of societies	Number of share accounts 000s	Number of mortgage accounts 000s	Share balances £ million	Mortgage balances £ million	Total assets £ million	Advances during year Number 000s	Advances during year Amount £ million
1890	2 795	659						
1900	2 289	585			46	60		9
1910	1 723	626			60	76		9
1920	1 271	748		64	69	87		25
1930	1 026	1 449	720	303	316	371	159	89
1940	952	2 088	1 503	552	678	756	43	21
1950	819	2 256	1 508	962	1 060	1 256	302	270
1960	726	3 910	2 349	2 721	2 647	3 166	387	560
1970	481	10 265	3 655	9 788	8 752	10 819	624	1 954
1971	467	11 568	3 896	11 698	10 332	12 919	769	2 705
1972	456	12 874	4 126	13 821	12 546	15 246	893	3 630
1973	447	14 385	4 204	16 021	14 352	17 545	720	3 513
1974	416	15 856	4 250	18 021	16 030	20 094	546	2 945
1975	382	17 916	4 394	22 134	18 802	24 204	798	4 908
1976	364	19 991	4 609	25 760	22 565	28 202	913	6 183
1977	339	22 536	4 836	31 110	26 427	34 288	946	6 745
1978	316	24 999	5 108	36 186	31 598	39 538	1 184	8 808

Source: Building Societies Association, *BSA Bulletin*

being wound up when repayments on the properties were complete. By the mid-nineteenth century societies became permanent institutions and were more and more involved in financing the purchase of existing properties. In the period 1890–1978 the number of societies decreased from 2795 to 316 mainly due to merger. The five largest societies in 1978 (in order of ranking, the Halifax, Abbey National, Nationwide, Leeds Permanent and Woolwich) owned 55.2 per cent of total building society assets (compared with only 39.1 per cent by the five largest in 1930); the value of total assets increased from £60 million to £39 583 million; the number of their share accounts from 659 000 to 24 999 000; and the number of their mortgages accounts from 720 000 to 5 108 000 (table 2.7). The main periods of expansion were between the World Wars and after 1960. Between 1920 and 1940, there was an eight-fold increase in the value of share balances despite the depression. That proportion of the working population in employment (nationally never less than 76 per cent) enjoyed rising real earnings (as retail prices slumped below money earnings) and their marginal propensity to save consequently increased. Building society shares were particularly attractive—being very liquid, having a fixed capital value and offering a high degree of security during a period of wildly fluctuating share prices. The substantial increase in owner-occupation in the 1930s was particularly attributable to the supply of mortgages from these funds. In the period 1960–70 total assets trebled, and almost quadrupled by 1978, but not in real terms because of inflation.

In the period 1967–78 total building society assets overtook those of the banking sector (personal deposits) and the National Savings movement, only being exceeded by the assets of insurance companies. But the societies' share of annual personal net savings was not maintained due to competition from life assurance and superannuation funds, and national savings (table 2.8). Nevertheless, whereas in the 1930s building societies were comparatively isolated from the rest of the capital market and were seen to be instrumental in expanding the total volume of personal savings, since the Second World War they have absorbed an increasing volume of savings, have become major competitors in the capital market, and have become increasingly aware of the response of investors to changes in interest rates.

Building Society Rates of Interest, Funds and Lending

The ability of building societies to provide mortgage loans relies upon the inflow of funds from savers, which in the first instance depends upon societies being able to offer rates of interest which are competitive with those offered by other institutions. The differential between building society rates and competing rates as indicated by Bank Rate (to October 1972) and Minimum Lending Rate (MLR) is of significance in indicating the likely level on inflow. Table 2.9 shows that Bank Rate/Minimum Lending Rate fluctuated substantially during 1970–9 reaching a peak of 17 per cent in Novem-

Table 2.8 Personal Savings in United Kingdom Financial Institutions, 1967 and 1978

Personal savings institutions	*Total Assets*			
	1967		*1978*	
	Amount (£ million)	*%*	*Amount (£ million)*	*%*
Insurance companies	11 802	28	46 809	31
Building societies	7 523	17	39 692	26
Banking sector (personal deposits)	8 250	19	24 490	16
All National Savings	8 472	20	16 424	11
Private superannuation funds	3 719	9	15 345	10
Trustee Savings Bank	2 272	5	4 999	3
Unit Trusts	788	2	3 873	3
	42 556		151 632	

Personal savings institutions	*Net Savings from Personal Sector*			
	1967		*1978*	
	Amount (£ million)	*%*	*Amount (£ million)*	*%*
Building societies	1 099	30	4 879	27
Life assurance and superannuation funds	1 372	37	7 705	42
All National Savings	125	3	2 121	11
Banking sector deposits	740	20	3 239	18
Trustee Savings Bank	121	3	465	2
Unit Trusts	84	2	116	1
Local Authorities	165	5	−166	1
	3 706		18 359	

Source: Bristol and West Building Society, *Factual Background*

ber 1979, and falling to 5 per cent in September 1971 and October 1977; but the gross rate of interest on building society shares fluctuated far less frequently, and reached a peak of 15 per cent in November 1979, and fell to a low of 7.77 per cent in January 1972 (table 2.9). Building societies tend to attract short term savings but lend over the long term, therefore to stabilise interest rates on mortgages as much as possible (whilst offering adequate rates to investors) there are far fewer fluctuations in society rates of interest than in Bank Rate/Minimum Lending rate, and the fluctuations are not so extreme. Societies are also slower to adjust their rates than the Bank of England—delays causing quite major 'differentials' among competitive rates of interest. Building societies may be reluctant to alter rates until it is fairly certain that market rates have settled because the frequent recalculation of mortgage repayments (resulting from a change in the share rate)

Table 2.9   Bank Rate/Minimum Lending Rate and Building Society Ordinary Share Interest, 1970–9

Year	Bank Rate/Minimum Lending Rate Month of change	%	Building Society Share Rates Month of change	Gross %	Net %
1970	March	7.50	(April 1969	8.51	5.00)
1971	March	7.00			
	April	6.00			
	September	5.00			
1972	June	6.00	January	7.77	4.75
	October	7.25	October	8.57	5.25
	October	7.50			
	December	7.75			
	December	8.00			
	December	9.00			
1973	January	8.75	February	8.00	5.60
	March	8.50			
	April	8.00	April	9.00	6.30
	May	8.25	May	9.64	6.75
	May	8.00			
	June	7.50			
	July	7.75			
	July	9.00			
	July	11.50			
	October	11.25	October	10.71	7.50
	November	13.00			
1974	January	12.75			
	February	12.50			
	April	12.25			
	April	12.00			
	May	11.75			
	September	11.50			
1975	January	11.25			
	January	11.00			
	February	10.75			
	February	10.50			
	March	10.25			
	March	10.00			
	April	9.75			
	May	10.00	June	10.77	7.00
	July	11.00			
	October	12.00			
	November	11.75			
	November	11.50			
	December	11.25			

Table 2.9   (continued)

| Year | Bank Rate/Minimum Lending Rate | | Building Society Share Rates | | |
	Month of change	%	Month of change	Gross %	Net %
1976	January	11.00			
	January	10.75			
	January	10.50			
	January	10.00			
	February	9.50			
	February	9.25			
	March	9.00			
	April	10.50			
	May	11.50	May	10.00	6.50
	September	13.00			
	October	15.00			
	November	14.75	November	12.00	7.80
	December	14.50			
	December	14.25			
1977	January	14.00			
	January	13.25			
	January	12.25			
	February	12.00			
	March	11.00			
	March	10.50			
	March	9.50			
	April	9.25			
	April	9.00			
	April	8.75			
	April	8.25			
	May	8.00	May	10.61	7.00
	August	7.50	July	10.15	6.70
	August	7.00			
	September	6.50			
	September	6.00			
	October	5.50			
	October	5.00			
	November	7.00	November	9.09	6.00
1978	January	6.50	February	8.33	5.50
	April	7.50			
	May	8.75			
	May	9.00			
	June	10.00	July	10.00	6.70
	November	12.50	December	11.94	8.00
1979	February	14.00			
	April	12.00			
	June	14.00	July	12.50	8.75
	November	17.00	December	15.00	10.50

Note: Share rates are those recommended by the Building Societies Association.

is an inconvenient and costly process, and most mortgage contracts require three months notice before existing mortgagor's rates can be raised. In 1977 for example MLR changed 17 times, but most society share and mortgage rates changed only three times. Also, when there are falling interest rates, building societies prefer to keep their rates relatively high in order to attract a large inflow of funds (at the expense of mortgagors); for example MLR dropped from 15 to 5 per cent in 21 stages between October 1976 and October 1977, whereas the building society gross share rate fell from 12 to 8.33 per cent in only four stages, during November 1976—Feburary 1978, with the mortgage rate falling simultaneously from 12.25 to 8.50 per cent.

Composite Rates of Taxation and Capital Market Competition

By the late 1970s building societies were providing over 90 per cent of the loans for house purchase (table 2.5) having got to this dominant position by offering mortgages at the most competitive rates of interest. This was made possible because they could borrow in the capital market at lower rates than other institutions, mainly because they incur on behalf of their investors a special low 'composite rate' of taxation. Since 1894 the government has agreed to a concession, which in the view of the Community Development Project (CDP) (1976) amounts to the Inland Revenue saying to the building societies:

> If you can persuade a few million of your poorer investors to pay tax when they need not, then we will allow your richer investors to pay less tax than they should. Rich investors will not get these tax concessions when they lend money to your competitors. So on balance they will lend it to you even if you pay less interest. Indeed when they have weighed up the tax advantages of investing in a building society, they will accept an interest rate of about 1% less than they could get elsewhere.

The composite rate of taxation yields the equivalent of the total amount the Inland Revenue would have collected had building society investors paid income tax at the rates applicable to each individual divided by the number of investors. It is based on the average tax rate of a sample of investors—the sample being taken periodically. Table 2.10 shows that in the 1970s the composite rate ranged from 22.50 to 32.75 per cent compared with the standard/basic rate which ranged from 33.00 to 41.25 per cent. Regardless of the investor's income, he or she has the same composite rate of tax knocked off the interest before it is received.

With the composite rate of interest, the building societies have a competitive edge over other institutions. For example, if a building society pays interest (tax already paid) at 8.00 per cent, the society investor obtains the equivalent of 11.94 per cent if they pay tax at the basic rate of (say) 33 per cent, therefore a commercial bank would have to offer interest at 11.94 per cent to provide the investor with the same return; but since the society's interest is liable to tax at only a composite rate (say 22.50 per cent), it pays a

Table 2.10 Composite and Standard/Basic Rates of Tax

Financial year	Composite rate %	Standard/basic rate %	Composite rate as percentage of standard/basic rate
1970/71	32.75	41.25	79.4
1971/72	31.00	38.75	80.0
1972/73	30.00	38.75	77.4
1973/74	23.50	30.00	78.3
1974/75	26.25	33.00	79.5
1975/76	27.75	35.00	79.3
1976/77	27.75	35.00	79.3
1977/78	24.25	34.00	71.3
1978/79	22.50	33.00	68.2

Source: Building Societies Association, *BSA Bulletin*

rate of interest of only 9.25 per cent—8 per cent to the investor and the rest to the Inland Revenue. The building society is thereby competitive with the bank, although it pays out much less to the investor. It could even offer a higher rate of interest than the bank and still pay out less to investors. This competitive advantage is clearly at the expense of the low income investor. Nearly a quarter of building society interest was paid (net of tax) to investors below the tax threshold in the late 1970s, and a half of all society investors unwittingly and indirectly incur tax when they are not normally liable and thereby subsidise the richer investor. Why do they accept a net rate of interest which is usually a negative rate? For example in 1975 they received a only 7.00 per cent on building society shares, whereas the rate of inflation was 25 per cent, and even when this fell to 9.0 per cent in 1978, share interest was less than 8.00 per cent for most of the year. Why did investors accept even 8.00 per cent when local authorities paid 11.75 per cent, and the National Savings Bank 12.00 per cent? The reasons include convenience, liquidity and vigorous advertising, and possibly the belief that savings in a building society would secure a mortgage if ever one was required.

But the bulk of society funds is in substantial sums rather than small savings. Over 30 per cent of society accounts contain over £5000 and over 16 per cent of total funds consist of these larger amounts. Although investors (at the time of writing) could only keep a maximum of £15 000 in their account with any one building society and be eligible for tax at the composite rate, higher amounts could be deposited and the interest was taxed at the normal rate on behalf of the investor—the net interest consequently being lower. Corporate bodies such as limited companies, pension funds and trust funds also invest in building societies but usually negotiate interest rates and withdrawal terms, or they may spread small amounts around many building societies. It is these large investors that are particularly sensitive to differences in interest rates, and even tiny changes can result in massive injections or withdrawals. The bigger investors:

invest where they can get most money, switching easily from one investment to another. If building societies offer more than banks, they invest with building societies. If banks offer more than building societies, they invest with banks. Theirs is 'hot money' because it moves like a scalded cat and has increased substantially as a proportion of building society funds in recent years. Welcome in some ways . . . in the long term it undermines the building societies' stability. If other interest rates increase significantly, as happened in 1967 and 1974, building societies become uncompetitive and there is a dramatic outflow of cash. If market rates fall much below theirs, they are awash with money, as in 1975 and 1976, which they daren't lend out to home buyers in case the investors suddenly want it back again.   (CDP, 1976)

In 1974, the building society gross share rate was 10.71 per cent, but 11.50 per cent was being paid by the banks on deposits over £10 000 and local authorities were paying 14 per cent on seven day deposits. The result of these differences was that building societies suffered a net withdrawal of funds of £21 million—the first net outflow ever (this may also have been due in part to small investors withdrawing their savings to pay bills during the three-day working week). Building societies could have paid higher interest on large deposits (for example 13 per cent on savings over £8000) to attract more funds (if allowed), and this might only have increased the mortgage rate by 0.5 per cent, but instead the government offered the societies £500 million in loans to enable them to maintain their liquidity and mortgage interest rates at 11.00 per cent. In 1976 by contrast, the building society gross share rate was 10.77 per cent, which was highly competitive with other rates, and net receipts exceeded £1000 million during the first quarter of the year, but net advances remained at a relatively low level. This was probably advantageous because following a drop in the share interest rate to 10.00 per cent later in the year there was a large reduction in the inflow of funds, net receipts in the fourth quarter of the year being only £148 million. The House Builders Federation warned the government that unless building societies pushed up their rates there would be a mortgage famine in 1977. The societies duly increased their gross share rate to 12 per cent in November 1977, but the Wilson Report (1980) called for more competition between society rates; urged the ending of the composite rate of taxation to the benefit of the small saver, and proposed the payment of interest gross to depositors who do not pay tax.

Net Receipts, Net Advances and House Prices

From 1970 to 1979 building society receipts and withdrawals both increased substantially, but net receipts and net advances fluctuated wildly (table 2.11). This was largely in response to interest rates and the liquidity of societies. Because building societies attracted an increasing proportion of

Table 2.11 Building Society Shares and Deposits, Lending and Recommended Interest Rates, 1970–9

Quarter	Receipts	With-drawals	Net receipts	Net advances	Ordinary shares	New mortgages
	£m	£m	£m	£m	Rate %	Rate %
1970 Q.1	675	447	228	201	5.00	8.50
Q.2	737	468	269	269	(April	(April
Q.3	815	475	340	310	1969)	1969)
Q.4	853	477	376	308		
1971 Q.1	818	488	330	289		
Q.2	963	596	367	393		
Q.3	1094	640	454	468		
Q.4	1216	667	549	450		8.00 (Nov.)
1972 Q.1	1310	807	503	465	4.75 (Jan.)	
Q.2	1334	859	475	571		
Q.3	1289	930	359	632		
Q.4	1365	899	464	547	5.25 (Oct.)	8.50 (Oct.)
1973 Q.1	1460	1133	327	644	5.60 (Feb.)	
Q.2	1602	996	606	500	6.30 (April)	
					6.75 (May)	9.50 (May)
Q.3	1558	1231	327	503		10.00 (Aug.)
Q.4	1433	1181	252	352	7.50 (Oct.)	11.00 (Oct.)
1974 Q.1	1434	1455	−21	318		
Q.2	1497	1240	257	242		
Q.3	1680	1292	388	415		
Q.4	1759	1218	541	515		
1975 Q.1	2000	1270	730	534		
Q.2	2403	1491	912	653		
Q.3	2330	1547	783	768	7.00 (June)	
Q.4	2304	1538	766	813		
1976 Q.1	2699	1697	1002	802		
Q.2	2529	1884	645	974	6.50 (May)	10.50 (May)
Q.3	2567	2084	483	1008		
Q.4	2455	2307	148	834	7.80 (Nov.)	12.25 (Nov.)
1977 Q.1	2894	2330	564	781		
Q.2	3590	2228	1362	884	7.00 (May)	11.25 (May)
Q.3	3679	2522	1157	1180	6.70 (July)	10.50 (July)
Q.4	4162	2523	1639	1255	6.00 (Nov.)	9.50 (Oct.)
1978 Q.1	3812	2763	1049	1261	5.50 (Feb.)	8.50 (Feb.)
Q.2	3829	3135	694	1339		
Q.3	4098	3352	746	1275	6.70 (July)	9.75 (July)
Q.4	4150	3272	878	1221	8.00 (Dec.)	11.75 (Nov.)
1979 Q.1	4279	3502	777	1181		
Q.2	4581	3804	777	1260		
Q.3	4950	4047	933	1318	8.75 (July)	
Q.4	5100	4261	839	1155	10.50 (Dec.)	15.00 (Nov.)

Source: Building Societies Association, *A Compendium of Building Society Statistics* (1978), *BSA Bulletin*

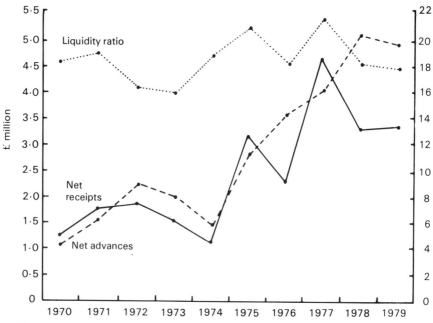

Figure 2.1 Building society net receipts, net advances and liquidity ratio 1970–79.

personal savings throughout the 1970s (50 per cent by 1977), they were able to keep the ratio of cash and government stock to their total assets (their liquidity ratio) very much higher than the 7.5 per cent required by the government. Figure 2.1 shows that although there was a positive correlation of net receipts and the liquidity ratio, there was only an erratic relationship between net advances and the liquidity ratio. The decrease in the ratio from 19.1 to 16.3 in 1971–3, was followed by a decrease in lending in 1972–4. Conversely decreases in the ratio in 1971–2, 1975–6 and 1977–9 did not result in a reduction in lending, quite the reverse. It could be assumed that it was a combination of falling net receipts and increased net lending which caused the ratio to drop. Tables 2.11 and 2.12 show that very generally net receipts tend to be relatively high when share interest rates and liquidity ratios are also high, and at other times all three are relatively low.

Because the composite tax arrangements normally enable large investors in building societies to get more than the market rate of interest, mortgagors can borrow more cheaply than the market would allow, for example in 1978 and most of 1979 they borrowed at a lower rate than that offered to investors, 9.75 and 11.75 per cent compared with 10.00 and 11.94. Nevertheless rising rates of share interest are ultimately passed on to the borrowers although as table 2.11 shows this does not occur every time the share rate increases. Higher rates of mortgage interest result in either larger monthly repayments or an extended repayment period—sometimes to

Table 2.12   Net Receipts, Share Interest and Liquidity Ratios, 1970–9

Year	Net receipts	Ordinary share rates of interest %	Liquidity ratio %
1970	1213	5.00	18.4
1971	1700	5.00	19.1
1972	1801	4.75–5.25	16.5
1973	1512	5.60–7.50	16.3
1974	1165	7.50	19.2
1975	3191	7.00	21.1
1976	2278	6.50–7.80	18.3
1977	4722	6.00–7.00	21.6
1978	3367	5.50–8.00	18.4
1979	3326	8.00–10.50	18.0

Source: Building Societies Association, *BSA Bulletin*

infinity. In 1972, for example, existing borrowers with a 25 year 8 per cent mortgage were faced with a choice of increasing their repayments or extending their mortgage to 29 years when the interest rate rose to 8.5 per cent in October of that year. In April 1973 they had an option of paying even bigger monthly amounts when the interest rate rose to 9 per cent, or extending their mortgage to infinity—a pattern repeated several times later in the 1970s when interest rates increased to over 12 per cent. New borrowers did not have this choice, they had to pay higher monthly repayments. Higher interest rates also prevented many housebuyers from spending sufficient on repairs and maintenance. Because of the extra costs incurred by mortgagors, building societies were often reluctant to raise mortgage rates until the share rate of interest had increased appreciably. But conversely, a decrease in the interest rate paid to investors could have signalled the need to increase the mortgage rate if liquidity was in danger of falling. In the second half of 1975, for example, the net receipts of building societies fell following the reduction in the share rate of interest from 7.5 to 7 per cent, but rather than increase the general mortgage rate to ration the supply of loans, some societies charged higher rates on larger mortgages—the Cheltenham and Gloucester Building Society, for instance, charging up to 12.5 per cent on loans in excess of £12 000, compared with the basic 10 per cent on mortgages up to £10 000.

Figure 2.2 shows that there is a strong relationship between bank rate/minimum lending rate (MLR), the rates of interest on building society shares and mortgages, building society net receipts and net advances, and the price of houses. When MLR is lowered a new equilibrium occurs in the capital market and building society rates usually appear relatively attractive to the marginal investor. Unless building societies immediately decrease their share rates, funds flow into the societies, more money is available for

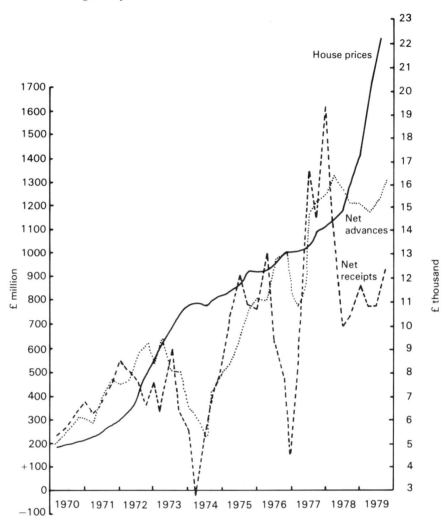

Figure 2.2 Interest rates, building society net receipts and advances (£ million), and
house prices (£ thousand).
Note: House prices refer to all houses at mortgage completion stage.

advances, and because of the consequent increase in effective demand for
housing, house prices spiral. This was evident in the period 1971–2 and
again in 1977–9. The inflow continues until building societies cut their rates
to lenders to restore the original equilibrium. Lower rates to investors are
followed by lower rates to mortgagors, therefore more capital can be raised
for house purchase and house prices spiral (as in 1972–3 and 1978–9). When
bank rate/MLR rises (for example in 1974 and 1976) the process works in
reverse, and the rate of increase in house prices decelerates. There are also
clear inverse relationships between changes in rates of interest and housing

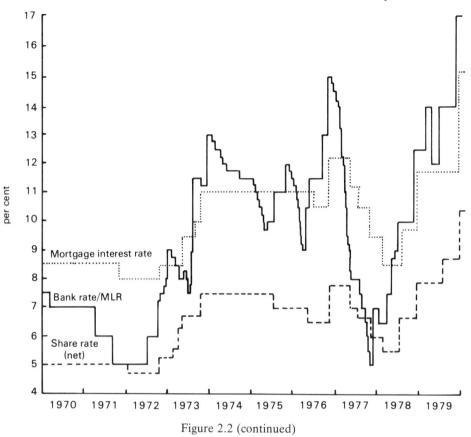

Figure 2.2 (continued)

starts (chapter 7). If investors received more competitive rates (as urged in the Wilson Report 1980), mortgage interest rates and MLR would probably converge with dramatic effect of housing starts.

Near the end of this chapter government policy towards the owner-occupied sector will be discussed, but at this point it is appropriate to note that the 1970–4 Conservative government was faced with a decline in building society lending in its last two years of office, a mortgage famine being inherited by the incoming Labour government in 1974. Labour managed to bring lending up to a high level and sustained it throughout the period 1975–8 (table 2.13). The reduction in the mortgage rate under the Labour government from 12.25 per cent to 9.75 per cent (October 1976 to January 1979) resulted in substantial reductions in monthly repayments (table 2.14)—savings in real as well as money terms.

Building Societies and the Community

In the 1970s building societies came under increasing public criticism. Forester (1976) outlined the form of this criticism, much of which originated

Table 2.13   Building Society Advances, 1970–8

Year	Gross advances (£ million)	Change in gross advances per annum %	Number of advances (000s)
1970	2021		540
1971	2758	+36	653
1972	3649	+32	681
1973	3540	− 3	545
1974	2950	−17	433
1975	4965	+68	651
1976	6117	+23	715
1977	6889	+13	737
1978	8734	+27	801

Source: Building Societies Association, *BSA Bulletin*

Table 2.14   Repayments on a 25 Year Mortgage, 1976 and 1979

Size of mortgage	Gross monthly repayments		Savings (£)
	at 12.25% (1976)	at 9.75% (1979)	
£10 000	£108.10	£90.05	£18.05
£15 000	£162.15	£135.07	£27.08

from the Labour Party. An obvious line of attack was that by increasing their branches, building societies were duplicating their efforts and costs; another was that they indulged in expensive persuasive advertising, and offered savers rates of interest below the rate of inflation—giving them a negative return. A greater cause of concern was that building society practice acted as a regressive redistributor of wealth—benefitting disproportionately the better-off and existing home owners. Building societies have been accused of being rigid and inflexible in their lending policies, and unwilling to lend on older properties, in inner cities, on converted flats, or to non-professional workers. They were criticised for advancing only £4965 million out of net savings and repayments of £6419 in 1975, and for sitting on liquid assets of £5049 million. There was also evidence that societies were 'red-lining' inner city areas (for example in Birmingham, Leeds and Liverpool); and at a national level, the Building Societies Association's own figures showed that whereas only 22 per cent of all mortgages (in the 4th quarter of 1975) were on pre-1919 properties, 33.4 per cent of all dwellings date from that period. (By the third quarter of 1978, building societies were responding to this criticism by allocating 32 per cent of their mortgages to first-time buyers purchasing pre-1919 dwellings.)

A more than proportionate number of mortgages went to high-income borrowers—in the 3rd quarter of 1975, 55 per cent went to applicants with earnings over £4000 per annum, yet only 22 per cent of households in the United Kingdom earned more than that. Likewise a disproportionate number of mortgages were on expensive houses—in 1975, 47 per cent were on houses costing more than £11 000, yet in seven out of twelve regions the average house price was below that figure. And whereas first-time buyers earning more than £6000, and buying houses costing on average £14 000, only had mortgage repayments equal to 16.9 per cent of their income; those earning only £2500–£3000 could only afford to buy houses costing on average £8050 and had to repay the equivalent of 27.2 per cent of their income. Forester suggested that:

> Despite their self-congratulatory image, building societies [appeared] to have abdicated their social responsibility.

He believed that there was a strong case for relaxing the income qualifications on mortgage applicants, and doubted whether this would increase default and re-possession rates.

The Labour government in the 1970s recognised that it could not directly control the number and size of mortgages, the type of borrowers who received them, nor the type of houses on which the building societies would lend. Although regulated by Act of Parliament, the growth and development of the building society movement owed more to the response of societies to market forces than to any liaison between the societies and the government. The Labour Party however was opposed to the continuing social unaccountability of the building societies, and in *Labour's Programme* (1976) proposed the setting up of a Housing Finance Agency to play a positive role in promoting the rationalisation of the building society movement, and to sponsor a searching inquiry into the operations of individual societies. The Party was concerned that the benefits of these operations were enjoyed disproportionately by the better-off and existing owners, whilst the societies had been extremely rigid and inflexible in lending on older housing and towards non-professional workers.

Incomes and Finance

The maximum demand for home ownership among first-time buyers is determined by the largest mortgage which can be raised plus any personal savings. For existing owner-occupiers wishing to move, the maximum demand is determined by the same factors plus the net value of the existing property. For both categories of buyer, the size of the mortgage is normally set at a multiple of the mortgagor's gross annual income. Table 2.15 shows that the ratio between average mortgages and average incomes (1969–79) ranged from 1.77 to 2.24 (first-time buyers), and from 1.64 to

Table 2.15   Mortgages and Incomes of House Buyers, United Kingdom, 1969–79

Year	First-time buyers			Existing owner-occupiers		
	Average mortgage (£)	*Average income* (£)	*Mortgage–income ratio*	*Average mortgage* (£)	*Average income* (£)	*Mortgage–income ratio*
1969	3204	1617	2.00	3460	1987	1.74
1970	3464	1766	1.96	3854	2168	1.78
1971	3914	1996	1.96	4407	2466	1.79
1972	4954	2281	2.17	5538	2748	2.02
1973	6115	2734	2.24	6273	3118	2.01
1974	6568	3231	2.03	6577	3618	1.82
1975	7292	3753	1.94	7409	4299	1.72
1976	8073	4285	1.88	8509	4997	1.70
1977	8515	4800	1.77	9101	5558	1.64
1978	9602	5283	1.82	10 611	6161	1.72
1979	11 281	6290	1.79	11 837	7101	1.67

Source: Building Societies Association and Department of the Environment: Five per cent sample survey
of building society mortgage completions

Note: The figures for average income should be viewed with caution because there is considerable variation
in the income recorded by different societies. For this reason the mortgage income ratios do not accord with
the societies' practice of advancing mortgages of up to $2\frac{1}{2}$ to 3 times the mortgagor's income

2.02 (existing owner-occupiers). It is notable that although existing owner-occupiers obtained larger mortgages, their mortgage–income ratios were less than those of first-time buyers, implying that they re-invested part or all of their capital gains on their old properties in their new accommodation.

Since maximum mortgages are geared to incomes, and mortgages are usually essential for house purchase, it might be expected that there is a fairly constant relationship between average incomes and average house prices. But fluctuations have occurred. Throughout the 1950s and 1960s the house prices/earnings ratio remained steady at approximately 3.75, but between 1966 and 1970 it fell to 3.25 before rising steeply to 4.60 in 1973 (the ratio being higher for the managerial and professional groups, and lower for manual workers). There is clearly a limit to the extent to which average house prices can rise at a greater rate than average incomes. Eventually high prices will decelerate towards equilibrium. This occurred in 1973–7 when the ratio fell to 3.49. Conversely low ratios of 3.25 in 1970 and 3.49 in 1977 indicated that house prices were due to accelerate, which they did in 1971–2 and again in 1978–9 (tables 2.2 and 2.16).

High ratios of house prices to mortgagor incomes can result if the borrower has a wife in paid employment, although societies are unwilling to take the full income of the wife into account since the continuity of that income may be deemed to be uncertain. By the late 1970s about 60 per cent of first-time buyers and 35 per cent of existing owner-occupiers applying for mortgages had working wives. Increased prices and the stretching of the house prices/earnings ratio can be expected to result in housebuyers having to initially repay a higher proportion of their earnings on their mortgage

Table 2.16   House Prices, Earnings and Mortgage Repayments, 1970–8

| Month of purchase | New House Prices | | Average earnings in month of purchase | House prices/ earnings ratio | Initial mortage repayments | Initial repayments as per-centage of average earnings |
| | Average price | Increase on same month of previous year | | | | |
	(£)	(%)	(£)		(£ p.a.)	(%)
April						
1970	5082	6.3	1560	3.25	398	25.5
1971	5630	10.8	1711	3.29	440	25.7
1972	6947	23.4	1908	3.64	521	27.3
1973	10 023	44.3	2179	4.60	850	39.0
1974	11 160	11.3	2480	4.50	1061	42.8
1975	12 273	10.0	3162	3.88	1166	36.9
1976	13 309	9.1	3743	3.56	1219	32.6
1977	14 274	7.3	4087	3.49	1381	33.8
1978	16 643	16.6	4702	3.54	1318	28.0

Source: Building Societies Association, *Facts and Figures*

loan. Table 2.16 shows that the rate of increase in house prices was greatest in 1972/73, the house prices/earnings ratio was highest in 1973, and initial payments as a percentage of average earnings was highest in 1974. Similar peaks were becoming evident in 1978.

Generally as incomes rise, owner-occupiers demand more and better quality housing. In 1978, 53 per cent of all housebuyers were existing owner-occupiers wishing to move—a high proportion of whom wanting to trade-up. But both cross-section analysis (which examines demand in rela-tion to households within various income groups in a given period) and time-series analysis (which measures the available data on housing in relation to income changes over time) suggest that in the United Kingdom, income elasticity ranges from 0.6 to just over 1.0. This suggests that there normally has to be a major increase (or decrease) in incomes before owner-occupiers trade-up (or trade-down); and, except where elasticity is more than 1.0, the proportionate change in income is greater than the price difference between the old and the new property. The price elasticity of demand for a dwelling is also inelastic, probably ranging from 0.26 to 0.60—less elastic than the demand for housing as a whole.

The implications of income and price inelasticity are as follows: Since existing owner-occupiers generally need to increase their incomes at a more than proportionate rate than the price divergence between their existing properties and the more expensive properties they wish to buy, the trading-up process functions slowly. There is great competition for houses in the lower and middle price range, making it difficult for low-income would-be buyers to get a footing on the housebuying ladder. Because of this competi-tion, and the inelasticity of demand for dwellings, vendors are able to push up prices—often faster than the rate of inflation. This in turn necessitates even larger increases in incomes if trading-up is to take place, and low-income households are to filter into the owner-occupied sector.

Tax Relief

A major incentive to owner-occupation has been tax relief on mortgage interest payments, an allowance geared to the standard/basic rate of income tax. During the inflation of the 1970s tax relief meant that the owner-occupier paid in effect a negative rate of interest—in 1975 being as much as 18.15 per cent and never less than 2.47 per cent (table 2.17). In addition, the doubling of house prices in the 1970s underlined the investment advantages of owner-occupation. If the increase in capital value is included, the effective rate of interest was even more negative.

Tax relief on mortgages for owner-occupation cost £1209 million in 1977/78 compared with £1283 million —the general subsidy to council housing (the respective amounts in 1972/73 being £802 million and £592 million). It was clearly advantageous to be a mortgagor repaying in depreciated pounds (with government assistance) in order to own a capital asset which was appreciating in value throughout most of the 1970s ahead of the rate of inflation. In addition, owner-occupiers were free from capital gains tax when they sold (an exemption generally limited to one property); and from 1963 Schedule A tax (on imputed net income derived from a dwelling by its owner) had not been applied, costing the Treasury initially £48 million in a full year, a cost nearer £300 million per annum by the late 1970s. In 1971 stamp duty on house sales was reduced and abolished on mortgages, and in 1973 new houses were zero rated for value added tax (VAT). Owner-occupiers could also qualify for improvement and standard/intermediate grants under the Housing Acts of 1969 and 1974—financial injections which normally increased the value of their property, assistance which was not then directly available to tenants.

Undoubtedly owner-occupation is the most privileged sector and has been for some time. Nevitt (1966) emphasised that the system of housing finance discriminated in favour of the owner-occupier; the Family Expenditure Survey (1966) showed that owner-occupiers not only received the greatest assistance but on average received the highest incomes, were better-off than council tenants and substantially better-off than private tenants—conclusions further supported by Aaron (1972) and Harrington (1972). Mr. Anthony Crosland (1971a), Shadow Minister for the Environment, seemed to be stating the view of the Labour Party when he argued that:

> If our object is not simply to eliminate the worst housing, but more generally to reduce inequality, then the present distribution of financial aid is strikingly perverse. The biggest share goes to owner-occupiers, and

Table 2.17   Rates of Mortgage Interest, 1970–79

Quarter		*Recommended mortgage rate*	*Standard/Basic Rate of tax*	*Net rate of interest after tax relief*	*Annual rate of inflation*	*Net real rate of interest*
		%	%	%	%	%
1970	Q.1	8.50	41.25	4.99	7.7	−2.71
	Q.2	8.50	41.25	4.99		−2.71
	Q.3	8.50	41.25	4.99		−2.71
	Q.4	8.50	41.25	4.99		−2.71
1971	Q.1	8.50	41.25	4.99	9.2	−4.21
	Q.2	8.50	38.75	5.21		−3.99
	Q.3	8.50	38.75	5.21		−3.99
	Q.4	8.50	38.75	5.21		−3.99
1972	Q.1	8.00	38.75	4.90	7.7	−2.80
	Q.2	8.00	38.75	4.90		−2.80
	Q.3	8.00	38.75	4.90		−2.80
	Q.4	8.50	38.75	5.21		−2.49
1973	Q.1	8.50	38.75	5.21	10.3	−5.09
	Q.2	8.50	30.00	5.95		−4.35
	Q.3	9.50	30.00	6.65		−3.65
	Q.4	11.00	30.00	7.70		−2.60
1974	Q.1	11.00	30.00	7.70	18.2	−10.50
	Q.2	11.00	33.00	7.37		−10.83
	Q.3	11.00	33.00	7.37		−10.83
	Q.4	11.00	33.00	7.37		−10.83
1975	Q.1	11.00	33.00	7.37	25.3	−17.93
	Q.2	11.00	35.00	7.15		−18.15
	Q.3	11.00	35.00	7.15		−18.15
	Q.4	11.00	35.00	7.15		−18.15
1976	Q.1	11.00	35.00	7.15	14.9	−7.75
	Q.2	10.50	35.00	6.83		−8.07
	Q.3	10.50	35.00	6.83		−8.07
	Q.4	12.25	35.00	7.96		−6.94
1977	Q.1	12.25	35.00	7.96	13.0	−5.04
	Q.2	11.25	34.00	7.31		−5.69
	Q.3	10.50	34.00	6.93		−6.07
	Q.4	9.50	34.00	6.27		−6.73
1978	Q.1	8.50	34.00	5.61	9.0	−3.39
	Q.2	8.50	33.00	5.61		−3.39
	Q.3	9.75	33.00	6.53		−2.47
	Q.4	9.75	33.00	6.53		−2.47

continued

Table 2.17   (continued)

Quarter	Recom-mended mortgage rate %	Standard/ Basic Rate of tax %	Net rate of interest after tax relief %	Annual rate of inflation %	Net real rate of interest %
1979 Q.1	11.75	33.00	7.87	17.2	−9.33
Q.2	11.75	33.00	7.87		−9.33
Q.3	11.75	30.00	8.23		−8.97
Q.4	15.00	30.00	10.50		−6.70

Source: Bristol and West Building Society, *Factual Background*; Department of the Environment, *Housing and construction statistics*
Note: In 1973–74 the standard rate of tax was replaced by the basic rate. The 15 per cent mortgage rate only became effective for new borrowers from 24 November 1979. Existing mortgagors incurred this rate from the 1 January 1980.

takes the form of mortgage tax relief ... It is clearly a subsidy, since it reduces the cost of buying a house below the economic price. And it is highly inegalitarian in its effects. It brings no help to those on the lowest incomes, who cannot afford to buy in any case; generally it goes to a group which is better off, on average, than either council or private tenants; and within this group it gives the most relief to those on the highest incomes.

The CDP (1976) clearly outlined the effect of tax relief upon the owner-occupier, the Exchequer and the financial institutions:

Owner-occupiers are allowed to knock each year's interest off their taxable income. For example in 1975 each new owner-occupier paid on average over £1000 interest. So the Inland Revenue didn't tax them on their last £1000 of wages. If they paid tax at the (then) basic rate of 35 per cent, £350 was effectively knocked off the money they paid to the money lenders, and paid to the state instead. Those who earned more and paid tax at 50 per cent on the last £1000 had £500 marked off..... In 1974/75 actual tax relief for owner occupiers borrowing from banks, insurance companies and councils as well as building societies was £780 million (and it didn't appear as public expenditure). Left to itself, the market fails to meet the basic need for shelter. A would-be house buyer offering to pay 7 per cent interest for a loan in 1975 ... would be told to go away. The state is forced to top up the interest to 11 per cent to make it competitive. This system of dual interest rates brings mortgage payments down to a level some workers can afford, yet induces money lenders to finance housing they would otherwise avoid.

This system became increasingly attractive to prospective house purchasers as a result of the Housing Finance Act of 1972 and inflation throughout the

1970s. Under the Act (which introduced fair rents in the public sector), rent rebates became based on 'need', but tax relief on mortgage interest was automatic and increased with the purchasers rate of income tax liability and the size of the mortgage, but even average subsidies tilted the balance in favour of owner-occupation. In 1971/72 the average central and local government subsidy to council housing was £50 per dwelling, compared with an average tax relief of £70 per mortgaged house. Despite the cut in the standard rate of income tax from 41.25 per cent to 38.75 per cent in 1971, with the increase in the annual rate of inflation from 7.7 to 9.2 per cent the net real rate of interest on mortgages became more negative—from 2.71 per cent to 3.99 per cent. With rising basic rates of tax in subsequent years, and/or higher rates of inflation the negative cost of house purchase became even greater.

These advantages of owner-occupation were increasingly highlighting the considerable inequality of assistance provided for different tenure groups, and the subsidy to housebuyers was itself highly regressive, for example a basic rate taxpayer in 1978 paid net mortgage interest of 6.53 per cent, whereas a taxpayer on the highest rate (83 per cent) paid only 1.7 per cent in net interest. This produced some remarkable anomalies, for example a basic rate taxpayer buying a £10 000 house with a 100 per cent 25 year mortgage would have to have repaid £1081 (gross) in the first year reduced to £759 (net) or £14.60 per week; but a single man on the highest tax rate (earning say £24 985) buying a £25 000 property would only have to have repaid £680 (net) (or £13 per week) on a gross mortgage repayment of £2703.

Tax relief on mortgage interest not only discriminates in favour of the highest income groups, especially those with the most expensive houses, but inflates house prices; encourages existing housebuyers to trade-up to larger and more expensive properties; and has been a major cause of the decline of private rented housing (chapter 3). The Conservatives favoured tax relief as a means of propagating a 'property-owning democracy', but the Labour Party has for long been opposed to the regressive nature of this assistance. Labour's *Programme for Britain* (1972), the Trade Union Congress's (TUC's) *Economic Review* (1972), and *Labour's Programme* (1973) all proposed the abolition of relief at higher levels of tax to 'bring about a fundamental and irreversible shift in the balance of wealth', and the Labour—TUC 'social compact', *Economic Policy and the Cost of Living* (1973) declared that a Labour government would:

end the scandal whereby the richer the person and the more expensive the house, the greater is the tax relief.

In *Labour's Programme* (1976), the party confirmed its support for a Universal Mortgage Subsidy Scheme, first proposed in 1973. This would limit interest relief to that enjoyed by basic rate taxpayers, and in addition the ceiling for this subsidy would be lowered from £25 000 to a figure equivalent to the average level of house prices, varied on a regional basis. (With the average price of houses rising to over £20 000 by 1979, the reduction would not have been very great had this proposal been implemented in the late 1970s.) The Universal Mortgage Subsidy Scheme would be based on the single annuity principle, whereby a first time buyer would receive the full subsidy (of basic rate tax relief) for 25 years, and if he moved after (say) seven years, his future assistance would be limited to 18 years, and so on. This would limit the extent to which the buyer could gear up at the Exchequer's expense.

It was thought by the Labour Party that these proposals would not be electorally unpopular since the proportion of first time housebuyers in the high tax categories and buying at prices above the average would be very small. It was estimated that £100 million could be saved by these changes—the savings could then be spent on loans and grants to first time housebuyers (under the Home Purchase Assistance Act of 1978), and used to keep local authority mortgage interest rates down to those of the building societies. In 1974 Mr. Anthony Crosland, Secretary of State for the Environment had set up a Housing Finance Review to deal with the main shortcomings in the 'dog's breakfast' as he described the prevailing system of financial support. The Universal Mortgage Subsidy Scheme was submitted to the Review for consideration, but the Review's conclusions, contained in the Green Paper, *Housing Policy* (1977) proposed that the *status quo* should be largely maintained. The Labour government (despite recommendations for reform by the party and Annual Conference) therefore rejected any major change in the system of housing finance in the owner-occupied sector. The Green Paper and the reform of mortgage finance are discussed more fully at the end of this chapter.

The Effects of Rising House Prices on Existing and Prospective Buyers

If inflation slowed down or stopped, there would still be an increase in house prices if public policy continued to stimulate demand for owner-occupation by offering tax relief on mortgage interest, if there was a lack of comparable housing in the other sectors, and if there were only limited increases in the supply of owner-occupier houses. But during inflation, two additional factors stimulate the demand for and therefore the price of houses. First: the mortgagor's debt decreases in real terms, and even if mortgage interest rates increased its real net rate could be negative. Second: because house prices normally rise at a faster rate than other prices during inflation, housing becomes a hedge against inflation—assuming an importance as an investment in addition to providing shelter. It is often argued that higher values are of little use to owner-occupiers as the capital gain cannot be realised—the owner having to face the high cost of an equivalent replacement property. But this argument is sometimes fallacious. Owner-occupiers can realise part (or all) of the gain if they take out a second mortgage; if, when they move to another house, they obtain a larger mortgage (or one with a longer repayment period than that on the terminated loan); if they move to a smaller and cheaper house; or if they migrate to lower price areas. If owner-occupiers realise capital gains greater than the mortgage interest incurred, they would effectively have lived 'rent free', paying only for repairs and maintenance—in stark contrast to tenants, public or private. But even if owner-occupiers do none of these things, they are accumulating wealth (which can be passed on as inheritance), in contrast to non-owners who acquire no property even though they may have paid more rent over the years than the mortgage repayments of owner-occupiers.

Many home owners trade-up for very sound economic reasons (apart from the intrinsic advantages of residing in larger and more expensive houses). For example a mortgage of £12 000 might initially have been obtained for the purchase of a £14 000 house, and if sold a few years later for say £27 000 (with £11 000 still owing on the mortgage), the owner could realise £16 000. If a new mortgage of say £17 000 was taken out and this was added to the £16 000 from the sale of the first property, a £33 000 house could be purchased (with conveyancing and commission paid out of savings or with a bank loan). The process could be repeated yet again in respect of an even more expensive property, assuming that a further capital gain could be made, and the credentials of the buyer and the type, age and condition of the house were appropriate. Existing owners clearly have an advantage over first time buyers. In the above example, a new owner would need a mortgage of £24 000 (which might in total have to come from a number of sources) to be able to buy the first house for £27 000—a much larger mortgage than the first owner-occupier would require to buy his second and more expensive property.

Existing owner-occupiers clearly have a vested interest in rising house prices (not least for the purpose of trading up), and in the continuing supply of mortgage funds at low interest to ensure a buoyant demand. The exchange professions (valuers, estate agents and solicitors) also have a vested interest in rising house prices (because fees go up proportionately), in increasing the mobility of owner-occupiers (because this increases the number of transactions they handle), and in increasing the number of owner-occupiers (because this increases the demand for professional services).

It is often argued that there would be no room at the 'bottom of the ladder' unless people there were moving upwards. But hardship for those at the bottom of the ladder often deters many would-be buyers from becoming owners. From August 1973 to November 1976 mortgage interest rates rose from 10 to 12.25 per cent (gross) imposing a very great strain on mortgagors, many of whom could not afford higher repayments, nor could the societies further extend the number of years over which repayments could be made. In 1976 a number of families were consequently forced to sell their houses, and others faced a lifetime of debt. The prospect of homeownership was receding for many low-income would-be purchasers. Meanwhile home-lessness was increasing. Of the 25 000 families registered as homeless in the United Kingdom in 1976, 14 per cent were former owner-occupiers, and generally councils refused to accept them as 'homeless' if they had sold-up. A high proportion of owner-occupied housing (much of it modern) is of poor quality—not being controlled by the Parker Morris standards (paradoxically the Conservatives in the 1980s have lowered local authority standards down to owner-occupied levels rather than the latter being raised to Parker Morris standards). Owner-occupiers thus often have to incur substantial expenditure on repairs and maintenance, many of whom cannot afford to do so. Up to half a million owners would have qualified for rent rebates if they were paying rents instead of mortgages (Parliamentary reply, *Hansard*, 10 July 1977)—low income mortgagors often facing the worst conditions and highest costs (in proportion to income).

But many would-be housebuyers are not deterred by the risk of house purchase or the condition of property, but they are barred by the high initial costs of deposits and legal fees, and by the difficulties of raising finance, or being able to meet repayments during the early years of the mortgage. These difficulties particularly face working class households. But the needs of all first-time buyers are in conflict with the interests of existing owners. Whereas first-time buyers want house prices to stabilise or fall, existing owners want them to rise; whereas first-time buyers want interest rates to be low, existing buyers who have bought their houses outright are not interested in government measures aimed at reducing mortgage rates; and whereas first-time buyers would like the supply of houses to increase, existing owners have a vested interest in the reverse or in anything else which maintains housing scarcity and residential values. The conflict must not however be exaggerated, as first-time buyers can be expected to change their view of these constraints, after a number of years of ownership, especially when they wish to trade-up.

The preceding sections of this chapter have shown that house prices are determined by what buyers can afford, and this in turn depends upon levels of income, credit and subsidy. If incomes rise, credit becomes easier to get and is cheaper, and subsidies increase—house prices go up. In the period 1971–3, though wages rose, they rose more slowly than house prices, the main stimulant to demand being the explosion of credit with mortgage interest rates being as low as 8.0—8.5 per cent (gross)—effects of the government's Competition and Credit Control Policy of 1971. When the house price boom collapsed at the end of 1973 mortgage rates increased to 11 per cent, and there was a drying up of mortgage funds as investors withdrew their money from building societies to reinvest elsewhere where net returns were higher than the 7.50 per cent being paid by the societies. The rise in house prices decreased dramatically from 36.2 per cent in 1973 to 6.1 per cent in 1974. This, and rapidly rising wage and material costs squeezed builders' profits and brought housebuilding in the private sector down to the lowest level since the early 1950s—leaving thousands of prospective buyers with little chance of acquiring property and thousands of construction workers unemployed.

In the period 1977–9, house prices again rose more quickly than wages, but unlike 1971–3 mortgage interest rates were high and credit was controlled, making it costly for some households to acquire property and to repay their mortgages, and difficult for others to obtain mortgages at all. In the 1970s it became evident that as soon as a not insignificant proportion of low income households came within reach of owner-occupation, the market process pushed house prices beyond their means. Although it might be argued that because the owner-occupied sector has grown from 28.6 per cent of the housing stock in 1953 to 54.5 per cent in 1979, it will continue to grow—possibly reaching 70 per cent by the 1990s, it is clear that very great obstacles remain. The rate at which owner-occupation is increasing is slowing down. In the period 1963–70, there was an 11.4 per cent increase in the owner-occupied stock, but in 1971–9 the increase was only 7.1 per cent. In the absence of a radical change in housing policy, the imperfections of the economic system may make it impossible for many more households to buy a decent home of their own.

Government Policy

Following a steady increase in housebuilding after 1945, the largest number of private sector completions—221 993—was achieved in 1968—a reflection of a high level of demand supported by tax relief on mortgage interest. But there were two obstacles to a further expansion of owner-occupation. First the leasehold system, and second the difficulties faced by low income would-be housebuyers in raising finance.

As early as 1884 a Royal Commission on the Housing of the Working Classes recommended 'leasehold enfranchisement'—the right of a lease-holder to buy the freehold of the land on which his house stands. But proposed legislation to implement this right was continually blocked. The Landlord and Tenant Act of 1954 left the leaseholder in a hopelessly weak position compared with the power of the ground landlord. It allowed a household to go on living in a dwelling after the lease had expired but as a tenant paying a market rent and not as an owner-occupier. In most cases when ground leases expired households could be evicted with no compensation for the home which they had saved over the years to buy. The anxiety and insecurity which had been created by the leasehold system had been obvious for decades. The Leasehold Reform Act of 1967 therefore ended this insecurity by giving leaseholders the right to buy the freehold of their houses or to extend the lease for 50 years providing: the house had a rateable value not exceeding £400 (in Greater London) or £200 (elsewhere); the lease was originally granted for more than 20 years; the lease is of the whole house; the lease is at a low rent (equivalent to less than two-thirds of the rateable value of the house), and the leaseholder was occupying the house as his only or main residence and had been doing so for five years.

To assist housebuyers in general who were not standard rate taxpayers, the Labour government introduced the Option Mortgage Scheme in 1968. The Option Mortgagor is charged a lower rate of interest on his loan (since he would not qualify for a full tax allowance), the difference between the option rate and the prevailing mortgage rate being paid by the government to the institution or local authority providing the loan. When introduced, the rate of subsidy on a fixed instalment mortgage was 2 per cent when the rate of interest was 6–6.4 per cent. But the subsidy increases in line with mortgage interest rates and could be as high as 5.1 per cent if the rate of interest ever exceeded 14.8 per cent. On endowment or standing mortgages the subsidy ranges from 1.75 to 4.85 per cent.

Also in 1968 the Option Mortgage Guarantee Scheme was introduced whereby the government with insurance companies would guarantee the difference between the valuation of the house and the amount building societies would normally lend. By offering 100 per cent advances this was intended to assist those who could offer either only a small deposit or no deposit for a low price house.

In net terms this assistance was not as beneficial as it seemed. Cuts in public expenditure had reduced the amount of local authority lending (especially 100 per cent mortgages) for house purchase from £191 million in 1965/66 to only £30 million 1969/70, and the Option Mortgage Scheme presented housebuyers with difficulties. Although high income buyers were better-off claiming tax relief on mortgage interest, and buyers with incomes of less than £1200 per annum benefitted from an option mortgage, according to Lapping (1970):

> most people near the margin ... seemed to have thought 'May be next year I'll earn more' and decided against the option mortgage. Anyway, for whatever reason, only some 7 per cent of housebuyers (1968–70) borrowed the necessary money by means of the option mortgages.

But summing up the period 1964–70, Mr. Anthony Crosland (1971b) stated that the government:

> gave much increased help to owner-occupiers and enabled lower income families to join their ranks through the option mortgage scheme and the provision of 100 per cent mortgages. In 1970, for the first time—and

under a Labour Government—more than half the households in England and Wales were owner-occupiers.

As a proportion of total mortgages granted, option mortgages reached their peak in 1972 and declined throughout the rest of the 1970s (table 2.18). This can be explained by the increasing number of people who became liable for income tax as a result of large reductions, in real terms, in the tax threshold. Option mortgages were also of less importance in high income, high house prices areas such as the South East of England and Greater London where they accounted for respectively 7.3 and 10.6 per cent of all mortgages allocated in 1977, in contrast to the Northern region where they accounted for 33.6 per cent.

Table 2.18   **Building Society Option Mortgages, Great Britain, 1970–7**

Period	Option		Non-option	
	Percentage of all mortgages granted	*Number (000s)*	*Percentage of all mortgages granted*	*Number (000s)*
1969	6.2	28	93.8	423
1970	6.5	35	93.5	496
1971	8.7	56	91.3	588
1972	20.6	138	79.4	533
1973	19.3	104	80.7	433
1974	16.9	72	83.1	355
1975	15.7	98	84.3	544
1976	15.3	108	84.7	598
1977	14.1	103	85.9	183

Source: Building Societies Association, *BSA Bulletin*

Soon after returning to office, the Conservatives greatly modified the system of housing finance in both the public and private rented sectors. The Housing Finance Act of 1972, by imposing fair rents on local authority tenants, and disqualifying households from rent rebates if their incomes were too high and their dependents insufficiently numerous—indirectly made owner-occupation more economically attractive to a greater number of people (chapter 5).

To assist would-be housebuyers to obtain mortgages at a price they could afford it was essential to keep interest rates down to an acceptable level. In May 1973, the government provided building societies with a £15 million grant to prevent the mortgage interest rate rising from 8.5 to 9.5 or 10 per cent— assistance which may have seemed inequitable to council tenants faced with rent increases up to the fair rent level under the 1972 Act. But in spite of the grant, societies increased the mortgage rate to a (then) record 11 per cent by the end of 1973—an increase that the government further attempted to postpone by persuading commercial banks in September of that year not to pay interest at more than 9.5 per cent on savings of less than £10 000 (to deter the transfer of funds from building societies to the banks).

The government thought that first-time housebuyers would benefit from the introduction of 'pay as you earn' (PAYE) or low start mortgages. Proposed in January 1971 the PAYE scheme (which would have geared mortgage repayments to salary increases) was superseded by a proposal of the Building Economic Development Council—a low start mortgage scheme operated by local authorities under the Housing (Financial Provisions) Act of 1958. This would have involved option mortgagors initially paying (say) £22.36 servicing a 25 year £5000 loan at 5.5 per cent (compared with £31.10 on a traditional scheme), but after 11 years the repayment would have become higher than with the traditional method. In 1973 a further scheme was proposed by the government based on the principal of a mortgagor paying low interest payments of (say) 8.5 per cent to a building society during the first five years rising thereafter by 0.5 per cent over five stages until it reached 11 per cent. The difference in interest charges would be added to the outstanding debt and would have to be paid off over the period of the mortgage. Although first-time buyers would be able to raise up to three times their annual salary (instead of the traditional $2-2\frac{1}{2}$ times), the Building Societies Association was sceptical of the proposal as it recognised that family commitments usually increase rather than decrease with age and that real incomes cannot be guaranteed to increase. By restricting the proposed scheme to houses of less than £9500 in the South East of England and £7000 elsewhere, and to buyers with incomes of less than £3000–£2300 the scheme would have been of only limited use. But none of these proposals took into account that the number of house completions in the private sector had decreased from about 180 000 in 1970 to 108 000 in 1973, and that even greater demand would have escalated prices beyond the means of many would-be recipients of PAYE or low start mortgages. A similar criticism can be made of the government's removal of the local authority ceiling on home loans in March 1971, but this was at a time when house prices had not begun to rise as rapidly as they did throughout the rest of 1971 and in 1972–3.

The increased concern about fluctuations in the provision of house purchase finance, provoked the government to set up a Joint Advisory Committee on Building Society Mortgage Finance in December 1973 (consisting of the Department of the Environment, the Treasury and the building societies) to consider the possibility of creating a Stabilisation Fund. Various possibilities were considered such as using Eurodollars and commercial bank Special Deposits to 'top up' building society funds when they were at a low level, as well as societies being permitted by the Bank of

England to operate with lower cash reserves—measures which in total would have mobilised at least £3000 million for home loans.

The Conservative government thus increasingly intervened in the owner-occupied sector. This emphasised the political significance and social importance of home-ownership, and reflected the government's belief that more resources should be attracted into this sector.

In February 1974, the incoming Labour government was faced with the possibility of the mortgage interest rate rising above 11 per cent. To improve the liquidity of the building societies and to ensure the continuing supply of mortgage finance at a stable (11 per cent) interest rate the government provided a £500 million loan in five £100 million instalments during April–August 1974. The Bank of England charged the building societies 10.5 per cent net interest on the loans, 1.5 per cent below minimum lending rate—the Department of the Environment paying the difference. The supply of mortgage finance consequently increased from £154 million in April to £261 million in June, and the building societies were also able to invest the government loan in the City—making a profit of £150 000 out of public funds—ostensibly to improve their long term liquidity. But like the Conservatives' 'bridging grant' to the societies in 1973, the loan only delayed an increase in interest rates. But this time the increase was not so sudden, the mortgage rate rising to 12.25 per cent, a (then) record, in October 1976. Although both the Conservative and Labour measures may have helped to have ameliorated a politically and socially difficult situation, they did little to solve the underlying instability of mortgage finance.

Whenever interest rates are low and funds are widely available private housing takes care of itself—although the government may be concerned with demand-induced price escalation. But when interest rates are high and funds are not available, the government is forced to assume responsibility. Although there are regular meetings between the Building Societies Association and the government, the government cannot compel societies to hold mortgage rates, cannot firmly control the number and size of mortgages, nor the type of borrower who can receive them, nor the type of house on which societies will lend. But an agreed approach can be reached within the Joint Advisory Committee, for example in March 1978 the government—in an attempt to stop house prices spiralling—pressed the Building Societies Association to reduce lending targets for the second quarter of 1978 by 10 per cent from £680 million per month to £610 million (an amount subsequently increased to £640 million per month in the third quarter).

Despite its willingness to intervene, the Labour government did not however implement the party's 1974 Manifesto proposal to establish a Housing Finance Agency. The agency would have set up a mortgage stabilisation fund to regulate the supply of funds from all lending institutions (including the commercial banks and local authorities) to the housing market. Local authorities as well as the main subscribers—the building societies—would have been able to have drawn on the fund to lend particularly to lower income borrowers, and on older and inner city properties. The fund could also have been used by building societies to maintain liquidity when inflows were low. The government instead relied upon its membership of the Joint Advisory Committee to achieve stabilisation, and upon local authority involvement and legislation to extend home-ownership 'down-market' and to help first time housebuyers.

'Down-market' Home Ownership

The Option Mortgage Scheme (discussed above) continued to be of assistance to low income mortgagors throughout the 1970s—in 1979 16 per cent of all housebuyers took out option mortgages. With the introduction of the 25 per cent band of income tax in 1978, mortgage interest relief became less for low income earners and option mortgages became more attractive, for example the (then) 8.5 per cent mortgage rate dropped to 6.38 per cent with tax relief at 25 per cent compared with a 5.6 per cent option mortgage rate. But the major initiative of the 1974–9 Labour government with regard to down-market housing was the encouragement of local authority lending. Circular 67/74 of the Department of the Environment guided local authorities in the operation of their lending powers and urged them to assist:

(1) Existing local authority tenants; households high on waiting lists and people displaced by slum clearance.

(2) Homeless households, those threatened with homelessness and those living in conditions which are detrimental to health.

(3) Members of self-build groups on completion of their dwellings.

(4) Households wishing to buy older and smaller properties (perhaps with a view to rehabilitation) who would not normally obtain finance from a building society.

(5) Applicants who wish to buy large properties for only partial occupation by themselves—but with conversion into flats proposed.

(6) Households wishing to reside in a Development or Intermediate Area, or overspill area.

(7) Needy local authority tenants who are unlikely to obtain alternative finance.

The highest proportion of local authority mortgages have generally gone to local authority tenants wishing to buy their own council houses. Otherwise advances have been made mainly to low income borrowers for the purchase of older and cheaper property. Local authorities generally charge a higher rate of interest than building societies, but 100 per cent mortgages are more forthcoming. Table 2.19 contrasts local authority and building society lending.

Table 2.19 Local Authority and Building Society Mortgage Lending, 1976

	Local authorities	*Building societies*
Average price paid (£)	6 190	10 181
Average advance (£)	5 640	8 073
Average income of mortgagor (£)	3 400	4 285
Average ratio of advance to price	91%	79%
Average ratio of advance to income	1.66%	1.88%
Proportion of first-time buyers	92%	49%
Proportion of mortgages of 100% of valuation	37%	negligible
Proportion of option mortgages	48%	15%
Proportion of pre-1919 properties	74%	23%
Proportion of purchasers under 25	43%	34%

Source: Local Authorities: Department of the Environment 20 per cent sample survey of local authority mortgages, Press Notice 21, 17/1/78. Building Societies: Department of the Environment and Building Societies Association 5 per cent sample survey of building society mortgages, reported in *Housing and construction statistics*

But local authorities tended to act as 'lenders of the last resort'. As table 2.20 shows, there was a substantial increase in lending in 1973/74–75 (largely because of the drying up of building society funds, and because of social policy), but lending diminished dramatically in the late 1970s. This resulted from cuts in public expenditure—Circular 64/75 withdrawing the general consent to lend to anyone in the previously specified priority groups.

Table 2.20 Local Authority Mortgage Lending, 1973/74–1977/78
(£ million)

	1973/74	*1974/75*	*1975/76*	*1976/77*	*1977/78*
Gross lending	475	789	443	210	157
Repayments	−282	−184	−260	−257	−251
Net lending	193	602	183	− 47	− 94

Source: *The Government's Expenditure Plans, 1978/79 to 1981/82* (1978)

Lending thenceforth became controlled by cash limits. But some councils were able to maintain or increase their level of lending for house purchase. The Conservative-controlled Greater London Council, for example, provided an additional £13 million (out of its total budget for home loans of £36 million 1978/79) in mortgages for house buying in the inner boroughs—100 per cent mortgages becoming available on houses costing up to £12 000 instead of the previous £11 000. In an attempt to offset the general decline in local authority lending, and to revitalise home ownership in the inner areas of up to 200 local authorities, the government introduced the Support Lending Scheme. Under this scheme, building societies earmarked a small proportion of their funds for local authority nominees—£163 million being advanced October 1975–March 1977, £176 million in 1977/78 and £300 million 1978/79, but there was growing concern that the scheme was not working. In 1977/78 only £105 million was lent out of an available £176 million, and only one in three applicants were offered a full mortgage and one in six were refused altogether. This was at a time when local authorities were having to charge mortgage interest at 2 per cent above the recommended rate of the Building Societies Association making it very costly or impossible for low-income households to borrow. The scheme was more successful in 1978/79, with £276 million (of the £300 million available) being allocated. Since the introduction of the scheme, building societies have become increasingly important contributors of finance for the purchase of pre-1919 houses (table 2.21), the local authorities' traditional area of support, but not surprisingly the average support scheme loan was some 15–24 per cent less than the average building society loan (1975–8).

Table 2.21   Loans on Pre-1919 Houses, England and Wales, 1974–8

| Period | Loans on pre-1919 houses | | | | | |
| | Proportion of all building society loans | Number of building society loans | Proportion of all loans | Number of local authority loans | Proportion of all loans | All loans |
	(%)	(000s)	(%)	(000s)	(%)	(000s)
1974	18.7	74	61.2	47	38.5	121
1975	19.2	115	64.6	63	35.4	178
1976	22.9	152	88.4	20	11.6	172
1977	23.5	160	89.4	19	10.6	179
1978	24.0	177	88.5	23	11.5	200

Source: Building Societies Association, *BSA Bulletin*

In 1978, the Labour Party's Home Policy Committee proposed a scheme whereby building societies would make the equivalent of 5–10 per cent of their advances available as loans to local authorities. Authorities would then use this facility to grant mortgages to households not normally eligible for building society assistance such as low income buyers wishing to buy older and cheaper properties. The scheme would replace support lending, whereby building societies lent directly to local authority nominees. It was calculated that the scheme would increase the amount available for low income purchasers from £157 million (the amount of local authority gross lending 1977/78) to £600 million. A similar scheme already exists in Northern Ireland where building societies lend 6 per cent of their advances to the Northern Ireland Housing Executive for re-lending. Block lending of this sort was proposed in the Labour Party's 1979 Manifesto.

Further attempts to expand down-market home ownership included the encouragement of equity sharing and local authorities building for sale— either directly or in partnership with private developers.

Assistance for First-Time Housebuyers

During inflation prospective housebuyers often face both rising house prices (with the possibility of gazumping) and high interest rates, and at times of relative price stability interest rates may again be high if anti-inflationary monetary policy is being applied. In both circumstances, a housebuyer normally incurs a substantial burden of repayment in the early years of a mortgage.

The Conservative's Local Government Act of 1974 enabled local authorities to grant low-start mortgages from June 1975 whereby early repayments were reduced by deferring payments of capital and interest until the later years of the mortgage life. Repayments were to start at about 20 per cent below the current normal rate rising to the normal rate in the sixth year and to 17 per cent after 11 years. The scheme was limited to mortgagors with incomes of less than £4800 (in the South East of England) and £3800 (elsewhere), and on properties of less than £14 000 and £11 000 in the South East and elsewhere respectively. The 1974 Act also made provision for maturity loans whereby only interest is paid throughout the length of a local authority mortgage, and capital is repaid as a lump sum on termination.

The principal measure introduced by the Labour government to assist first-time housebuyers was the Home Purchase Assistance Act of 1978. The Act was not only intended to help first-time buyers who might otherwise be unable or find it very difficult to purchase, but to give them more 'money in the pocket' during the first few years of a mortgage. A cash bonus up to a maximum of £110, and a loan of £600 (interest free for five years) became available. Under the Act those who had saved for two years with a recognised savings institution and had kept a minimum of £300 in their account would have received a tax-free bonus of at least £40. For every additional £100 kept in that same year, there was an additional bonus of £10 (up to a maximum of £110 for savings of £1000 or more. To qualify for the loan the same conditions applied, and when applying for a mortgage the applicant would have to have had a total of at least £600 in savings—an amount which would be matched by the lending institution with a government loan (interest free for five years). After five years the institution repays the government, and the mortgagor repays the £600 over the remaining life of the mortgage. Further conditions attached to the loan included a stipulation that the mortgage should have been for at least £1600 (inclusive of the loan), that it should have covered at least 25 per cent of the selling price of the property, and that the price was below a regional limit set by the Secretary of State. It was hoped that about two-thirds of first-time buyers would be able to qualify for assistance, amounting to over 200 000 households per annum. The minimum savings period began on 1 November 1978, with the benefits of the scheme being available from late 1980s (assuming that the Conservative government operates the scheme).

In November 1978, all first-time borrowers (and particularly those on low incomes) were adversely affected by an increase in the mortgage interest rate from 9.75 to 11.75 per cent. This was in part a response by building societies to the flow of funds into National Savings. In July 1978, the government raised the minimum holding of the 14th issue of National Savings Certificates from £1000 to £3000 (the building societies experiencing a record withdrawal of £1193 million in that month), and in August the Treasury announced improved National Savings provisions—including an increased rate of interest (from 8.5 to 9.5 per cent from 1 October); a new issue of $9\frac{1}{2}$ per cent British Savings Bonds, and a new weekly premium bond prize of £75 000 and an increase in the top level of holdings from £2000 to £3000. As savings institutions, the societies would have become uncompetitive if their rates of interest had not been increased.

The Green Paper

The Green Paper, *Housing Policy: A Consultative Document* (1977) was critical of the lending policy of building societies—especially the over cautious approach to older and cheaper properties in the inner urban areas. It proposed help for lower income first-time buyers in ways which were selectively and broadly adopted by the Labour government. It recommended that interest free loans of £500 should be available to home buyers (if they had saved the same amount for two years and wished to buy a house within a specified price limit); cash bonuses should be awarded to savers; new public and private finance agencies should be set up to raise extra funds for building societies; more low-start and high percentage mortgages should be granted and lending should be extended on older property especially in the inner urban areas, and that the rate of interest on local authority mortgages should be the same as the building society rate—the local authority being subsidised from the general rate fund. Local authorities should keep building societies informed of plans for their areas; provide top-up loans, mortgage guarantees, and improvement and repair grants on older properties on which society mortgages had been granted.

The instability of building society funds was a major concern of the housing finance review body responsible for the Green Paper. They recommended that the societies should achieve a greater degree of stability by such methods as:

(1) Building up large stabilisation funds when interest rates fall. Up to 1977 these funds did not exceed 7 per cent of total building society assets.

(2) Keeping interest rates paid to investors more closely in line with the market so as to reduce fluctuations in the inflow of savings.

(3) Adopting a flexible relationship between interest rates paid on savings and those charged on mortgages, so that (2) could be achieved without frequent disturbance of the mortgage rate.

(4) Raising short term loans on the money market when interest rates rise so that interest rates to investors (and mortgagors) could be left largely unchanged.

The Green Paper did not propose that a stabilisation fund should be set up and run by the government, but that the government could accept the building societies' own stabilisation funds for investment in the National Loans Fund at an interest rate which would guarantee the societies against incurring a loss as a result of complying with Joint Advisory Committee decisions on stabilisation. The Green Paper suggested that in order to increase the supply of mortgage funds, societies should require a mortgagor who moves to transfer the net proceeds of the sale to the purchase of his next property—reducing the size of the new mortgage required, and that societies should be prepared to borrow from insurance companies, pension funds and other financial institutions possibly through a new intermediary body set up and controlled either by the building societies or the government.

A major consideration of the Green Paper was the extent of tax relief on mortgage interest. Table 2.22 shows that the total tax relief and option mortgage subsidy to owner-occupiers is broadly comparable to the subsidy (Exchequer grants and rate contributions) to council housing. The Green Paper reported that in 1976/77 the average subsidy to a mortgagor was £205 and the average subsidy to a council tenant was £210. But whereas the amount of assistance to mortgagors increased with income, assistance to council tenants remained fairly constant over a wide range of incomes

Table 2.22   **Mortgage Tax Relief and Option Mortgage Subsidy, and General Subsidies to Council Housing, Great Britain, 1972–8**

	Owner-occupiers (£ million)	Council housing (£ million)
1972/73	802	592
1973/74	1044	722
1974/75	1213	1188
1975/76	1239	1236
1976/77	1333	1320
1977/78	1209	1283

Source: The Government's Expenditure Plans, 1978/79 to 1981/82 (1978)

Table 2.23 Financial Assistance to Mortgagors and Council Tenants, Great Britain, 1974/75

Income (£)	To mortgagors (£)	To council tenants (£)
Less than 1000	59	120
1000–1499	73	132
1500–1999	91	152
2000–2499	104	137
2500–2999	101	147
3000–3499	129	154
3500–3999	129	148
4000–4999	148	164
5000–5999	179	} 154
6000 and over	369	

Source:Housing Policy: A Consultative Document (1977) Tech. Vol. part 1

(table 2.23), but increased inversely between income bands £2599–£3000 and £1500–£1999.

It is often argued that a tax allowance on mortgage interest is not a subsidy, whereas proponents of this view are in no doubt that council tenants receive subsidies. Whether or not tax relief is a subsidy is purely a semantic argument, but it has all the characteristics and effects of a subsidy. First, the government had £1209 million less in revenue (1977/78)—the same as if it had spent that amount on grants to housebuyers. Second, the government would have needed to have raised that money in other ways (either by higher rates of taxation or by borrowing). Third, housebuyers had £1209 million more to spend. Most of this went on inflating the price of existing houses as only 1 in 5 houses purchased are newly built—80 per cent of £1209 million therefore had no effect on stimulating housebuilding. Although tax relief to mortgagors is undoubtedly a direct benefit, subsidies to tenants are indirect. They are paid to local authorities as Exchequer grants (and are supplemented by rate contributions) to assist them in covering building costs and interest charges, and in some areas tenants cross-subsidise other tenants to a greater degree than the Exchequer or ratepayers assist the local authority.

Prior to its publication, it was thought that the Green Paper would recommend that tax relief should be substantially reduced to mortgagors on high incomes and that the £25 000 limit on mortgages eligible for tax relief should be lowered. The extra tax burden would have probably amounted to £200–£500 million per annum. A mortgagor with an income of, for example £9000 (paying income tax up to 60 per cent) and paying-off a mortgage of (say) £20 000 could have been faced with an increased tax liability of £500–£550 if tax relief were to be restricted to the standard rate. As one-fifth of the 715 000 mortgages granted by building societies in 1976 went to people earning more than £6000, and as 24 per cent of all new mortgages were for houses costing over £15 000 (38 per cent in the South East), decreases in tax relief and a lowering in the £25 000 limit on mortgages subject to tax relief would have affected a very large number of housebuyers. But the Green Paper was a very conservative document, favoured by both the Building Societies Association and the House Builders Federation. It left mortgage interest relief alone on the grounds that the construction industry depended upon it; that tax relief gives help when it is most needed (in the early years of a mortgage when interest payments normally account for 95–100 per cent of repayments); that the high amount of relief which could be claimed by mortgagors on high incomes and with large mortgages was not inequitable in view of progressive income tax; and that changes might be politically hazardous in view of an increasing number of households becoming owner-occupiers and with house prices steadily rising. The Green Paper did not wish to upset 'the household budgets of millions of families', but it seemed to have discounted the fact that reduced tax relief is an essential political counterpart to increased council house rents.

The Reform of Mortgage Finance

Both the White Paper, *Fair Deal for Housing* (1971) and the Green Paper, *Housing Policy* (1977) recommended the reform of the system of financing council housing but largely left the owner-occupied sector alone. But partly because council house rents were increased in response to these recommendations, and partly because many problems in the owner-occupied sector remained unsolved, a plethora of proposals were forthcoming for the reform of finance in the private sector.

Many of these proposals, such as action by the government in ironing-out the glut and famine of funds, the setting up of a stabilisation fund, the imposition of a ceiling on tax relief and no relief on second homes, providing finance for equity sharing, and offering low-start mortgages have either been implemented or incorporated into party policy for implementation should the opportunities arise.

But other proposals have not been adopted or met with favour politically. Shelter (1972) suggested that Schedule A tax should be reintroduced (it was abandoned in 1962) to collect a proportion of imputed rent enjoyed by owner-occupiers. This would provide the Exchequer with a share of betterment, and could lower rates of income tax to compensate most owners, although house prices might begin to fall. The *Sunday Times* (10 March 1974) was more concerned with the supply of funds for house purchase. It proposed that 'fat banks', insurance companies and pension funds should be encouraged to put money into the building societies; the government should also inject money (on a temporary basis); the liquidity reserves of building societies should be freed for lending in return for the government granting societies special drawing rights with the Bank of England so as to ensure a minimum acceptable level of liquidity; and the societies by being integrated into the Bank's monetary controls would enable the Bank to iron-out cyclical fluctuations rather than accentuating them when minimum lending rate fluctuates. It was also proposed that building societies should become more financially sophisticated by offering higher rates of interest on long term savings, charging higher rates of interest to larger borrowers, and providing longer term mortgages during 'times of plenty'. But the *Sunday Times* conceded that it was important that more houses should be built, otherwise increased supplies of finance—as in the past—would only inflate the price of second-hand houses.

Wilson and Braham (1974) suggested that the rate of mortgage interest could be stabilised if building societies were exempted from corporation tax and the composite tax paid on behalf of investors. The shortfall in revenue could be offset by the imposition of a 10 per cent capital gains tax on all house sales.

Mrs Margaret Thatcher, Shadow Minister for the Environment in 1974, promised 9.5 per cent mortgages if the Conservatives won the autumn General Election of that year. Low interest mortgages would have been possible, thought the Shadow Minister, if the rate of tax payable by the societies was adjusted accordingly. Mrs Thatcher also proposed a new home savings grant scheme in which for every £2 saved by the building society investor in an approved scheme the government would provide a grant of £1. The societies considered that pegging the mortgage rate at $9\frac{1}{2}$ per cent would have cost the government £300 million per annum in lost revenue, and Mr Anthony Crosland, Secretary of State for the Environment, thought that the scheme was 'wildly and hopelessly expensive' and costed it in excess of £500 million per annum. But the Shadow Minister had taken into account that there would have been reciprocal cuts in government spending on municipalisation and public sector housebuilding.

The Fabian Society (1974) proposed a new state-controlled body which would have control over the building societies and other mortgage lenders, and would have funds of £2000 million. It would fix interest rates for society borrowers and investors, secure long term deposits from traditional building society savings, and set up a substantial stabilisation fund to remove the 'feast' or 'famine' of mortgage finance.

Mr Bruce Douglas Mann (1977), MP, suggested that emphasis should be placed on helping first-time buyers, giving assistance with repairs, expanding the scope and level of improvement grants, and possibly giving direct subsidies for new house construction. He believed that the government could not have afforded to do this whilst owner-occupiers receive approximately £1200 million in tax relief on mortgage interest.

Except for the latter proposal (and suggestions relating to Schedule A and Capital Gains Tax) all of the above recommendations are essentially concerned with increasing the liquidity of lending institutions and promoting the stabilisation of funds—all ostensibly aimed at ensuring a steady increase in demand for private housing. But the effects of market lubrication are not always as intended. With ordinary consumer goods the market reacts to increased demand and rising prices with a quickly increased supply. But housebuilding may take many months—supply cannot be rapidly increased relative to the existing stock. Thus market forces work by scaling down effective demand by rising prices which absorb extra credit available. The rise in prices may cause some existing houses to be offered for sale sooner rather than later but this simply shifts some of the excess demand and rise in price to a later date. In time, sustained price increases will bring forth a supply of new houses, but by then prices may have escalated generally imposing increasing difficulties for first-time buyers—with a marked excess of demand over supply at the lower end of the market.

The most far-reaching proposal for the reform of housing finance—which fully took into account the above repercussions of extending finance—was offered by Kilroy (1978). He argued that the Green Paper had rejected the fundamental reform of the current system of tax relief on mortgage interest because:

the case for it was dammed by equating fundamental with *sudden*— although the constant theme of evidence submitted to the review had been gradual reform over a long transitional period.

Kilroy advocated 'organic reform' which would involve the following action. First, interest rate relief would be phased out at high income levels eliminating about 10 per cent of total relief and raising £110 million in revenue (at 1976/77 rates of taxation). Only one in nine mortgagors would be affected. A 'universal option mortgage' could be introduced simultaneously, whereby mortgagors pay back interest net of relief. Second, the ceiling for mortgages on which relief is granted could be lowered, the Exchequer saving £5 million if it were lowered to £15 000; £50 million if it were £10 000, and £100 million if it were £8000. Third, for existing owners of long standing whose mortgages have fallen to a far smaller proportion of their incomes than recent buyers, relief could be given at some 'reckonable mortgage rate' or as a fraction of the interest charged. A tapering or sliding scale could be introduced. Fourth, a single annuity mortgage could be introduced to prevent exchange buyers from reverting to the most favourable end of the relief staircase. Mortgage relief would be for a total of 25 years regardless of how many times a mortgagor moved house, for example if he moved after eight years from a £7000 mortgage house, he would be entitled to relief on say a £11 000 mortgage on the new house but only on the ninth year of the mortgage. If he moved after another eight years, he would receive relief on say a £15 000 mortgage as if it were the 17th year of the loan. A single annuity system would preserve the housing ladder but reduce its angle of slope. It would not harm the filtering process, indeed by reducing the rate at which house prices increase it would particularly benefit first-time buyers. Over a period of five years, Kilroy's proposals, if applied, would save the Exchequer a minimum of £250 million per annum.

In the long term the principle of tapered relief would be maintained, but the reckonable rate of interest (or the proportion of the tax rate eligible for relief) would be reduced year by year for all mortgagors, but some relief would be preserved for first-time buyers as they would still be at a disadvantage compared with exchange buyers. To pay for tax relief on mortgages, capital gains tax would be imposed during the life cycle of home-ownership, and capital transfer tax would be applied at the end of the cycle. The sector would become self-financing and there would be considerable savings to the Exchequer. Relief could be diverted to housebuilding and renovation (leading to cheaper housing); could lead to reduced income tax, and would in general ensure that house prices would increase only in line with other investments and so not attract a disproportionate amount of funds away from other sectors of the economy. Owner-occupiers would eventually be on a more equitable footing in terms of assistance *vis a vis* council tenants.

Figure 2.3 shows how Kilroy's proposals could be expected to reduce the level of demand (from DD to D_1D_1), and hence lower house prices in real terms. But supply would be contracted with resulting scarcity. This could only be remedied if housebuilding increased (from SS to S_1S_1)—a distinct possibility if investment funds were injected, and land became available at an economic price for development.

Organic reform would not be incompatible with the proposals of the Wilson Report (1980). If interest subsidies were to replace tax relief, they too could be adjusted to income and be tapered.

Conclusion

Although home ownership has always been a central plank of Conservative policy, it was difficult for the party (when it regained office in 1979) to introduce any major measures to assist house purchase. The Labour governments of 1966–70 and 1974–9 had brought in leasehold reform in 1967, the option mortgage scheme in 1968 and a home purchase assistance scheme in 1978, and (contrary to Labour Party policy) had retained tax relief on mortgage interest up to £25 000. Labour had also stabilised the supply of mortgages—most notably in 1974 and 1978—constraining in turn soaring mortgage interest rates and spiralling house prices.

The Conservatives were therefore forced to concentrate upon trying to increase the rate of housebuilding in the private sector—a task of almost

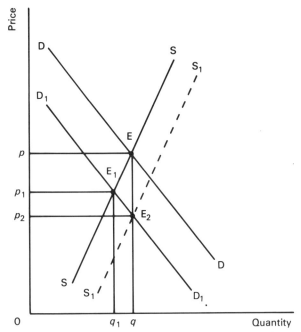

Figure 2.3 The possible effects of 'organic reform' upon the price and supply of owner-occupied houses.

Note: E = Initial market equilibrium.
      E_1 = Equilibrium if demand decreased from DD to D_1D_1.
      E_2 = Eventual equilibrium if supply increased from SS to S_1S_1.

unprecedented proportions as the number of housing starts was running at an annual rate of only 240 000 in June 1979, the lowest number since the early 1950s. In the Budget of the same month—in an attempt to hasten the rate of building—development land tax was cut from 80 and 66.66 per cent to a single rate of 60 per cent, and the threshold was raised from £10 000 to £50 000—a prelude to the repeal of the Community Land Act of 1975. But an alleged motive for dismantling the community land scheme—the shortage of development land—was a myth. In 1975 there were some 850 000 plots with planning permission for private housebuilding (the total not being very different in 1979), and of this figure speculative builders owned 270 000 plots—enough for over two and a half years output at 1979 rates of housebuilding. With this supply of immediately developable building land, it could not have been argued that planning delays were a major constraint on development. But the Conservatives, by increasing MLR from 12 to 14 to 17 per cent within six months of regaining office (with corresponding increases in base lending rates), imposed a devastating burden on housebuilders, offsetting many of the tax benefits of the June Budget and impeding any increase in housebuilding which might otherwise have occurred.

Many potential first-time housebuyers had their dreams shattered in November 1979 when building societies (in response to a MLR of 17 per cent) raised mortgage interest rates to 15 per cent—an all time high. It was ironic that the Conservatives in opposition had only a few months earlier condemned a rate of 11.75 per cent. Unlike previous governments in 1973 and 1974, the government had no intention this time of subsidising the mortgage rate, Mr Michael Heseltine, Secretary of State for the Environment (1979a) argued that:

> there is no purpose ... in attempting to isolate mortgage interest rates from the prevailing economic climate. To subsidise them would simply encourage house price rises and switch the burden from those who have just bought to those who are saving to buy.

It was estimated that a 2.5 per cent reduction in the mortgage rate (as a result of a subsidy to the building societies) would cost £600 million over twelve months. But the prevailing economic difficulties (it could be argued) were the direct result of the government's attachment to monetarism as the almost exclusive means of economic control. Cuts in public expenditure had forced the Conservatives in September 1979 to scrap their manifesto pledge to aid first-time buyers by a Home Savings Grant Scheme, and by the end of the year, the increase in the mortgage rate meant that:

> there would be hardship and anxiety ... Many young couples having or hoping to buy their first homes are probably amongst those with modest incomes who have managed their present repayments only after sacrifices. They will find that the new increases are literally beyond them.
> Mr Roy Hattersley, Shadow Environment Secretary (1979).

With or without the mortgage rate subsidy, young couples were doomed to be the principal sufferers of mismanaged policy. With entry into the owner-occupied sector barred, there was inevitably an increase in demand for local authority housing, and this was at a time when housebuilding in the public sector was at a post-war low and councils were being compelled to sell-off their housing stock (chapter 5) and inflate rents. Britain was without doubt facing its gravest housing crisis for at least four decades.

3 Private Rented Housing

The supply of private rented accommodation has declined from approximately 90 per cent of dwellings in 1914 to about 12 per cent in 1979, and unlike other west European countries and North America there has been virtually no housebuilding for private renting since the Second World War.

Private rented housing includes a high proportion of the oldest and poorest dwellings. The *General Household Survey* (1973) showed that 68 per cent of unfurnished private tenants and 51 per cent of furnished tenants lived in dwellings built before 1919, and that 44 per cent of unfurnished tenants lived in terraced housing and 69 per cent of furnished tenants lived in non-purpose built flats and rooms (considerably higher than the proportions in the other housing sectors). The *House Condition Survey of England and Wales* (1971) reported that of those privately rented dwellings built before 1919, 23 per cent were statutorily unfit compared with 7 per cent of all tenures nationally.

The *General Household Survey* showed that in Great Britain, 45 per cent of private unfurnished tenants and 58 per cent of furnished tenants lacked exclusive use of a fixed bath/shower; the unfurnished sector had the second highest percentage of heads of households aged 65 and over (owner-occupiers who had purchased their properties outright had the highest); the furnished sector had the highest percentage of heads of households under the age of 30; unfurnished heads of households had the lowest median incomes, and 67 per cent of unfurnished dwellings and 41 per cent of furnished accommodation were occupied by manual workers (in this latter tenure the percentage was only exceeded by intermediate and junior non-manual workers).

In Greater London, private rented accommodation is a far larger proportion of the housing stock (35 per cent 1971) than in the country as a whole. In Inner London 49 per cent of the stock was privately rented. The Milner Holland Report (1965) classified the many different types of households renting from private landlords in London. The household characteristics were as follows:

(1) Single people, very young families, the elderly, newcomers, unskilled workers and the very poor. The proportions were higher than in any other sector.

(2) Families with children were concentrated in multi-occupied dwellings.

(3) Families living in a whole house or flat were mainly elderly people who had occupied the accommodation for many years.

(4) Half the private furnished tenants had moved in during the year of the survey (1963) and 32 per cent were attempting to move out. This indicated the extent of the transient sector.

Young families tried to move out of privately rented housing as soon as they could because of the low standard of accommodation and because a high percentage of self-contained dwellings were occupied by controlled tenants and the elderly. In the mid-1960s:

> hardship due to the lack of security of tenure for tenants of privately rented housing in the London area [was] serious and substantial in nature. (Milner Holland Report)

Those who suffered most were families with young children, those with low incomes and newcomers to the metropolis. The Greve Report (1971) further stressed that hardship, and particularly homelessness, was due to the lack of the security of tenure and soaring rents in the furnished sector. The Francis Report (1971) stated that in London, even in the regulated (unfurnished) sector conditions were far from satisfactory. Over 85 per cent of regulated tenancies were in flats or tenements, or in rooms in unconverted houses lacking self-contained amenities, and at least 18 per cent of regulated tenancies had occupancy rates in excess of 1.5 persons per room.

The *National Movers Survey* (1972) reported that 54 per cent of new households had entered the privately rented sector in Greater London in 1972, compared with only 31 per cent in England and Wales. In the capital this was the main sector to attract new households, whereas nationally it was owner-occupation (50 per cent). However unsatisfactory, the privately rented sector, at least in London, provided a stepping stone to other forms of tenure.

Reasons for the Decrease in Supply of Private Rented Housing

During the nineteenth century almost all working class housing was privately rented. Landlords needed to raise about two-thirds of the value of their property on mortgage, and if interest rates increased, landlords passed on the cost as much as possible in higher rents in order to maintain profitability. Gauldie (1974) has shown that rents rose steadily in the period 1780–1918 (even when the general price trend was downwards), and that in the nineteenth century the average working class family paid 16 per cent of their income in rents in contrast to 8–9 per cent paid by middle class families. The majority of private landlords were relatively small capitalists content with a secure return on their capital. An 8 per cent gross return was possible which compared very favourably with for example 3.4 per cent Consols and less than 3 per cent on gilt-edged securities (in the late 1970s a return in excess of 15 per cent would have been necessary to compare favourably with returns on government stock). Until the extension of limited liability in the late nineteenth century, investment in joint stock companies was unattractive to those with modest means. But with the development of the stock exchange and building societies, the expansion of government and municipal stock, and increased investment opportunities overseas, private rented property became much less attractive as an investment. Increased public intervention further reduced the attraction of housing investment. The appalling quality of rented housing led the government (from the Public Health Act of 1848 onwards) to increase its control over housing in an attempt to improve standards. These controls resulted in *either* higher rents (to compensate landlords for improvement costs incurred) *or* a decrease in the supply of accommodation if investment became no longer profitable. In the twentieth century the factors which have led to the decline of the private rented sector have been numerous:

(1) *Slum clearance* Since the end of the nineteenth century and particularly since the 1930s many hundreds of thousands of houses have been demolished, with demand being diverted from the private to the public rented sector, or to owner-occupation.

(2) *Policies aimed at dealing with overcrowding* The Housing Acts of 1961, 1964 and 1969 increased controls over multi-occupation, and consequently reduced the number of private tenants. Landlords often diverted supply to the owner-occupied sector as a response to the constrained rent income, and demand was diverted mainly to the public sector.

(3) *Housing rehabilitation* Particularly in the early 1970s, housing improvement grants were often taken-up by landlords for the purpose of 'gentrifying' property. In Inner London, for example, tenants were displaced, the dwelling improved with the aid of a grant, and the rehabilitated building sold for owner-occupation. The combination of the provisions of the Housing Act 1969 and the housing price boom of 1971–3 led to a substantial diversion of supply away from the private rented sector (see chapter 8).

(4) *The unattractiveness of investing in private rented housing*   It has already been stated that there was an aversion to invest in this sector towards the end of the last century. In this century investment in private rented housing has been even less attractive. Greve (1971) recorded that 130 000 houses per annum were built in England and Wales in the period 1901–6, and the number fell to 100 000 (1907–10) and 60 000 (1911–14)—almost all the houses being built to rent. Rising standards, the higher cost of construction and rent control adversely affected production after the First World War. The price of new houses increased fourfold between 1914 and 1920, and economic rents would have been beyond the means of most would-be tenants. The Housing and Town Planning Act of 1919 enabled local authorities to partly make good the deficiency of supply by giving them powers to provide subsidised housing for the needs of the working class.

(5) *The cost of repairs and maintenance*   Inflation since the Second World War has increased these costs and driven many landlords out.

(6) *The desire to own ones own house*   Home ownership became a reality for an increasing proportion of the total population in the 1930s as interest rates were low, and land, materials and labour were cheap. Planning legislation did little to impede extensive residential sprawl.

(7) *Subsidies and tax allowances*   The benefit of subsidies to council tenants and tax advantages to building societies and mortgagors put local authority tenants and owner-occupiers in a comparatively privileged position compared with the private tenant and landlord. Only since 1973 have private tenants received rent allowances, yet landlords were not able to set a 'depreciation allowance' against taxation as it was assumed that a property lasts for ever. The lack of an allowance encourages landlords to sell for owner-occupation and this was even apparent when rents were decontrolled, 1957–65.

It has been argued, however, that rent control and regulation has been the major cause of the decline of this sector.

The Unfurnished Sector

Rent Control and Decontrol, 1915–39

Rent control was introduced in 1915 by the Increase of Rent and Mortgage Interest (War Restrictions) Act. Rents were controlled at 1914 levels on property where rateable values were less than £35 in London, £30 in Scotland and £26 elsewhere in the United Kingdom (table 3.1). If

Table 3.1 Legislation Controlling Rents, 1915–38

Year of Rent Act	*Major provisions*		*Rateable value £*		
			London	Scotland	Elsewhere
1915	Rents controlled at 1914 levels	Not exceeding	35	30	26
1920	Rent controls continued	Not exceeding	105	90	78
1923	Decontrol by possession; letting freed from control when tenant left				
1933	(a) Decontrol of houses	Not below	45	45	45
	(b) Decontrol by possession	Not below	45	35	35
	(c) Decontrol on registration of possession	Not below	35	20	20
	(d) No decontrol by possession unless decontrolled 1923 to 1933, and registered	Not below	20	20	20
1938	(a) Decontrol of houses	Not below	35	20	20
	(b) No decontrol by possession or self-contained dwellings	Not exceeding	35	20	20

improvements were made or the rates increased landlords were partly exempt from this control. Mortgage interest rates were also fixed and building societies had restrictions placed on foreclosure. It was hoped that these emergency measures would protect tenants from high rents or displacement during a national housing shortage, and that the legislation would be repealed within six months from the end of the war. The effect of the Act upon the landlord's profit is not clear. It may not have been substantial as mortgage interest costs were pegged, but the measures indicated to landlords that government was prepared to respond to the immediate needs of the majority—the tenants—and that rent control even during 'normal' economic times could not be ruled out. The Act therefore discouraged investment in rented property. The Increase of Rent and Mortgage Interest (Restrictions) Act of 1920 substantiated these fears. Rent control was continued into peacetime and applied to properties with rateable values of less than £105 in London, £90 in Scotland and £78 elsewhere, but the increase was more a reflection of increased property values and re-rating than any significant extension of control. Protection was extended however to any relative of the statutory tenant who had been resident in the dwelling for six or more months at the time of the tenant's death, but there could be no further extension after the death of the relative. The Onslow Report (1923) confirmed that rent control deterred investment in new housing. It stated that the 1915 and 1920 Acts had made private enterprise reluctant to perform its traditional function of supplying working class housing, but warned that instant decontrol would cause hardship.

The Rent and Mortgage Interest (Restrictions) Act of 1923 generally continued the policy of rent control, but there was immediate decontrol if the landlord gained possession, or if sitting tenants accepted a lease of two years or more, or if a lease was granted fulfilling certain conditions. The Act remained in force for ten years. The Marley Report (1931) investigated the working of the Act, and showed that of the 1.5 million houses built from 1918 to 1931, 600 000 local authority dwellings constituted virtually all the new accommodation for the working classes. Rent control was clearly deterring investment in low-income housing, although the 1923 Act had worked well for middle-income housing where a large measure of decontrol had not caused hardship to tenants, whilst it encouraged private developers/landlords to increase supply. The Report proposed that rents should be immediately decontrolled where supply exceeded demand (usually in the case of large houses); rents should be decontrolled when landlords obtain vacant possession (in the case of medium size houses where supply equalled demand), and rents should continue to be controlled where demand exceeded supply (usually in the case of small houses). Following these proposals, the Rent and Mortgages Restrictions (Amendment) Act of 1933 divided houses into three classes. Class A houses (the most expensive properties) were decontrolled immediately: Class B houses (those inter-mediate in price) were decontrolled on vacant possession, and Class C houses (those with rateable values less than £20 in london and £13 else-where) remained controlled, regardless of whether there was a change of tenant. The Act was to remain in force until 24 June 1938 and no longer.

The Ridley Report (1938) examined the working of the 1933 Act and was critical of the effects of the control of Class B houses. The Increase of Rent and Mortgage Interest (Restrictions) Act of 1938 consequently decontrolled the higher rent houses in Class B (those with rateable values above £35 in London and £20 elsewhere), but abolished decontrol by vacant possession of the lower rent self-contained dwellings in that class.

In the period 1923–38 approximately 4.5 million dwellings had been decontrolled, and investment in the development of medium and high rent housing had become attractive. There were still however 4 million controlled dwellings, and at the lower end of the market properties were mainly pre–1914 in origin, usually terraced, in poor condition and lacking basic amenities.

Rent Control 1939–57

With the outbreak of the Second World War, the Rent and Mortgage Interest Restriction Act of 1939 abolished decontrol by vacant possession and extended rent control to over 10 million dwellings with rateable values

Table 3.2   Legislation Controlling and Regulating Rents, 1939–65

Year of *Rent Act*	*Major provisions*		*Rateable value £*		
			London	*Scotland*	*Elsewhere*
1939	Rents controlled	Not exceeding	100	90	75
1957	Rents decontrolled	Not below	40	40	30
	Owner-occupied houses partly let				
	New unfurnished dwellings				

	Remaining tenancies had rents
	   fixed at twice their 1939
	   rateable value				

1965	Rent regulation	Not exceeding	400	200	200
	Rent control continued	Not exceeding	110	80	80

of less than £100 in London, £90 in Scotland and £75 elsewhere (table 3.2). Until 1957 the rents of these properties were frozen at their 1939 level but the general price level had increased by 97 per cent by 1951. The principal economic effects of government intervention in the private rented sector were clear:

(1) Rent restriction at the time it was introduced was at the market level, but over a period and with inflation hypothetical market rents rose further and further above controlled rents and created scarcity ($q_1 - q$ in figure 3.1).

(2) The scarcity of private rented accommodation diverted demand to other sectors of the housing market. Unsatisfied low income households increased demand for local authority housing or (until the Rent Act of 1974) for uncontrolled furnished accommodation, and higher income households increased demand for owner-occupied housing. One wonders what proportion of the 54 per cent of households which are now owner-occupiers would have preferred to have been private tenants if satisfactory rented accommodation had been available. Scarcity also rendered many households homeless, especially when inflation widened the scarcity gap, impeded the increase in the supply of local authority housing and put owner-occupation further out of reach of low-income families.

(3) During inflation, there was a transfer of income from landlords to tenants, as the formers' money rent was fixed and fell in real terms, and the latters' money wage or salary normally rose and usually also increased in real terms. Because of rising costs, the landlords ability and incentive to repair and maintain his property was reduced. Housing consequently deteriorated in quality and whole areas of rented accommodation degenerated into slums. But as a house was considered to last for ever, landlords could not

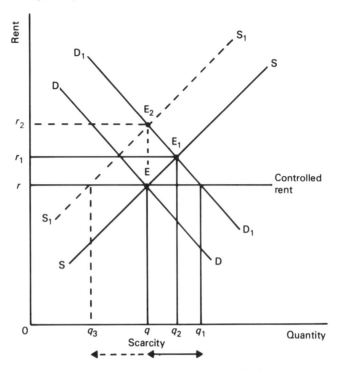

Figure 3.1 The effect of rent control upon the supply of private rented dwellings.
    Note: E = Initial market equilibrium.
         E_1 = Hypothetical market equilibrium after demand
              increased from DD to D_1D_1.
         E_2 = Eventual hypothetical market equilibrium
              after supply decreased from SS to S_1S_1.

claim a depreciation allowance to set against taxation, and even payments into a sinking fund to replace the dwelling were not tax deductable.

(4) Because of the above factors, investment in the building of private housing to rent has been negligible since 1939, but it was difficult to quantify to what extent rent restriction was responsible in view of the high returns on investment elsewhere, for example, office and shopping development competitively attracting long term capital.

(5) There was an inducement for landlords with vacant possession to sell their properties for owner-occupation. This reduced the supply of rented accommodation (from SS to S_1S_1 in figure 3.1) and increased the degree of scarcity (to $q_1 - q_3$). Landlords also converted their properties to uncontrolled furnished accommodation.

(6) Rent control led to an under use of the housing stock. Many small households clung to large dwellings, and many high income tenants benefitted from very low rents. Conversely some large families often with

low incomes had to settle for small furnished dwellings at high uncontrolled rents. There was thus little relationship between household size, income, housing space, amenities and standards. Sometimes a single room in an unfurnished tenancy was let furnished at a rent higher than the controlled rent for the whole.

(7) Rent control produced a number of nefarious results such as key money, premiums, licences and 'furniture and fittings' payments—all ways of increasing the landlord's revenue and control over his tenants without infringing the letter of the law.

(8) Rent control may also have impeded the mobility of labour. Even if the householder was unemployed, secure and low rent accommodation was often preferable to employment opportunities but problematic housing elsewhere.

Rent Decontrol 1957–65

Landlords obviously wanted the 1939 Act to be repealed, and within the Conservative government there was a desire to return to free market rents. The Housing (Repairs and Rent) Act of 1954 permitted landlords to raise controlled rents if proof of recent repair expenditure could be produced and the dwelling was subsequently in a good state of repair. But the Act was complex and generally not successful. The Rent Act of 1957 consequently decontrolled some 5 million dwellings. Its aims were to enable landlords to afford to repair and maintain their properties and to remove the incentive to sell for owner-occupation. The main provisions of the Act were as follows:

(1) Dwellings with rateable values greater than £40 in Greater London and Scotland and £30 elsewhere were completely decontrolled. It was forecast that this would free approximately 750 000 dwellings but the Act actually decontrolled only 400 000.

(2) Owner-occupied houses (about 4.75 million) and any houses falling vacant were immediately decontrolled.

(3) New unfurnished dwellings were freed from control.

(4) The remaining controlled dwellings had rents fixed at twice their 1956 gross rateable value if the landlord was responsible for repairs. Rents therefore only increased to twice the 1939 rateable value (since rateable values were still at pre-war level), but by 1957 the general price level was 156 per cent higher than in 1939 and house prices were 200 per cent higher. Thus, as the Milner Holland Report (1965) pointed out, landlords after a rent freeze of 18 years were only able to increase their rents in real terms by 78 per cent above the level of 1939.

The 1957 Act brought about the decontrol of 2.5 million rented houses between 1957 and 1965 leaving a further 3 million controlled. The Act was intended to increase the supply of privately rented accommodation but caused a gross loss of 3 million dwellings from this sector—1.8 million were sold for owner-occupation and the rest were demolished. There was very little construction for private letting. It is ironic that the average annual loss in 1957–60 was 290 000 dwellings per annum, in contrast to a loss of only 180 000 per annum in 1951–6 during rent control. It was probable that the reduction during decontrol was due to landlords anticipating that there would be some future reversion to control, but this can hardly explain why the loss was in fact *greater* than during the previous period of control.

The Act attempted to correct the distortions in the market such as the under-occupation of large, formerly controlled dwellings by small and often high income households or the elderly. It was hoped that these households would either move out into small dwellings or pay a decontrolled rent, and that large households would move out of cramped (usually furnished) accommodation and into the vacated and larger dwellings. But the properties which became decontrolled were mainly the large sub-divided houses or blocks of purpose built flats and these were sold for owner-occupation. Young and low-income married couples were particularly affected because they could neither afford to buy their own home nor easily find a vacant controlled dwelling.

Tenants of decontrolled accommodation were often faced with either higher rents which led to a diversion of demand to other sectors of the housing market (often to cheaper but less adequate housing) or notices to quit and threats if other accommodation could not be found. Tenants of controlled properties, usually the poorest housing, were frequently subjected to notices to quit, false accusation of rent arrears, deceptive offers of cash or alternative housing, smoking out and other forms of harassment.

Greve (1965) argued that evictions were particularly a result of rent decontrol. The Rent and Mortgage Interest (Restrictions) Act of 1923 which brought about limited decontrol, necessitated the provisions of the Prevention of Eviction Act of 1924, and similarly the 1957 Act brought forth the need for protective legislation—the Landlord and Tenant (Temporary Provisions) Act of 1958 which was applied to tenants of certain decontrolled properties. But slum landlords were able to exploit the scarcity of low rent housing in the inner areas of large cities often by criminal means. The plight of the private tenant was eventually acknowledged by the government, and it appointed the Milner Holland Committee in 1963 to investigate the housing market and particularly the private rented sector in Greater London. Its report paved the way for the repeal of the 1957 Act and the introduction of new rent legislation.

Rent Regulation 1965–70

The Rent Act of 1965 (consolidated by the Rent Act of 1968) was one of the most important pieces of legislation introduced by the 1964–70 Labour government. Rent regulation was to apply to unfurnished dwellings where the rateable value was less than £400 in Greater London and £200 elsewhere (table 3.2). Those properties which had not been decontrolled by the 1957 Act remained controlled. Regulated rents were 'frozen' at the amount payable in 1965 and for new tenancies rents were to be equal to the amount payable under the previous regulated tenancy. The Act implemented a proposal of the Milner Holland Report that there should be security of tenure for unfurnished tenants (this was to apply to both controlled *and* regulated tenancies).

Machinery was set up to fix and review rents for regulated tenants. Rents were to be assessed and registered by a Rent Officer after an application by a tenant, a landlord or both. The Rent Officer was to objectively assess a 'fair rent', although there was no fixed formula available to enable him to determine what was 'fair'. Officers were to have regard 'to all circumstances (other than personal circumstances) and in particular to the age, character and locality of the dwelling house and its state of repair'. Scarcity value had to be disregarded, therefore the 'fair rent' was to equal the hypothetical market rent which would result if supply and demand were in equilibrium in the area concerned. No account should be taken of any improvements carried out by the tenant or any damage caused by him. Rent Officers could also fix the rent of a new tenancy (where there had not been a regulated tenancy for the previous three years) if the parties were unable to agree amongst themselves. If the tenant, or landlord, or both disagreed with the Rent Officer's assessment of a 'fair rent' an appeal could be made to a Rent Assessment Committee. Safeguards were introduced to prevent harassment and eviction without a court order. It became a criminal offence to harass or evict a tenant illegally.

The idea of a 'fair rent' had been established some years before the 1965 Act. The Furnished Houses (Rent Control) Act of 1946 and Landlord and Tenant (Rent Control) Act of 1949 set up Rent Tribunals to determine what was a fair and proper rent mainly with regard to individual furnished lettings. But a fair rent policy extensively applied after 1965 to unfurnished tenancies produced consequences not envisaged by the government.

Although there were 192 360 applications to the Rent Officer between 1965 and 1970, these represented only 14 per cent of the total stock of regulated tenancies. Only 30 per cent of the applicants were tenants and 31 per cent of total applications resulted in rent reductions—the rest resulting in rent increases. But where tenants did apply, 86 per cent of their applications led to a reduction in rents. Landlords, often with professional assistance, also made much greater use of the appeal procedure. There were 12 819 assessments referred to the Rent Assessment Committees, and in most cases the committees accepted the landlord's plea and raised the level of fair rents. A high proportion of tenants may either have been unaware of the provisions of the 1965 Act or have been unwilling to oppose an increase in rent due to their fear of harassment or unlawful eviction, fear of the Rent Officer, satisfaction with their rent or they may have been more concerned with repairs rather than rents. Under the 1965 Act only 580 cases of harassment and 457 cases of unlawful eviction had been heard in the courts by 30 June 1969. Sentences of imprisonment were very few, only five between 1965 and 1970, and average fines were hardly punitive, falling from £26.50 in 1967 to £16.75 in 1970 for harassment, and from £22.75 to £15.75 for unlawful eviction.

During an inflationary period, Rent Officers had an enormous responsibility to ensure that their assessment of fair rents was as realistic as possible, and this was no easy task as rent levels had to be fixed for three years. There was almost inevitably a lack of consistency, and it was a doubtful advantage that many officers lacked professional qualifications and had to rely on their impartial but non-expert judgement.

The Rent (Control of Increases) Act of 1969 ensured that there would be an element of control over the Rent Officer's power to increase rents. For a rent increase registered in 1970, only a third (or 37.5p if greater) could be added at once, another third (or 37.5p) a year later, and the balance paid in 1972. For an increase registered in 1971, one-third had to be paid at once and the balance in 1972. Landlords of controlled tenancies (with rents pegged to 1939 or 1957 levels) were permitted to increase their rent if they rehabilitated their properties up to a 12 point standard with the aid of improvement grants under the Housing Act of 1969 (see chapter 8). They could *either* charge an annual rent equal to the new gross rateable value plus 12.5 per cent of their share of the authorised improvement cost *or* in consultation with the local authority fix a rent equivalent to a hypothetical market rent less the inflationary effect of any local shortage of similar accommodation. But the rent could be subsequently assessed by the Rent Officer (if the tenancy was unfurnished) or the Rent Tribunal (if it was furnished). Although most local authorities preferred to award grants in respect of unfurnished dwellings, landlords favoured the improvement of furnished lettings where returns on investment were greater and where security of tenure was least. Alternatively landlords sold rehabilitated property for owner-occupation.

The 1965 Act was intended to benefit both tenants and landlords, and to enable the market to function without producing the adverse effects of the 1957 Act. Donnison (1967) explained that:

unlike rent control, which was designed to freeze a market, thus eventually depriving its prices of any systematic or constructive meaning, rent regulation was designed to recreate a market in which the overall pattern of prices responds to changes in supply and demand, while the local impact of severe and abnormal scarcities is kept within bounds. .. The first task of those responsible for regulating rents is to bring down some of the highest to a level that is rationally related to those that are freely determined in the open market.

But within the major cities, fair rents were being assessed at well below hypothetical market rents. Rent regulation failed to take supply and demand into account. Because of the resulting low returns on investment in unfurnished rented housing, landlords were deterred from continuing to supply accommodation in this sector. On obtaining vacant possession, or by means of harassment and 'winkling' (offering deceptive cash sums to tenants to quit), landlords sold their properties for owner-occupation or to larger landlords, or converted them into uncontrolled furnished dwellings. Outside of the luxury and controlled sectors, private rented housing was becoming almost extinct. The 1965 Act, like the 1939 and 1957 Acts, failed to safeguard this sector for the working classes. Scarcity had resulted from the same demand and supply interrelationship which had characterised controlled rents (figure 3.1), and unfurnished properties were being diverted to other sectors no less rapidly than during the period 1957–65.

Rent Policy 1970–4

In order to review and report on the working of the 1965 Act and to consider any possible amendments to the legislation, the Francis Committee was constituted in 1969 and its report was published in 1971. The Report showed that by 1970, 320 Rent Officers and 450 supporting staff had been appointed in England and Wales, and the service was costing £1.6 million per annum. It found that whereas initially Rent Officers assessed the scarcity element as a percentage of market rent and made the proportionate deduction to establish the fair rent, this had been discontinued. It had been replaced by an analysis of comparables involving an appraisal of market rents (where no scarcity existed) and a consideration of a reasonable return with regard to capital value, economic cost and gross value. On average, registered fair rents were determined at about 20 per cent lower than market rents. Nevertheless in 40 per cent of the upward rent assessments there had been increases of more than 50 per cent, and in only 10 per cent of downward assessments were rents reduced by more than a half.

Although the Francis Report found that 50 per cent of the regulated and furnished tenancies in the conurbations were managed by landlords or agents with more than 100 tenants, and that the large landlord extracting high rents was very much extant, it confirmed the belief that the supply of private rented unfurnished accommodation was drying up, presumably because other forms of investment were more attractive. It referred to the *London Weekly Advertiser* where advertised unfurnished dwellings had fallen from 90 per cent in 1963 to 5 per cent in 1970 of the total available to let. To help slow down this reduction or prevent the further deterioration in the quality of these dwellings, the Report recommended that the 1.3 million controlled tenancies in England and Wales became regulated, and that landlords and tenants should agree to a rent or be free to apply to the Rent Officer for a fair rent assessment and registration.

The Conservative government's White Paper, *Fair Deal for Housing* (1971) accepted the broad recommendations of the Francis Report and claimed that its proposals presented a radical change in housing policy creating conditions for:

> a final assault on the slums, the overcrowding, the dilapidation, and the injustice that . . . scar the housing scene.

It proposed that controlled rents should be brought up to fair rent levels. The concept of a fair rent remained virtually unchanged, that was:

> the likely market rent that a dwelling could command if supply and demand for rented accommodation were broadly in balance in the area concerned.

Controlled rents had been barely covering the cost of insurance and maintenance, and many landlords of controlled tenants receiving 1957 rents were poorer than the tenant who enjoyed a very low rent at the landlord's expense. Rent control had undoubtedly accelerated the deterioration of older houses. The White Paper stressed that if control continued, the effort involved in removing slums would be offset by the drift into slumdom of the controlled dwellings.

The Housing Finance Act of 1972 implemented the major proposals of the White Paper. It too acknowledged that:

> more and more private dwellings [had] fallen into disrepair, to the serious disadvantage of the tenant. Some [had] become unfit and [had] been lost to the housing market altogether.

In an attempt to remedy this, the Act stipulated first that most controlled tenancies were to become regulated. Rents were to rise up to fair rent levels by £2 per week from 1 January 1973, and up to a further £2 per week in each of the succeeding two years. If a tenant and landlord agreed between themselves to a rent increase, the rent would have to be registered with the local authority, but if they failed to agree, the Rent Officer would have to assess the fair rent level. Alternatively local authorities could refer proposed registered rents to the Rent Officer if they seemed unreasonably high. The higher rateable value properties were to be the first to be converted to regulated tenancies, and only those dwellings statutorily unfit and scheduled for clearance were to remain controlled. After three years, the landlord or tenant could apply for the cancellation of the registration, and a new fair rent could either be negotiated or assessed by the Rent Officer—in either case being subsequently registered. The provisions of the 1965 Act still applied to existing regulated and exempt tenancies (table 3.3).

Table 3.3 Legislation Regulating Rents, 1969–75

Legislation	*Major provisions*		*Rateable value £* *London Elsewhere*	
Housing Act of 1969	Controlled dwellings rehabilitated up to a 12 Point Standard to be de-controlled and regulated	Not exceeding	400	200
Housing Finance Act of 1972	All controlled tenancies to be decontrolled and regulated	Not exceeding	400	200
1973	Rent regulation extended to higher rateable value properties	Not exceeding	1500	750
Rent Act of 1975	Rent regulation extended to furnished tenancies	Not exceeding	1500	750

The second main provision of the Act was that from 1 January 1973 unfurnished private tenants were able to apply to local authorities for rent allowances. A tenant was assessed as having a 'needs allowance' for himself and his wife of £13.50, and £2.50 for each child. When this was the same as his gross income he would pay 40 per cent of the rent on his dwelling. If his income was more than the needs allowance he would pay 40 per cent of his rent plus 17p for every pound his income exceeded his allowance. If his income was less, he paid 40 per cent of his rent minus 25p for every pound it fell below the allowance. Some families would pay no rent at all and even tenants with an income of £50–£55 per week would receive allowances if they had five or more children. In addition, supplementary benefits were extended. Already there were 250 000 tenants (both in the private and public sectors) receiving supplementary benefits, and a further 500 000 in the unfurnished private sector might become eligible. Benefits were calculated on the tenant's weekly rent, net of any amounts paid in rates, water rates, furniture or services unless these were an integral part of the tenancy. It was not necessary for landlords to be told that their tenants were receiving allowances/benefits, and the Act was intended to ensure that because of these payments families would no longer face eviction because thay could not afford the rent.

It was argued that the legislation would not only bring about an improvement in the quality of former controlled dwellings but that:

> the many elderly, relatively poor, one-house landlords who are stuck with sitting tenants in their own homes will be rescued from what has become an intolerable situation.

(Rogaly, 1971).

In attempting to achieve these aims the Conservative government was able to do what previous Labour legislation had been inhibited from doing—subsidising the private tenant. Lapping (1970) had suggested that:

> to subsidise the poorest tenants . . . was an unacceptable policy for any . . . [Labour] . . . Minister of Housing if he was likely to face the accusation within his own party that 'subsidising these tenants merely enabled them to pay higher rents and so subsidised the private landlord'. It was because of arguments like this that the government [in the period 1965–70] failed to respond to the Milner Holland report's statement that insufficient private money was going into housing—especially housing to let.

In West Germany, France and parts of the United States, private landlords are directly subsidised to enable them to provide cheap rented housing, and in return they are prepared to abide by conditions laid down by the government regarding security of tenure, type of household, and the standard of accommodation. In Britain, local authorities had not had full responsibility for the total rented housing stock in their areas, only for that which they owned. This administrative inadequacy was partially tackled by the 1972 Act with the introduction of rent allowances. By providing landlords with a higher return, these 'subsidies' may have been seen as the first stage in attracting private capital back into rented housing (or at least discouraging it from leaving the sector). But although the Conservatives saw the legislation (which also included some radical changes in the financing of local authority housing) as:

> the most important reform in housing this century.
> (Mr Peter Walker, Secretary of State for the Environment, 1971).

it met with considerable opposition, being condemned as a reactionary and socially divisive measure by Mr Anthony Crosland, Shadow Minister for the Environment. Such different interpretations reflected more than a difference of opinion over detail, they represented a polarisation of basic principles.

The adoption of 'means testing' (on a hitherto unprecedented scale) in determining rent allowances provoked much criticism. It would have seemed logical for rents to have been assessed at a level at which the majority of tenants could afford to pay without an allowance. But rents were likely to be assessed at a level so high that most tenants were eligible for an allowance. Crosland (1971c) referring to the public sector where a comparable system was to operate, forecast that:

> an army of bureaucrats will be employed to pay back part of the excessive rent in rebates. There is a risk of a low take-up of rebates with consequent family hardship. And the creation of yet another means-tested benefit aggravates the increasingly serious problem of working class incentives.

The same could have been said about private sector rent allowances. But accepting that these allowances were to be introduced, Crosland argued that their cost:

> should fall on the State and not, as the government propose, in large part on . . . local ratepayers. The relief of poverty is a national, not a local, responsibility; and its cost should be borne by central government and the national taxpayer.

It was probable that the average rent allowance paid to decontrolled tenants would have been larger than the average rebate to local authority tenants, since decontrol meant that there could have been increases in rents of 400 per cent or more. The average controlled rent in England and Wales had been 90p per week (and £1.50 in London) in 1971, whilst the average fair rent had been £4 per week (and £7.25 in London). Whereas council tenants faced increases of only £1 per week during the first year, private tenants could have faced increases of twice this amount and during each of three years (see above).

The 1972 Act took little account of housing scarcity in the inner areas of the major cities, especially London. An inadequate supply of accommodation enabled landlords to make excessive demands, and high rent levels were negotiated far above the comparables of existing tenancies. The Act allowed landlords to double or treble existing fair rents if a new tenant accepted an alleged market rent. Landlords could then persuade Rent Officers and Assessment Committees to use these rents as comparables. For tenants, this was one of the most disadvantageous aspects of the Act. It was a nonsense to assume that such agreements were voluntary, the terms were dictated by the landlord.

Under the Act it was not an offence for a rent to be charged in excess of the regulated rent. Landlords reported to be doing this merely had to repay the excess rent which had been charged over the previous two years. Tenants paying the excess for more than that period would receive no additional repayment. 'Leapfrogging' was a further aspect of rent regulation which operated against the tenant. If a registered rent was for example £10, but the landlord charged £18, and a new tenant subsequently paid £20, he could only reclaim £2 per week rather than £10 per week.

Although rents of unfurnished tenancies increased at 10 per cent per annum, 1972–3 (compared with 3 per cent per annum, 1965–71), there were marked regional variations. In Lanarkshire, for example, rents rose by 1000 per cent from £34 per annum to £340 per annum (1972–3), and that was on houses built under the Housing Act of 1924 which cost only £300 to build and were financed by a 40 year public subsidy.

But in the period 1971–3, house prices were accelerating at a faster rate than rents. Landlords were increasingly eager to sell their properties (even their high rent luxury flats) for owner-occupation. Tenants were consequently being displaced by winkling and harassment. Sums of up to £4000 were being offered by landlords to tempt tenants to leave, although the average inducement was far less. Lloyd (1972) reported that:

> offers of £500 have become common place to people to leave controlled tenancies for which they have been paying low rents. Lesser sums are offered to higher paying occupants to vacate valuable flats. Such inducements are frequently meaningless to pensioners, widows and the lowly paid who are unable to raise a mortgage or pay market rents elsewhere.

With the severe housing shortage, landlords needed possession to be able to realise substantial capital gains. Short leases were therefore not renewed and flats were left empty for up to 18 months to allow the property to deteriorate so that remaining tenants would leave. Alternatively high rent luxury accommodation (much of which had been recently rehabilitated) was being sold leasehold to former tenants, the freehold often being acquired by property speculators. If leaseholders were unacceptable to the new freeholders, they were winkled out.

The 1972 Act was thus clearly not preserving the stock of private rented housing, nor was it likely to have a favourable effect on the quality of rented housing. Whereas the Housing Act of 1969 permitted landlords to decontrol a property if it was rehabilitated up to a 12 point standard (and about 80 000 tenancies were decontrolled in this way), the 1972 Act would have made decontrol virtually automatic, and not dependent upon the condition of the dwelling, except in the case of very poor housing.

Supporters of the free market also criticised the 1972 Act. They believed that fair rents were often much more than 20 per cent below the market level, and that the scarcity discount was assessed very subjectively as it was difficult to find examples of market rents for private unfurnished property. For this reason, and because of political uncertainty (the 1972 Act possibly being repealed with a change of government), little private capital was attracted back into rented housing—there were more attractive opportunities elsewhere, and not necessarily in property.

The 1972 Act came into force during a period of rapid inflation and at a time when the Conservative government was attempting to introduce a prices and incomes policy. As part of its anti-inflationary legislation, rent increases were frozen in 1973. As Crosland (1971c) had argued:

> rent policy cannot be divorced from prices and incomes policy as a whole. Rents are a particularly sensitive aspect of the cost of living, and their behaviour has a powerful influence on wage claims and cost of living.

Even before the Conservatives lost the General Election of February 1974 their 1972 Housing Finance Act seemed doomed.

Rent Policy Since 1974

On the return of the Labour government, rents were further frozen in March 1974, and imprisonment became a penalty for illegal eviction. The freeze, nevertheless, led to more harassment, and properties became neglected as less was spent on repairs and maintenance. Between April 1966 and March 1974 the number of private tenancies had decreased from 3.4 million to 2.4 million and most of the decline was in the unfurnished sector. The trend was likely to continue as landlords were being increasingly squeezed. Simultaneously, the increased pressure of demand for owner-occupation at a time when house prices were high and rising rapidly made it increasingly difficult for lower-income households (the traditional tenants of private rented housing) to become owner-occupiers.

The Housing Rent and Subsidies Act of 1975 replaced the 1972 Act and introduced new measures concerning fair rents. Rents were to be raised in three stages spread over two years, but landlords could apply for a further increase in the third year. In 1973, the upper limit to Rent Act protection was raised to £1500 in Greater London and £750 elsewhere in England and Wales. This was incorporated into the 1975 Act. Only about 2000 privately rented dwellings in Greater London and fewer elsewhere were above these limits. Rent Officers and Rent Assessment Committees retained their previous functions.

The Furnished Sector

The General Lack of Control up to 1974

Until 1974, furnished accommodation had not been subject to the same control or regulation as unfurnished rented housing. Under the Furnished Houses (Rent Control) Act of 1946, and the Landlord and Tenant (Rent Control) Act of 1949, Rent Tribunals were set up to provide an independent assessment of a 'reasonable rent', but they were not specifically directed to disregard scarcity. Thus the differential between the assessed rent and the market rent was often negligible. Furnished tenants did not have the same security of tenure as unfurnished tenants. At the most, Rent Tribunals would grant six months security to a tenant after the hearing of a dispute, but most extensions of tenure were for less than four months. There was thus no disincentive for landlords to supply furnished accommodation.

Although there was rent control on some furnished lettings if the rateable value was under £400 (in London) and under £200 (elsewhere), it was much looser than in the unfurnished sector. If there was a fixed term tenancy, the tenant had no negotiating rights at the end of the lease, and the landlord was then free to charge the market rent. But if the landlord was willing to accept the rent offered by the tenant when a lease expired, the new agreement became an 'intermediate contract' and the rent became controlled. If the landlord demanded a higher rent, and the tenant objected, the latter could appeal to the Rent Tribunal which would establish a Registered Rent; however, the Tribunal dealt mainly with threats of eviction.

With the introduction of fair rents to the unfurnished sector by the Rent Act of 1965, landlords of unfurnished dwellings were induced to convert to furnished tenure. The Housing Act of 1969 gave a further encouragement to let furnished (rather than unfurnished) after a property had been rehabilitated with the assistance of an improvement grant matched by at least an equivalent amount of expenditure by the landlord (see chapter 8). There was also a tax advantage of letting furnished, as the provision of domestic services such as cleaning and laundering, and breakfast (unlikely to be provided by the landlord in unfurnished accommodation) permitted rent to be taxed as earned rather than unearned income. Also, depreciation allowances in furniture and fittings could be negotiated with the Inland Revenue, or a capital allowance could be made in respect of total cost to be offset against income in the first year of the tenancy.

By the early 1970s, the supply of furnished accommodation was increasing at a rapid rate in contrast to the diminishing supply of unfurnished tenancies. There had been 530 000 households in furnished lettings in England and Wales in 1966, but by 1971 the number had increased to 760 000. Some examples of this increase at a local level are shown in table 3.4. The swing away from unfurnished accommodation was notable. In Wandsworth for example, there was a decrease of 9000 unfurnished tenancies (1966–71), but a gain of 4000 furnished tenancies (demolition and sale for owner–occupation resulting in a net loss of rented accommodation), and

Table 3.4   **Households in Furnished Dwellings, Selected Boroughs, 1966–71**

Borough	Furnished households as a % total households		% increase
	1966	1971	1966–71
Bristol	5.9	10.6	79.7
*Wandsworth	10.0	15.5	55.0
Coventry	2.9	3.9	34.5
Leeds	5.6	7.5	33.9
*Hammersmith	17.1	21.7	26.9
*Brent	12.7	16.1	26.8
*Lambeth	12.1	15.2	25.6
*Islington	16.1	19.2	19.3
*Camden	22.4	26.1	16.5
*Kensington and Chelsea	35.0	38.0	8.6
*Westminster	24.5	26.1	4.9

Source: Census, 1966, 1971
*London borough.

in Bristol there was a decrease of 1000 unfurnished tenancies and a gain of 5000 furnished tenancies (a net gain due to conversion into smaller units).

But because of the scarcity of housing in other sectors, the demand for furnished accommodation also increased. In Inner London in particular, where the proportion of furnished households was generally higher than elsewhere (16 per cent in contrast to 3.7 per cent in England and Wales overall), this gave cause for concern. Figure 3.2 shows the demand for furnished accommodation increasing from DD to D_1D_1, and supply increasing from SS to S_1S_1—demand and to a certain extent supply being diverted from the unfurnished sector. Rents are shown to increase from r to r_1.

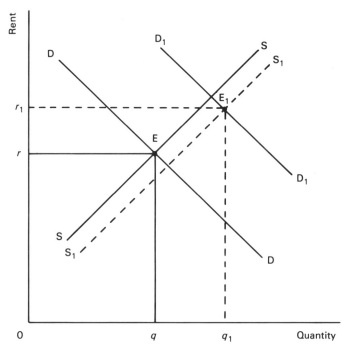

Figure 3.2 The effect of increased demand and supply upon the market for private furnished accommodation.
Note: E = Initial market equilibrium.
E_1 = Equilibrium after demand has increased from DD to D_1D_1 and supply has increased from SS to S_1S_1.

The Francis Committee paid considerable attention to the furnished rented sector. It reported that furnished dwellings tended to be smaller than unfurnished units, 30 per cent of the former in England and Wales consisting of only one room. In Greater London 53 per cent of furnished households occupied only two rooms or less, and in the Housing Stress Areas of London 65 per cent occupied accommodation of this size. Twice as many furnished tenants than unfurnished tenants shared the same building as their landlord, and 26 per cent were living at over 1.5 persons per room as opposed to 4 per cent in unfurnished lettings. In the Housing Stress Areas of London, 100 per cent of dwellings let furnished were built before 1919, and in general furnished accommodation suffered from inferior amenities—58 per cent of furnished households in London shared a WC as compared with 30 per cent of unfurnished households. Rents for furnished accommodation were higher than for unfurnished lettings. In Greater London, 57 per cent of furnished rents exceeded £120 per annum in 1970, and the average rent for this tenure was £200—high when compared with unfurnished rents, and equivalent to as much as 24 per cent of the average net income of heads of households.

There were also distinctions in the characteristics of the households of furnished dwellings as compared to unfurnished. They are generally younger with 43 per cent of heads of households under 25 as compared to 15 per cent; they have smaller families and smaller incomes. They are also more mobile—61 per cent had moved into their 1970 accommodation within the previous 18 months, and only 10 per cent had occupied their dwellings longer than five years, in contrast to 58 per cent of unfurnished households. Furnished tenants were generally less satisfied with their accommodation, with dissatisfaction being greater among families than single persons.

The Francis Report warned that furnished tenancies should not be brought into the fair rent system. It was suggested that as the supply of unfurnished accommodation had diminished following the Rent Act of 1965, so the supply of furnished dwellings would dry up if rent regulation were extended into this sector. It would be even easier for landlords of furnished accommodation to sell their properties for owner-occupation or to convert to some more dubious form of (non-regulated) tenure, as there was greater tenant mobility than in the unfurnished sector. The Committee found that as rents and rates of return on furnished property were higher than on unfurnished tenancies, furnished dwellings (despite their poorer amenities) were in a significantly better structural condition than unfurnished dwellings. It predicted that if rent regulation were extended, those furnished properties which remained would no longer be maintained, repaired or renovated to the same standard, thereby shortening the physical life of these buildings and exacerbating the whole housing problem particularly in the inner cities and especially in Inner London.

These warnings were severely criticised. Des Wilson (1971) of Shelter referred to the Francis Report as:

> one of the most reactionary documents ever to come from a Ministry of Housing Committee,

and he thought that:

> everyone concerned with helping the homeless [Housing Aid Centres, Housing Associations, Rent Officers and Social Workers] in our major

cities will be stunned to hear that the committee has decided not to recommend that the 1965 Act's clauses of security of tenure should be extended to furnished lettings.

The Francis Report clashed with Greve's report, *Homelessness in London* (1971), which attributed the increase in homelessness to the increase in furnished accommodation with its insecurity of tenure. The furnished sector had seen continued eviction of tenants with minimal delay while Court Orders were obtained and implemented. Alternatively, furnished tenants experienced harassment and bad conditions, and were apprehensive about approaching Rent Tribunals. Greve consequently argued that there was a strong case for extending protection to the furnished sector, although exceptions could be made if landlords lived in part of their property. Greve felt reform was particularly necessary in the case of multi-occupied properties owned by absentee landlords.

The Francis Committee based its misleading argument on the assumption that the Rent Act of 1965 *caused* the decline in the number of unfurnished rented dwellings, and that without regulation there would have been no decline. But although the number of unfurnished lettings had diminished by an average of 3 per cent per annum (1965–70), they had declined by 3.5 per cent per annum in the years immediately prior to regulation. The Committee's analysis (illustrated in figure 3.3) may therefore have seemed syllogistic to critics in 1971. *DD* and *SS* are the demand and supply of furnished dwellings, and their intersection determines the market rent (r) and availability of accommodation (q). If a regulated rent (r_1) is introduced at say 20 per cent below the market rent, scarcity will result ($q_1 - q_2$). The scarcity gap would widen to $q_1 - q_3$ if landlords reduced supply to S_1S_1 by withdrawing from the ordinary furnished rented sector. Critics of the Report argued that this would not happen as landlords would not wish to divert their properties to the unfurnished sector (many had originally been unfurnished), nor would furnished accommodation be easily sold off as the Committee feared. However, critics did not take into account that the supply of furnished accommodation might decline because landlords faced with rent regulation would prefer to either occupy the whole of the property themselves or leave it empty, and it was probable that given a house price boom, deconversion for owner-occupation would be feasible.

It was no surprise that following the Francis Committee's recommendations, the Housing Finance Act of 1972 excluded furnished tenancies from rent regulation and the security of tenure enjoyed by unfurnished tenants. The consequent problems of furnished tenants were centred in London which disproportionately contained 40 per cent of the 760 000 furnished lettings in England and Wales in 1971. In London the hotel boom of the early 1970s was displacing furnished tenants, especially in Kensington and Chelsea, Westminster and Camden where 'creeping conversions' were

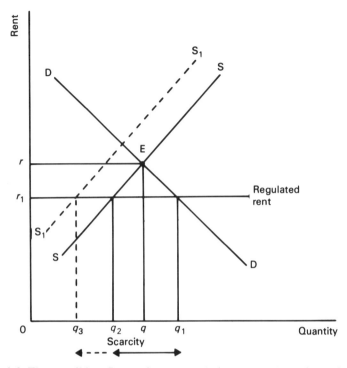

Figure 3.3 The possible effects of rent regulation upon the private furnished sector—according to the Francis Report (1971).
Note: E = Initial market equilibrium.

taking place (the conversion of furnished accommodation into hotels by hotels acquiring adjoining residential property). Landlords were selling off their properties for this and other reasons, evicting about 20 000 tenants per annum. Many furnished tenancies were also being converted into 'bed and breakfast' boarding houses. There was also the continuing conversion of unfurnished into furnished tenancies, providing landlords with higher rents and greater control. Furnished accommodation was getting beyond the means of young families or single people wishing to live alone. It was being increasingly shared by for example three or four wage earners all of whom contributed to the rent. A quarter of all furnished tenants were however the poorest in the country and were under the growing threat of eviction. Shelter reported that of the total number of tenants seeking help (March–September 1972) those paying over £6 per week increased from 43 to 85 per cent. But this rent was low compared with rents exceeding £50 per week for two bedroom furnished accommodation in the 'less desirable' parts of central London.

Tenants were also initially excluded from rent allowance. Although it was recognised by the Conservative government that the furnished rented sector contained many of the poorest and downtrodden households, rent allowances were omitted from the 1972 Act ostensibly because of the administrative difficulties involved in making provision for the high percentage of transient tenants. The Furnished Lettings (Rent Allowances) Act of 1973 was an attempt to remedy this deficiency, although Birmingham had already begun its own scheme. The Act required local authorities to extend allowances to certain categories of furnished tenants by the 1 April 1973 (England and Wales) or the 1 October (Scotland). The cost of the scheme was estimated to be £5–£8 million per annum.

Although the Labour Party had been pressing for months for allowances to be made available to furnished tenants, Crosland (1972a) condemned the legislation (at its Bill stage) as:

> a most disappointing measure, bordering on the fraudulent. First . . . the allowance is based not on the *actual* rent the tenant pays, but on a much lower *hypothetical* rent plus 25 per cent. . . Secondly, the Bill fails to give the furnished tenant what he needs more than anything else—*security of tenure*. . . . Finally, administering the complex Bill will require yet another large expansion of Local Authority bureaucracy.

Many furnished tenants would not have been able to have coped with the complexities of the measures, and as in the unfurnished sector the take up of allowances by those in need was probably low. Where demand was high, landlords were able to push up rents by an amount equal to the allowance, and if the tenant protested by going to the Rent Tribunal he would have received security for up to six months, or he might have been harassed out.

Rent Policy Since 1974

As in the unfurnished sector, rents on furnished dwellings were frozen from the 8 March 1974 to the end of the year, and landlords were prohibited from evicting tenants in order to be able to charge higher rents to new tenants. The incoming Labour government also extended rent regulation to the furnished sector. The Rent Act of 1974 (consolidated by the Rent Act of 1977) enabled tenants to apply for a fair rent and security of tenure was granted—both provisions applying to properties with rateable values of up to £1500 in London and £750 elsewhere. The Rent Tribunal's rent assessment function was taken over by the Rent Officer. In 1974, these provisions covered nearly 90 per cent of the 764 000 furnished lettings in the United Kingdom. A landlord could only regain possession (through the courts if necessary) if he had been temporarily letting his own home, or eventual retirement home; letting holiday accommodation out of season; letting student accommodation out of term; and temporarily letting accommodation to a number of different categories of occupiers such as agricultural workers. Possession can also be regained if the tenant fails to pay rent, damages the property or furniture, causes a nuisance to neighbours, and undertakes unauthorised sub-letting.

However, many groups of occupiers did not qualify for full Rent Act security of tenure. They comprised:

(1) Tenants of resident landlords. But where a dwelling is part of a purpose-built blocks of flats of at least two storeys, the tenant has full protection if the landlord lives in one of the flats, and a landlord previously not a resident cannot reduce his tenants' security by moving in with them after the tenancy has been created.

(2) Occupiers of dwellings where a substantial part of the rent is for board and attendance; student and holiday lettings; and licensed premises. In these situations, occupiers (like all lawful occupiers) can only be evicted with a Court Order.

(3) Business tenants under the Landlord and Tenant Act of 1954, and farmworkers under the Rent (Agricultural) Act of 1976.

(4) Persons with a 'licence to occupy'—usually where accommodation is not exclusively their own, for example shared flats; or where no rent is paid, for example housing tied to employment.

The 1974 Act was clearly intended to alleviate the growing problems faced by furnished tenants (or would-be tenants), and was a belated response to the recommendations of the Greve report of 1971. But although it generally benefitted existing tenants, the Act may have aggravated the problems faced by people seeking accommodation. Indications suggested that Rent Officers were setting 'fair' rents often as much as 40–50 per cent lower than 'reasonable' rents which Rent Tribunals previously set. The effects of this, as had been predicted by the Francis Report, was that the supply of furnished accommodation began to dry up. Even before the legislation was enacted in July 1974, Shelter reported 500 cases of eviction from furnished dwellings, and Mr Hugh Rossi MP, the Conservative housing spokesman reported that 150 000 furnished lettings had been withdrawn from the market by March 1976. A Department of the Environment-sponsored survey of advertisements in *The Times*, *Evening Standard* and 20 local London newspapers suggested that the 1974 Act had led to a 20 per cent drop in the number of advertised furnished lettings in 1973–6. This was not an altogether surprising finding, as security of tenure doubtless resulted in a slower turnover of tenants, and the drop did not prove that landlords were withdrawing their properties from the rented sector *because* of the Act. There was evidence of property companies selling off their blocks of flats to sitting tenants (possibly to realise capital gains), and smaller landlords were selling their properties to local authorities intent on municipalising. In the London borough of Camden, most of the council's acquired stock was obtained in this way during 1974–6. Other landlords increasingly granted fixed term tenancies or let as 'holiday accommodation' especially to the growing number of visitors from overseas.

Landlords may have misinterpreted the Act. Nick Raynsford, Research Officer for SHAC (Shelter Housing Aid Centre) claimed that many resident landlords were no longer letting for fear of not being able to get full possession when required, yet under the Act the power of the resident landlord improved, as tenants (both furnished and unfurnished) no longer had security of tenure. Raynsford also stated that landlords often relied on the tenant's ignorance of the Act in order to minimise security of tenure, for example many landlords were converting ordinary tenancies into 'service tenancies'by providing breakfast or sheets, or they claimed to be resident landlords by occasionally living in part of the property, and having mail delivered there.

In Inner London, because of the shortage of properties to buy in relation to demand, the price of flats accelerated, for example a four bedroom flat in a 'desirable' location may have sold for £65 000 in 1977, but would have fetched £200 000 by 1978, and prices of £50 000–£100 000 were unexceptional for one or two bedroom flats in 1978. With values like these, landlords of furnished accommodation would have been tempted to sell even if there had been no 1974 Rent Act. The scarcity of rented accommodation, due partly to properties being sold off, led to soaring rents. Foreign visitors were prepared to pay up to £250 per week for two bedroom flats which would have normally been let at £80. Rent Officers began to use as market rent guidelines the rents which foreign tourists or companies were prepared to pay. Young couples who hoped to live near their work found it impossible to find accommodation which they could afford, and long-established and middle income tenants were increasingly squeezed out as rents were frequently raised by as much as 80 per cent at the end of a lease. Concerned with this trend, the London borough of Kensington and Chelsea set up a property company in 1979 to acquire rented housing in Earls Court for the purpose of selling the dwellings to the existing tenants—a remarkable example of intervention in the property market by a Conservative council which (because it has the smallest proportion of council housing in London) is inhibited from selling council houses.

It was thought that the furnished dwellings market had reacted to rent regulation in much the same way as unfurnished lettings had responded to control and regulation, but the 1974 Act if anything slowed down the decline in the private rented sector (table 3.5) by making it more difficult for landlords to gain possession and sell off for owner-occupation. It is significant that the number of dwellings in the private rented sector declined by 10.1 per cent (and the average decline per annum was 3.3 per cent) in 1971–4, whereas the number declined by only 8.8 per cent (and the average decline per annum was only 3.1) in 1975–8.

**Table 3.5   Households Renting Privately, United Kingdom
1971–8**

	% housing stock	*Change from previous year %*
1971	18.9	−2.7
1972	18.0	−3.5
1973	17.2	−3.4
1974	16.4	−3.5
1975	15.7	−3.3
1976	15.0	−3.1
1977	14.4	−2.6
1978	13.8	−3.3

Sources: Social Trends, Housing and Construction Statistics

One considerable advantage of the 1974 Act was that the number of households made homeless due to repossession by the landlord was greatly reduced. Table 3.6 details this reduction in London. But the number of households made homeless through not being able to abtain private rented accommodation probably more than offsets this decrease.

Table 3.6   Households Accepted as Homeless, London, 1974–7

	Total accepted	*Homelessness as result of repossession by landlords*	
		% total	*Number*
1st half 1974	5760	28	1601
1st half 1975	6280	17	1090
1st half 1976	6520	13	820
1st half 1977	5410	9	510

Source: Department of the Environment, *Housing and Construction Statistics*

The Rent Act of 1974 (and often the misinformed reaction to it by landlords) undoubtedly had an effect upon the market for private rented accommodation, but it is difficult to differentiate the effects of the Act from the effects of soaring property prices which tempted landlords to sell off their housing. Although there was an annual loss of about 100 000 private rented dwellings in 1975–8, this must be contrasted with the annual loss of 290 000 units in 1957–60—a period of decontrol and insecurity of tenure.

Conclusion

Much concern was expressed about the effects of regulated rents upon the quantity and quality of both unfurnished and furnished dwellings to let and the differences in rent between the two sectors. *Labour's Programme* (1976) proposed that in order to obtain equitability between rents paid for unfurnished and furnished accommodation and between localities, a new Housing Tribunal be established to take over from Rent Assessment Committees and Rent Tribunals. The Programme also saw a need for the reform of the system of rent allowances (and rebates in the public sector). Because of the stigma of means-testing, there was a less than 25 per cent take-up of allowances. The Programme proposed (like Mr Anthony Crosland in 1971) that:

> allowances should be entirely financed by the Exchequer, since they form a part of the complex pattern of benefits which provide income support for poor families.

The Rent Act Review Committee (1977) reported that:

> Fair rents do not necessarily take direct account of the actual costs incurred by the landlord in providing the accommodation and this discourages the provision of improved services and good maintenance and repair. In addition the 3 year review system has been strained by the recent high rates of inflation, and the phasing system which cushions tenants against the full effects of that inflation can exacerbate the feelings of landlords that their expenditure is outstripping rents.

It also stated that anomalies often occur because:

> the fair rent in one area may not enable the landlord even to cover his immediate costs whilst in another large increases in the registered rent may cause hardship for tenants of limited means who have been living in the same house for many years.

This partly explains why fair rent policy is criticised by both landlord and tenant.

In giving evidence to the Committee, the National Consumer Council called for tax allowances to be given to landlords as an inducement to maintain properties adequately, and penalties for harassment should include increased fines up to £1000 (this was implemented in 1978), or imprisonment for up to two years. Shelter proposed that all private tenancies should be compulsorily registered with local authorities as a means of ensuring that rent regulation was equitably applied, and the Citizens' Advice Bureau—in its evidence—criticised lazy landlords who forced tenants to endure leaking roofs, blocked drains, damp and darkness.

The Labour Party's Housing sub-committee was particularly concerned with the unwillingness of landlords to do repairs. In 1977 it proposed that where this happened, local authorities should do the work instead, taking in payment a share of the value of the house which it could realise when the property was sold.

The Conservative Party in the late 1970s had no intention of removing security of tenure from tenants of absentee landlords, and recognised that rent regulation was necessary. But under the Housing Act of 1980, the Conservative government introduced shorthold tenancies—believing that many properties stood empty because the Rent Acts of 1974 and 1977 had got in the way of landlords and tenants wishing to agree to a lease for a short fixed period. Shortholds are only applicable to new lettings, and at the end of fixed term agreements of 1–5 years landlords have the right to regain possession. Shorthold is in effect a form of decontrol. It encourages landlords to take all possible steps to ensure that existing rented accommodation becomes vacant so that it can be re-let on a shorthold basis, and, because of more frequent repossession of the property, landlords are able to sell it off more easily than under the Rent Acts of 1967, 75 and 77. According to Shelter (1979a):

> More tenants will become homeless, and tenants will be too scared of eviction to ask for essential repairs and improvements.

Shelter believed that there would be a recurrence of the situation which occurred after the Rent Act of 1957 when decontrol led to a more rapid annual decline in the number of private rented dwellings than in the previous period of control.

The 1980 Act also introduced 'assured' tenancies, whereby approved landlords are permitted to let their new dwellings outside of the Rent Acts. Building societies, banks and other finance houses can be licenced by the government to build homes for rent, but although the Abbey National Building Society has already moved into this area, high interest rates may make this form of investment unattractive. Also under the Act, fair rents can be raised every two years instead of every three years as before, and remaining controlled rent tenancies are being converted to fair rent properties. As a result, rent allowances are going up by an estimated £72 million by 1982–3, partly in line with rent increases of up to 50 per cent.

The policies of both the main political parties over the years have done little to arrest the decline of the private rented sector. No government has been able to achieve simultaneously an adequate return for the landlord, and satisfactory rents and protection for the tenant. It has become clear that if the landlord is able to make a reasonable return it is at the expense of the tenant, but if the tenant is protected and pays only a controlled or fair rent the landlord is encouraged to withdraw his rented property from the market. In practice, even when restrictions are withdrawn (as in the period 1957–65), landlords may be faced with attractive alternative investment opportunities and a buoyant demand for owner-occupation, and consequently sell rather than let. Few people would mourn the disappearance of the private landlord. His reputation has generally been poor, but the housing which he owns must not be allowed to vanish from the rented sector. It is needed by those who stand little chance of being granted a mortgage, or a local authority dwelling—particularly young single persons; young married couples without children; transients such as students; businessmen and building workers; the elderly (many of whom may have been life-long tenants) and those at the bottom of the socio-economic ladder suffering from one or many forms of deprivation. It is unlikely that tinkering with rent legislation will ensure the continuation of the supply of private lettings, and deregulation (in the form of shorthold) will almost inevitably produce a recurrence of the results of decontrol. Social ownership is probably the only way of preventing the disappearance of this small but necessary stock of rented accommodation (chapter 4).

4 Social Ownership

The Rationale of Social Ownership

Within the Labour Party there has been a firmly held conviction that the social ownership of housing is not only desirable as a means of creating an egalitarian society but that it is necessary if the immediate problems of poor housing and an inadequate supply of rented accommodation are to be solved. A Party statement *Homes for the Future* (1956) explained in detail how municipalisation (a major form of social ownership) could be put into effect. In 1959, at the 'you've never had it so good' election, the Labour Party's election manifesto stated:

> At the last count there were seven million households in Britain with no bath: and over three million sharing or entirely without a WC. The Tories have tried to induce private landlords to improve their property by means of public grants with very small success. Labour's plan is that with reasonable exceptions, local councils shall take over housed which were rent controlled before 1 January 1956 and are still tenanted. They will repair and modernise these houses and let them at fair rents. This is a big job which will take time and its spread will vary according to local conditions.

A further cause for concern was the effect of the Rent Act of 1957 upon the supply of rented housing. Low income unfurnished tenants were being displaced by landlords selling off their properties for owner-occupation, and by the conversion of unfurnished dwellings into furnished (uncontrolled) bedsitters or into high rent luxury accommodation. Illegal and dubious means were used to evict tenants as was highlighted by the Milner Holland Report (1965). In the aftermath of the 1957 Act, 290 000 private rented units per annum were thereby lost in 1957/60.

But in the 1960s, the determination to end private landlordism by municipalisation diminished as the Rent Act of 1965 introduced rent regulation and reintroduced security of tenure at least for unfurnished tenants of properties with rateable values of less than £400 (London) and £200 (elsewhere). Also many local authorities, not least those under Labour control, found the costs involved in municipalisation were prohibitive. In the 1970s municipalisation again became a policy issue. The Rent Act of 1965 was being circumvented. Harassment and winkling led to displacement as landlords sought vacant possession for the same motives as those in the late 1950s–early 1960s. From 1966 to 1970 an average of 135 000 dwellings per annum were lost to the private rented sector, falling to about 100 000 per annum in the late 1970s.

Poor housing however remained a principal reason for municipalisation. In 1972 there were still one million dwellings in England and Wales which were unfit for human habitation, and this was the year when the housebuilding figures had reached their lowest since 1964 (319 100 completions in 1972 in contrast to the record number of 413 700 in 1968). The unfit houses were deficient in basic amenities and were probably unhealthy. Some would remain for a very long time. What was significant was that although only 2 per cent of council houses and 7 per cent of owner-occupied houses were unfit, the proportion in the private rented sector was as high as one third. It was thought that the provisions of the Housing Act of 1969 would accelerate improvement, and retain much of the stock of older housing in the inner urban areas. But desirable rehabilitated houses doubled or trebled in price, controlled and regulated tenants were often harassed or 'winkled' out of their homes, and long-established communities were broken up as developers took over (chapter 8). In 1972 over £60 million was paid out in improvement grants, but in the inner urban areas up to 80 per cent went to property developers and landlords—tenants often being displaced as a result. Because of the inelasticity of supply, the improvement grant could be added completely to the capital value/price of the dwelling and the profit of the speculator. Without adequate safeguards, improvement policy was demolishing communities as effectively as the bulldozer.

Public Control or Social Ownership

Although it could be argued that rent control failed after the Second World War and up to 1957, the alternative—free market rents—also failed in that homelessness and stress remained. Clearly there was one thing worse than rent control, and that was the *lack* of rent control. A compromise solution— fair rents, rent allowances and some security of tenure—is so fraught with difficulties, that like improvement grants, in the early 1970s, landlords rather than tenants or the homeless received the benefits. The question must therefore be asked: is there a need for greater and more diverse governmental control over private rented housing (the government has already extended fair rents and security of tenure to the furnished private rented sector by the Rent Act of 1974), or should local authorities and central government transfer into social ownership what is left of the stock of private rented accommodation? It is difficult to accept without criticism the first of these alternatives. No post-war government has produced a policy which has combined a profit for the landlord, and reasonable rents and protection for the tenant, and this sector has been the scene of continuous dispute and tension, not least after the Rent Act of 1974. In spite of the protection given by governments since 1939 (with the exception of the years 1957–65) tenants live:

> in constant insecurity, often not knowing who their landlord is, uneasily aware that their homes are being bought and sold above their heads, certain of only two things: the huge speculative profits being made at their expense, and the relentless pressure on them to pay up or get out.
>
> (Mr Anthony Crosland, 1972b)

This is as true of middle income tenants of large commercial landlords as of the poor, often immigrant, often uneducated underprivileged of the inner urban areas. Without social ownership there will be a further loss of rented accommodation to the owner-occupied sector. Social ownership would arrest this decline, and would be a far cheaper alternative to the construction of an equivalent number of new council dwellings—the latter being constrained by the availability of sites and cash limits.

The Advantages of Social Ownership

At a time when the Labour government was acquiescent in the field of private rented housing, Donnison (1967) argued that:

> it is plain that greater and bolder use must be made of public ownership and investment. . . . Public enterprise . . . has the advantages that it can give those with urgent needs and smaller incomes greater scope for choice and movement . . . it provides security of tenure and protects tenants from abuses that have sometimes arisen in private property; and it enables the community to acquire capital gains that arise in the course of time and apply them in a constructive fashion.

Whilst Shadow Secretary for State for the Environment, Mr Anthony Crosland (1972b) firmly committed the Labour Party to a thoroughgoing programme of municipalisation when it returned to office. Mr Crosland believed that only local authorities had the power, resources and experience to manage rented housing efficiently and that:

> municipalisation would bring other advantages in its train. Acquiring as they would a more diverse stock local authorities could offer all tenants a wider choice of accommodation—not just a home on a purpose built council estate, but a variety of sizes, shapes, ages and locations. Thus we would make a more advantageous use of our existing stock.

Wicks (1973) further discussed the advantages of municipalisation. He listed the following:

(1) Municipalisation would give local authorities powers over the allocation of former private tenancies, and this would help to solve the problem of gross overcrowding in some dwellings and under-occupancy in others. Although households should not be forced out, there would be the possibility of matching need with the supply of vacant housing if alternative accommodation was made available as families increase or decrease in size.

(2) Local authorities would become the main or sole supplier of rented housing and they would no longer provide just a 'welfare' service. Municipalised housing would provide homes for a cross section of society, and help to end the 'two nation' syndrome.

(3) There would be the possibility of large scale systematic repair and improvement work especially in the General Improvement Areas and Housing Action Areas. This would ensure that work would be speeded up and be for the benefit of existing residents rather than for speculators.

(4) In the private rented sector, tenants may be reluctant to go to the Rent Officer, or [until the Rent Act of 1974] to appeal to the Rent Tribunal for fear of receiving notices to quit. But if the sector were municipalised fair rents would be assessed over a single stock of rented property, thereby producing greater equitability. If tenants were eligible for rebates there would be a better chance of them receiving their entitlement, and it would be necessary to ensure that all local authority tenants received security of tenure.

Yet, many private tenants are sceptical of the idea of swapping private landlords for the council or other public bodies. It might be thought that all kinds of pettifogging restrictions on personal liberty would be imposed. But this belief should be rapidly losing ground. Such restrictions are not generally unreasonable (and are being relaxed where appropriate), are usually made solely to safeguard other tenants (rather than at the whim of the landlord), and are often trivial compared to those so often imposed in the private sector. The belief that there would be less freedom to choose where to live should be dispelled, as council tenants already move with surprising frequency; and with a larger stock of housing, mobility could be greater.

There may be no other effective way than social ownership of ensuring that public money and resources actually provide for those in greatest need, while simultaneously increasing the choice of housing for a cross section of society.

The Processes of Social Ownership

As the urgency of the problem of the diminishing supply of private rented housing varies from place to place being (in consequence to a larger excessive demand) greater in, for example, inner London than in Bath or Tunbridge Wells, a government sympathetic to social ownership would not wish to lay down a uniform national timetable for acquisition. In areas of severe housing stress, acquisition should be completed in say 18 months; in areas where there were major housing problems (for example where there were large numbers of slum dwellings) acquisition should take place within three to four years; but in areas where there were no housing problems of concern (the Housing Minister could keep a register of such areas), local authorities would be given the option of municipalising all, some or none of the private rented stock.

Wicks (1973) proposed a policy of social ownership rather than muni-cipalisation as a means of safeguarding the supply of rented housing, on the grounds that the former is more flexible and could cater for minority groups in addition to satisfying general housing need, while municipalisation is monopolistic and could lead to the abuse and victimisation of tenants who displease the council, and would promote few innovations in housing management. Social ownership could involve a variety of publicly respon-sible bodies. Wicks outlined these as follows:

(1) *Local authorities*   Under the Local Government Act of 1972 the major housing authorities are the District Councils. These together with the London boroughs and the Greater London Council (under the London Government Act of 1963) would be the municipalising bodies. County authorities could also be granted acquisition powers to allow a regional strategy to evolve, and to provide diversity of ownership. Where muni-cipalisation (or its equivalent in the counties) involves compulsory purchase, local authorities already have the necessary powers. The central government could support municipalisation by issuing a circular agreeing to allow all compulsory purchase orders on privately rented property. It could also introduce *safe notices* compelling any landlord wishing to sell his rented property to notify his council in advance, giving it first option to buy.

(2) *Housing Associations*   These would be offered dwellings acquired by local authorities and would then manage them themselves (chapter 6).

(3) *Co-operatives*   These would similarly be offered dwellings by the acquiring authority, but with the council providing financial and technical expertise (chapter 6). Both housing associations and co-operatives would play an increasingly major role in social ownership because in the medium and long term local authorities would reduce the proportion of their stock which had been municipalised.

(4) *A Social Housing Authority*   The central government would set up this body to acquire properties, and to either manage the dwellings itself or dispose of them to housing associations or co-operatives. A SHA would need to establish local administrative units possibly alongside the local

authorities, and initially its buying powers might be exercised by the local authorities. It would have the following functions:

(a) At the request of the Minister it would step in and acquire properties if local authorities were undertaking little or no municipalisation.
(b) In areas of difficulty it would acquire housing at the request of the local authority or Minister.
(c) It would provide advice to local authorities, housing associations and co-operatives on policy, procedure and methods of social ownership.

Although social ownership would be more complex than municipalisation alone, it would be a boost to tenant participation and local democracy. Although local authorities, housing associations, co-operatives and the SHA would probably charge different rents for similar dwellings, pay different rebates, and impose different responsibilities on tenants, the increase in choice would make the situation immeasurably preferable to the private rented sector and in some areas preferable to traditional council housing.

Wicks recognised that in certain circumstances private rented tenure should be exempt from the processes of social ownership. Where the landlord was resident in part of the property he could be given the choice of either selling his home to the local authority and remain in occupation as a tenant, or be rehoused by the council and given a capital sum. Alternatively the landlord should be able to enter into a tenancy agreement with the local authority, with the local authority assuming responsibility for management. If furnished tenants were given full security of tenure [as they were in part under the Rent Act of 1974] resident landlords could retain full control. Where temporary lettings occurred (for example owner-occupied houses let whilst their owners were abroad) there could also be an exemption.

The Cost of Social Ownership

Wicks in 1973 forecast that by 1975 there would be 2.3 million private rented dwellings in Great Britain of which (because of the exemptions noted above) only 1.7 million would be eligible for municipalisation. Taking into account both unfit and 'fit' dwellings, he calculated that the total cost of acquisition would be up to £3250 million (the 1.45 million 'fit' dwellings costing as much as £2900 million). The cost of acquisition by the late 1970s would not have been much greater despite inflation because the number of private rented houses had decreased since 1975.

The price at which the unfit dwellings could have been obtained would have been not much more than £1000 each (barely in excess of site value). But the price of 'fit' accommodation would have been much more and would be equivalent to a multiple of the landlords annual income (based on his fair rent) *less* tax, insurance, repairs and other authorised expenses. Compensation would not have been based on a speculative price with vacant possession. The multiple would have been as low as one or two on a house on the verge of unfitness, but would be generous on properties with long lives ahead of them although the ceiling on compensation would equal the market price of the property with a tenant in possession with full security of tenure.

Acquisition would need to take place over a number of years and costs need not exceed £800–£900 million per annum (at 1979 prices), less than that paid out in subsidies to council tenants or in tax relief (on mortgage interest) to owner-occupiers. Compensation could either be in cash, or in bonds with interest. Recipients could be given the option to cash the bonds right away, or hold them and draw tax-free interest. The interest would approximate to the fair rent, *less* expenditure on management, repairs and depreciation. It would probably be the intention of the local authority to pay off bondholders as soon as possible, say within ten years. A subsidy from the central government would increase the pace of municipalisation.

Obligations

With wider responsibilities, local authorities incur increasing obligations. There would have to be a powerful and imaginative commitment to provide for the old and the young, students and single people, those wanting to share, established residents and transients. There must be safeguards to ensure that with a greater number and variety of dwellings, allocation procedures reflect the increased scale of municipal responsibilities. There would have to be a rethink on conditions of letting as municipalised lettings may differ from ordinary council house lettings.

It would be essential to raise local authority standards of maintenance, and management would have to respond to the wider range of responsibilities. Municipalisation would become a catastrophe if newly acquired property was mis-managed in the way some local authority estates are today.

Local authorities would have to decide (given an option) whether to buy that which is good or move into areas of unfit housing or stress. They would also have to decide which sort of dwellings they would offer to housing associations and co-operatives.

Municipalisation in Practice

The reduction in public sector housebuilding from a record of 213 900 starts in 1968 to 112 800 in 1973 was not only accompanied by a shift of emphasis from redevelopment to rehabilitation (chapter 8), but also by an increase in the municipalisation of housing. At first this was possibly a response to pressures and advice from various groups and individuals, for example in 1972 the Notting Hill Housing Trust urged the London borough of

Kensington and Chelsea to purchase (compulsorily if necessary) housing mainly occupied by low income families, especially where the dwellings were badly managed. Douglas-Mann (1972) argued that local authorities should do even more than this and buy up as many houses as were necessary to ensure that waiting lists were cleared, and the National and Local Government Officers Association (1973) demanded the municipalisation of all private rented housing in stress areas. The wider possibilities of social ownership proposed by Wicks (1973) have already been described.

But in 1972–3 some local authorities (especially those under Labour control) needed little encouragement to municipalise on a large scale. The London boroughs of Camden, Haringey, Islington and Lambeth each spent between £3 million and £13 million acquiring dwellings (Lambeth municipalising more dwellings than it built). It was forecast that in total the Inner London boroughs would buy up 2000 properties in 1974/75 and that the Greater London Council (GLC) would acquire 7500 (a greater number than it would build) at a combined cost of approximately £100 million. But the Conservative government in 1973 and early 1974 was inevitably hostile to the extension of municipalisation, and Conservative local authorities showed little interest in acquiring private rented properties. The Conservatives hoped that housing associations (aided by the Housing Corporation and the professional expertise of the National Building Agency) would fill the gap left by the decline of private rented tenure.

Ironically, the Labour government returned in March 1974 imposed constraints on local authorities wishing to municipalise. In April 1974 the government announced that local authorities would be able to spend an extra £350 million on buying up flats from private landlords and taking over unsold private housing (as well as on building more rented housing), but that they were required to produce five year plans for municipalisation, and had to confine acquisition to where tenants were living in bad conditions; where there was harassment or homelessness; where properties were left empty for six months or more and where properties were coming on to the market (with vacant possession) in areas of severe overall housing shortage. Priority would have to be given to accommodating the homeless or essential public service employees. These yardsticks forced many authorities to revise downwards their plans for municipalisation—the GLC for example reduced its proposed expenditure on acquiring private properties from £57 million to £40 million. The GLC *Strategic Housing Plan* of 1974 nevertheless proposed that extensive municipalisation should take place up to the 1980s, and aimed thereby to raise London's council house stock by 250 000 to 300 000 dwellings. The Plan also proposed that compulsory acquisition should be widely used if landlords attempted to force tenants out in order to sell on the open market.

With the slump in the property market in 1974 a high proportion (often 100 per cent) of local authority acquisitions were not compulsory but by agreement, and there was much evidence that some authorities in their eagerness to acquire properties paid pre-slump prices. Booker and Gray (1974) reported that the London borough of Camden paid £240 000, £257 000, and £470 00 for residential properties which had been currently valued by estate agents at £150 000, £170 000 and £250 000 respectively. Booker and Gray also showed that although Camden had municipalised 3850 dwellings (January 1973–November 1974) at a cost of £25 871 000, more than 3000 of these needed to be improved/converted, and that only 150 had been brought up to that standard by the end of 1974. Similarly, in 1974/75 the GLC bought 2500 properties, but 1000 of them had to be kept vacant pending rehabilitation.

The White Paper, *Public Expenditure to 1978–79* (1975) introduced major cuts in public expenditure. Whereas £234 million had been spent on acquiring private rented housing in 1974/75, the amount fell to £56 million in 1977/78. The number of dwellings acquired fell from 25 200 to 9000 (table 4.1), and a high proportion of housing purchased by local authorities for improvement stood empty, much of it subsequently falling apart or being vandalised. Municipalisation as a major plank of Labour policy at national and local level seemed almost to have been abandoned. In the GLC area municipalisation virtually came to a halt especially after local government elections resulted in swings from Labour to Conservative control.

Table 4.1   Local Authority Acquisition of Dwellings, Great Britain, 1973/74–1977/78

	1973/74	1974/75	1975/76	1976/77	1977/78
Expenditure (£m)	90	234	135	104	56
Dwellings acquired	N/A	25 600	19 500	16 300	9500

Source; Department of the Environment

In submitting evidence to the Review of the Rent Acts (carried out by the Department of the Environment) in 1976, the Labour Party as distinct from the Labour government remained committed to the principle of municipalisation. It urged local authorities to introduce ten year programmes of municipalising all sub-standard private rented housing, and saw municipalisation as the only means of retaining as rented housing as many as possible of the 100 000 dwellings which are sold off by private landlords annually.

Conclusion

Mr Anthony Crosland (1972b) believed that municipalisation would both symbolise and encourage the wider view then being taken of the role of the housing authorities;

They are responsible not for just creating and managing council estates, but for the *total* housing situation in their area. And they are not in the business of rented accommodation solely to provide a welfare service for the poor; with the demise of the private landlord they must meet the demand for renting from whatever source it comes.

In a wider context, social ownership (in its many forms including municipalisation) would provide the maximum degree of choice, variety and self government in housing—features which have been largely absent throughout the last two hundred years of urbanisation. The Conservatives' support for home ownership on the one hand, and private landlordism and voluntary housing on the other, woefully fail to meet these provisions. More negatively, municipalisation was severely affected by the cuts in housing expenditure announced in June 1979. Although local authority acquisitions accounted for less than 10 per cent of public spending on housing, 28 per cent of the £300 million cut fell on municipalisation—perhaps the first phase of the Conservative's attempt to eliminate it altogether.

5 Local Authority Housing

By the late 1970s local authorities were the largest landlords in the country, accounting for 32 per cent of the United Kingdom housing stock in 1979, compared with 13 per cent in 1947 and less than 2 per cent in 1913.

Local Authority Housing: 1869–1939

The introduction of local authority housing in the nineteenth century was mainly a response to the economic and social legacy of the industrial revolution. The population of England and Wales increased from 8.9 million in 1801 to 32.5 million in 1901 and it had become largely urban. Poverty and squalor were manifested in the condition of housing in our towns and cities. The increase in the supply of labour enabled employers to keep wages to the minimum—often to the subsistence level—but urban landlords either in their desire to maximise profit on their property or to keep costs to the minimum developed housing at very high density and of abysmally poor quality. Overcrowding and disease were the inevitable results throughout the industrial areas of Britain.

The Artisans and Labourers Dwellings Act of 1868 (the Torrens Act) and the Artisans and Labourers Dwellings Improvement Act of 1875 (the Cross Act) were intended to promote slum clearance, but because ratepayers were reluctant to finance clearance and as most slum housing was sited on high value land in the inner urban areas the Acts were ineffectual. Authorities also had the problem of having little or no accommodation to offer displaced households. Local authority housebuilding however was beginning to take place. In Liverpool in 1869 a local authority first built dwellings for rent, and following the Housing of the Working Classes Act of 1890, the newly constituted London County Council and London's boroughs developed a number of large housing estates often with their own workforces—the direct labour organisations. The Public Health Act of 1875 ensured that new housing—both private and public—would conform to high standards and thereby had a marked influence on the emerging environment on the fringe of the inner urban areas or in what are now the inner suburbs.

It was not until after the First World War that local authority housing really 'took-off'. In 1919 610 000 new houses were needed in Britain as housebuilding had virtually ceased throughout the duration of the war, and at the 1919 General Election, Lloyd George promised homes 'fit for heroes' to attract the ex-serviceman's vote. After his election win his coalition government introduced a housing programme in which local authorities and public utility societies (akin to housing associations) were to build 500 000 houses within three years. This was incorporated in the Housing and Town Planning Act of 1919 (the Addison Act)—a watershed in British social history. The government appreciated that there was a stark contrast between election pledges and the fact that private enterprise could not supply the houses needed by the country either in sufficient numbers or at appropriate rents. It was also understood that wartime rent controls, the high cost of labour and building materials, high interest rates and the demand for higher standards of accommodation militated against any easy solution to the housing problem. Under the Act local authorities initially had the duty of surveying housing needs in their area (an innovation) and then, having quantified the shortage, to meet the needs of working class families— generous subsidies being introduced to help them achieve this. Local authority losses in housebuilding were limited to the product of a penny rate with the Exchequer automatically meeting all additional losses—losses which inevitably would be high as rents were to be pegged to the level of prevailing 'working class' rents in the area, adjusted to the means of the tenant. Many rents were therefore equal to controlled rents. The Act also fixed standards for new housing well above the normal conditions of working class houses. Addison:

> more than any other man thereby established the principle that housing was a social service, and later governments had to take up his task.
>
> (Taylor, 1965)

But the 1919 Act gave little incentive for local authorities to economise, and the capacity of the construction industry was strained—pushing up costs and exacerbating post-war inflation. Subsidies simultaneously increased as houses costing for example £400 to build in 1918 were costing over £900 by 1920. Exchequer grants were therefore sharply restricted in 1921 and stopped in 1922. The Addison Act nevertheless resulted in 213 000 houses being built.

A new subsidy system was devised and included in the Conservative's Housing Act of 1923 (the Chamberlain Act). Chamberlain believed that the rising cost of housing was the result of Addison's open-ended subsidies rather than a cause, and introduced a subsidy which in form was to continue through to the Housing Finance Act of 1972. It consisted of a fixed

Exchequer payment of £6 per dwelling for 20 years—available to both the public and private sectors. The government showed a preference for the latter sector as it built houses for sale, and local authorities could only qualify for the subsidy if they built houses in areas where private enterprise could not meet demand. The low subsidy resulted in the construction of small sub-standard houses. Thompson (1968) remarked that:

> Chamberlain's small subsidised houses were condemned as rabbit hutches.

and Taylor (1965) suggested that:

> Chamberlain was marked as the enemy of the poor, and his housing act lost the Conservatives more votes than they gained.

Soon after taking office for the first time, the Labour government—insisting that more and better houses be built—repealed the Chamberlain Act and replaced it with the Housing Act of 1924 (the Wheatley Act). The subsidy was raised to £9 for 40 years, and the Act transferred the main responsibility for housing back to local authorities who did not have to demonstrate that private enterprise could not meet local needs before they could proceed with building. Rents were to be equal to 'appropriate normal rents', interpreted as being equal to controlled rents in the private sector. The difference between this rent level and market rents was to be offset by a minimum rate fund contribution of at least half of the Exchequer subsidy. It was considered that the Act

> was a great personal triumph for Wheatley, and the main domestic achievement of the first Labour Government
>
> (Thompson 1968)

Altogether 503 000 dwellings were built under the 1923 and 1924 Acts. It was doubtful however whether the needs of the poorest working class families had been met. Council housing was regarded by many to be prestigous and it was going mainly to the lower middle classes such as clerks, teachers and shopworkers. The main working class areas—the inner cities—had an insufficient rate base to take advantage of Exchequer grants. It was also in these areas that slum clearance was necessary, but only 11 000 unfit houses were demolished in England and Wales in 1923–39. Although the 1924 Act provided 50 per cent Exchequer grants for slum clearance and rehousing, the complexity of the way in which this subsidy was calculated was an inhibiting factor, and in 1929 it was withdrawn by the Conservative government (Chamberlain again having responsibility for housing).

The return of a Labour government produced the Housing Act of 1930 (the Greenwood Act). Generous subsidies were granted for slum clearance, based not on the number of homes demolished or provided but on the numbers of persons displaced. Extra subsidies were available if displaced families were rehoused in blocks of flats (of over three storeys) on expensive sites within the inner urban areas. Rents, although still approximately based on controlled rents, were differentiated according to the means of tenants, and a system of rent rebates was introduced.

The National government's Housing Act of 1933 discontinued the Wheatley subsidies and all government provision for new public housing for general needs—even though the 1931 *Census* had shown that there was a deficit of one million dwellings in relation to households. The Conservative-dominated government believed that new council housing should be confined to those households displaced by slum clearance, and that the private sector should satisfy the needs of the rest. This was a confirmation of the Conservative Party's belief that council housing was a restricted welfare service and not a facility to meet a general need for rented accommodation—a view the party seems to have resurrected from time to time if indeed it was ever buried. The 1933 Act was based on the assumption that the private housebuilding industry was well equipped for its task—helped by low wages and material costs, and an available supply of cheap land on the urban fringe. Town and country planning legislation which did little to control development or constrain urban sprawl further assisted private housebuilding—most of it being speculative.

Under the Conservatives' Housing Act of 1935 the emphasis again shifted to the problems of low income housing. It may have been realised that market forces were incapable of ameliorating the housing conditions of the urban poor—most of whom were still living in private rented housing rather than in council dwellings. The Act charged local authorities with the duty of relieving overcrowding (defined as an occupancy rate of more than two persons per room), and further legislation—the Housing Act of 1936—pooled the subsidy and rent provisions of previous Acts under a statutory Housing Revenue Account and Equalisation Account. Local authorities thereby had greater discretion in fixing rent levels and giving rent rebates. From 1935 until the outbreak of the Second World War, local authorities concentrated on slum clearance and reducing overcrowding, 400 000 houses being constructed for these purposes in Great Britain in this period. Even more replacement houses may have been built, but the Housing Act of 1938 reduced the level of subsidy to local authority housing, though special grants were available for high flats. It may have been thought that the problems of low income urban housing had eased, and that 1.3 million council dwellings in 1939 (about 11 per cent of the total housing stock) was the maximum which should be developed, taking into account that the sector was not intended by the government to meet general housing needs.

It was evident that during the inter-war years, housing policy depended very largely upon the political philosophy of the government or dominant party in office. The Conservatives favoured keeping subsidies to a minimum and placed an emphasis on private sector building. The Labour governments of 1924 and 1929–31 extended subsidies and encouraged council housing. Only in a fairly limited welfare-sense did the former party pay 'lip service' to public sector activity. The level of subsidy at any time however depended upon costs. Post-war inflation, peaking in 1921, resulted in 'runaway subsidisation', but a period of relatively minor inflation in 1924–5 brought forth a controlled increase in subsidies. The 1929–34 depression in prices and money wages (but not real wages) may have made subsidisation more difficult and possibly less necessary—the underlying rationale for subsidy cuts in 1933. The level of subsidy was also dependent upon the capacity of the construction industry. During inflation, the industry worked at full capacity and was faced with rising costs; during the slump the industry operated at under-capacity and enjoyed low factor input costs—this was reflected in the price of housing and rents, and consequently subsidies. A final influence was the priorities which the central government and local authorities placed on housebuilding, slum clearance and the reduction in overcrowding—each need affecting the direction of subsidies in a specific way.

1939–1951

By 1938 the workforce in the construction industry in Britain exceeded 1 million and there were 12.5 million houses. But during the Second World War there was virtually no housebuilding, and 208 000 dwellings were completely destroyed, 250 000 made uninhabitable and over 250 000 seriously damaged (equal in total to 5 per cent of the housing stock)—but as much as 33 per cent of the stock had been damaged and, together with the rest, remained largely unrepaired or unmaintained throughout the six years of the war. In this period the population had grown by 1 million, the total housing shortage was therefore about 1 460 000—not including unfit and obsolete housing which needed replacing. The construction industry was unable to meet this demand in the immediate post-war years. The workforce had fallen to a third of its size in 1938, and materials (many of which had to be imported) were scarce and costly.

Public sector housebuilding was to dominate the period 1945-51. As in the years immediately following the First World War, the emphasis at first was on building for general need to meet an acute housing shortage—one which seemed likely to remain as marriages in the years 1945–8 increased by 11 per cent more than in the period 1936–9, and the number of births increased by 33 per cent over the pre-war rate.

The Housing (Financial Provisions) Act of 1946 was a personal triumph for the Minister of Health (and Minister responsible for housing), Mr. Aneuran Bevan. It provided a generous basic subsidy for local authority housing of £16 10s (£16.50) per dwelling per annum over 60 years, a sum which varied according to the needs of different authorities. Building licences were introduced in the private sector so that housebuilding would respond to 'need' rather than exclusively to the ability to pay. It was hoped that this would ensure that materials and labour would be available for local authority housebuilding—in contrast to the situation in 1919. It was necessary however for a system of building quotas to be imposed on public sector building.

From the outset of the post-war housing programme, it was stressed that council housing was intended for general need—it was not intended solely for the poor, the underprivileged or the population of 'traditional working class areas'. Neither was it intended to sustain the existence of a two-class nation. No one held this view more strongly than Bevan:

> In his first housing speech Bevan . . . protested against the whole pre-war system of building; it produced 'castrated communities'. The arrangement whereby the speculative builders built for one income group and the local authorities for another was 'a wholly evil thing from a civilized point of view, condemned by anyone who had paid the slightest attention to civics and eugenics; a monstrous infliction upon the essential psychological and biological one-ness of the community'.
>
> (Foot, 1973)

Bevan's Housing Act of 1949 incorporated this view into legislation. His Act removed the 'ridiculous inhibition' restricting local authorities to the provision of houses for the 'working class'. Instead they could attempt to meet the varied needs of the whole community.

> 'We should try', he said, 'to introduce in our modern villages and towns what was always the lovely feature of English and Welsh villages, where the doctor, the grocer, the butcher and the farm labourer all lived in the same street. I believe that is essential for the full life of a citizen . . . to see the living tapestry of a mixed community'.
>
> (Foot)

Bevan was also concerned with improving the quality and increasing the floor space of public sector housing. The minimum size of a three bedroom house had been fixed at 750 ft^2 in the 1930s, in 1944 the Ministry of Housing Manual prescribed 800–900 ft^2 and in the same year the Dudley Committee recommended 950 ft^2. Bevan accepted the latter proposal and encouraged local authorities to adopt even higher standards where this was possible. Although more houses could have been built if lower standards had been applied, Bevan argued against this view, and insisted that:

> To cut standards . . . was 'the cowards way out'. It would be 'a cruel thing to do. After all people will have to live in and among these houses for many years . . . If we have to wait a little longer, that will be far better than doing ugly things now and regretting them for the rest of our lives'
>
> (Foot)

—a sentiment regretably not shared by local authorities and central government in the 1950s–60s nor by the Conservatives in the 1980s.

Between 1945 and 1951 a total of 1.01 million houses were built in Great Britain—89 per cent being local authority dwellings. Output accelerated from 55 400 completions in 1946 to 284 230 by 1948. Overall this was a great achievement in view of post-war material shortages, the need to reconstruct industry, curb inflation and correct balance of payments deficits. More importantly, the quality of new housing was not sacrificed (indeed it was improved) and it was re-established that the public sector had a role to play in satisfying general housing need. The importance which the government and particularly Bevan attached to housing in the period of post-war austerity cannot be overestimated.

1951–1964

When the Conservatives returned to office in 1951, Mr Harold Macmillan was appointed Minister of Housing. At the Conservative Party Conference the previous year he had pledged that the party, if elected to power, would have a housebuilding target of 300 000 houses per annum—a figure cautiously included in the Conservative manifesto at the 1951 election. By 1953 this target had been achieved and the number of houses built continued to increase. In 1951 the number of completions in Great Britain had been 195 000 of which 88 per cent were in the public sector. In 1954 when Mr Macmillan was transferred to the Ministry of Defence, completions numbered 347 000, 74 per cent being council houses.

But the Conservatives' housing record was not as spectacular as it seemed. Housing came only second to Defence in the allocation of Exchequer funds—its high priority being supported by the Prime Minister, Winston Churchill, despite there being a feeling in the Cabinet that the housing programme was putting too great a strain on the economy. The emphasis on the number of houses built meant that quality and space standards became secondary considerations. Sampson (1967) records that in November 1951 designs for the 'People's House' were announced:

> each of which would save £150, and could be built more quickly. The People's House quickly helped to speed the flow of new housing: by May 1952 sixty per cent of the new houses were People's Houses, which saved 10 per cent of building materials. [In May 1952 it was announced] that 1000 more houses a week were being built than under the Socialists, and by August [there was] a big reduction in the time of construction and in cost.

Many other consequences of the government's housing policy in 1951–4 can be identified. Few of the new local authority dwellings were earmarked for the low income inner city dwellers—the 'upper working classes' and middle classes being the main beneficiaries; more slums were being created by poor maintenance and the lack of repairs than were being removed by clearance (extensive compulsory purchase, public sector redevelopment and local authority allocation could have helped with these problems but failed to do so); resources were tied up in housebuilding and insufficient were available for investment in industry or road construction (the United Kingdom road programme lagging behind that of most other industrial countries), and imports of timber and other building materials put a strain on the balance of payments. In total, the above may have been an acceptable price to have paid for an increase in the size of the housing stock—the greatest proportion of the increase being council housing. For the first and last time (to date) a housebuilding target had been achieved.

There was a minor shift of emphasis in 1953–6 towards the rehabilitation of unfit houses, grants being made available for this purpose, and private landlords were permitted to raise (controlled) rents in relation to their contribution to the cost of renewal (chapter 8). The 1930s provided a precedent for this when there was a switch to slum clearance away from local authority housebuilding for general needs. Between 1955 and 1961 subsidies to local authorities were reduced to decelerate the average rate of increase in the number of public sector houses, the proportion reaching only 35 per cent of new housebuilding by 1960.

The Housing Subsidies Act of 1956 reduced and eventually abolished Exchequer subsidies for general housing needs. But grants were still available for slum clearance schemes and redevelopment—increasing with the height of the new building—a stimulant for the construction of high rise blocks. Bevan's philosophy of classless and high quality council housing had been reversed within five years. The 1956 Act also released local authorities from mandatory rate contributions to their housing accounts, but imposed restrictions on borrowing from the Public Works Loans Board—making it necessary for them to borrow in the open capital market at rates of interest higher than they would have been charged by the loans board—with consequent pressure on rents.

There was a reversion to the general needs subsidy under the Housing Act of 1961, and more generous grants were made available for slum clearance and rehousing, the relief of overcrowding, provision for the elderly, and overspill or town development schemes. The subsidy for approved needs was set at either £8 or £24 per annum per dwelling, with the former amount being the normal sum. Local authorities were to charge 'realistic rents' defined as an annual amount equal to twice the Gross Value of the building (as determined in 1956). It was thought that these would be equivalent to private sector rents after the Rent Act of 1957 (chapter 3). Poorer authorities (with a small proportion of pre-war houses) would receive the higher subsidy if they incurred a shortfall in rent revenue.

In the early 1960s the high rate of inflation meant that rents based on 1956 values were no longer appropriate. Over 4.2 million local authority houses were let at rents which failed to cover the cost of repairs, maintenance and administration, or loan servicing charges. Rent subsidies by 1962 had reached £140 million, £88 million from the Exchequer, the balance from rates. A major reason for the subsidy was not the level of rent, nor rising building costs, but high interest rates. In 1951 when the Public Works Loans Board was lending at 3 per cent, a council house would have cost in total £3000 over 60 years, but in 1964 over the same length of repayment a similar house (although probably smaller) would have cost over £7000. High interest rates had an even greater effect on housing costs when local authorities were restricted from going to the Public Works Loans Board and had to seek finance from the capital market in 1956–63. In these circumstances it was inevitable that rents were pushed up, the extent of the increase depending on how many houses an authority had built and when. Authorities with large amounts of low cost pre-war housing could (by averaging the lower annual loan servicing charge with its more costly post-war houses) ask lower rents than others which had built most of their houses since the war. Rural authorities and the new town development corporations which had few or no pre-war houses had to charge the highest rents.

After the years in which Mr Harold Macmillan had been Minister of Housing, public sector activity diminished as the Conservative government placed increasing emphasis on owner-occupation (chapter 2). But as Mr Harold Wilson (1964), Leader of the Opposition argued:

> The primary housing need in this country is homes to let. And this is precisely what the Conservatives have failed to provide. The number of council houses built last year, in 1963, was 124 000, 66 000 less than were built when Aneuran Bevan was Housing Minister in 1948, only three years after the end of the war.

1964–70

After the Labour Party's General Election win in October 1964, Mr Richard Crossman (Minister of Housing and Local Government) was determined to achieve the party's manifesto pledge of building 500 000 houses per annum by 1970. There was an emphasis placed on increasing housebuilding in the public sector, and in the period 1964–70 nearly a half of the completions were in that sector (table 5.1). But output over the whole period was not at the expense of standards—in contrast to the Conservative period of office 1951–64. After 1964 Parker Morris standards became mandatory. The decrease in public sector completions 1967–9 can be mainly attributable to a change of power at local government level from Labour to the Conservatives— the latter party reacting against the cost of applying

Table 5.1   Housing Completions, Great Britain, 1964–70

Year	Public sector (000s)	(%)	Private sector (000s)	(%)	Total (000s)
1964	155.6	(42)	218.1	(58)	373.7
1965	168.5	(44)	213.8	(56)	382.3
1966	180.1	(47)	205.4	(53)	385.5
1967	203.9	(50)	200.4	(50)	404.4
1968	191.7	(46)	222.0	(54)	413.7
1969	185.1	(51)	181.7	(49)	366.8
1970	180.1	(51)	170.3	(49)	350.4
Total 1964–70	1265.0	(47)	1411.7	(53)	2678.8

Source: Ministry of Housing and Local Government; Scottish Development Department; Department of the Environment, *Housing and Construction Statistics*

higher standards with resulting reductions in the quantity of public development.

In an attempt to encourage housebuilding at a time of inflation, the Housing Subsidies Act of 1967 modified the basic form of subsidy which had been in its existence since 1924. The Exchequer subsidy would henceforth meet the difference between loan charges incurred by the local authority on borrowing for the financial year and charges which would have been incurred had interest rates been 4 per cent. At a time of rising interest rates, the local authorities commitment therefore remained stable. The Exchequer's commitment was however far from being open-ended (unlike its commitment under the 1919 Act). The central government was indirectly able to control spending through the 'approved cost element' measured by the 'cost yardstick', and subsidies were conditional on the adoption of Parker Morris standards. The 1967 Act also provided for additional subsidies where blocks of flats of four or more storeys were built.

Despite the new subsidies, many Conservative authorities failed to maintain their rate of housebuilding, and the number of public sector completions diminished nationally. Some authorities, for example the Conservative dominated Greater London Council and London boroughs of Westminster and Harrow proposed increasing rents by 38s 6d(£1.92½), 42s 3d(£2.11) and 31s(£1.55) respectively. The Prices and Incomes Act of 1968 therefore restricted increases to 7s 6d(37p)–10s(50p) per week over the following year. With the ending of prices and incomes control, the Rent (Control of Increases) Act of 1969 required local authorities to obtain Ministerial approval if they wished to increase rents on more than 10 per cent of their stock by an average of more than 7s 6d(37p) per week in any 52 week period.

From 1946 to 1970 public sector housing policy passed through three phases. First, from 1946 to 1954, there was an emphasis on housebuilding and rents were generally stable. This was followed by a shift of emphasis to rehabilitation and slum clearance, with less housebuilding and increased rents. From 1964 rents were stabilised and there was a reversion to an emphasis on housebuilding, with a record number of public sector houses completed in 1967 (203, 918).

1970–1974

In its White Paper, *Fair Deal for Housing* (1971), the Conservative government (elected to office in 1970) claimed that its proposals presented a radical change in housing policy, and created conditions for:

> a final assault on the slums, the overcrowding, the dilapidation, and the injustices that still scar the housing scene.

It was argued in the White Paper that although policies for subsidising new buildings prevented an averall shortage of houses, they hindered a solution to the problems which remained. They took too little account of the need to keep the existing stock of houses in good heart. They provided too little help for people in need. The method for controlling rents was fundamentally unfair (claimed the White Paper), and took from people who could ill afford to give to others who often had no need for help. The government consequently laid down three objectives:

(1) A decent home for every family at a price within its means.

(2) A fairer choice between owning a home and renting one.

(3) Fairness between one citizen and another in giving and receiving help towards the cost of housing.

It was argued that the prevailing system of housing finance thwarted these objectives because:

(1) Subsidies for new buildings were indiscriminate—in 1970–1, 90 per cent of the Exchequer subsidies of £157 million and local authority housing subsidies from rates of £65 million went to reduce general rent levels regardless of need, and only 10 per cent went as rent rebates.

(2) Many housing authorities received subsidies but did not need them, whilst authorities with the worst problems got too little.

(3) Some rate and tax payers made a disproportionately high contribution to the housing costs of others—often being poorer and worse housed than the council tenants whom they subsidised.

(4) An unfair pattern of rents existed between different authorities, partly due to historical accident—depending upon when council housing was built.

(5) Housing subsidies from tax and rates which cost £222 million in 1970–1 would rise to at least £300 million by 1980 without even reducing scarcity or removing the [alleged] injustices of the system.

To achieve the objectives of their policy the government proposed in its Housing Finance Act of 1972:

(1) Fair rents for all local authority tenants who could afford them (the same measure being applied to all unfurnished private lettings).

(2) A rent rebate for those who cannot afford fair rents.

(3) The concentration of Exchequer subsidies on authorities with the worst housing.

The legislation was heralded by Mr Peter Walker (1971), Secretary of State for the Environment as 'the most important reform in housing this century', but Mr Anthony Crosland (1971d) Shadow Secretary condemned it as:

the most reactionary and socially divisible measure that was likely to be introduced in the entire lifetime of [that] Parliament . . . [representing] . . . fundamentally a social philosophy of the thirties rather than the seventies.

There was more than just a difference of opinion over detail—there was a polarisation of basic principles. The 1972 Act was abandoning a system of housing rents and Exchequer subsidies which had been used to a greater or lesser extent by governments of different political philosophies since 1923. Although Britain had the largest public housing sector in the western world—giving the greatest degree of freedom to local authorities—the sector was threatened by the Act.

Fair Rents for All Tenants who Could Afford Them

The crux of the government's proposals was the fair rent system. A fair rent was defined by the 1971 White Paper as:

the likely market rent that a dwelling could command if supply and demand for rented accommodation were broadly in balance in the area concerned.

Fair rents were to reflect the value of the accommodation—

by reference to its character, location, amenities, and state of repair—

but not its scarcity value. The rents of most council dwellings were currently below the fair rent level and equal annually to $1.1 \times$ the Gross value of the property. If fair rents were charged local authorities would have been able to make large surpluses.

Fair rents were assessed by the local authority (within a six month period), and provisional assessments were then published. Tenants then had one month to make representations to the authority for consideration. Assessments were then submitted for approval to a special committee of an independent Rent Scrutiny Board—with the local authority having a two

month appeal period if the board imposed a rent different from the submitted assessment. The board tested assessments by inspecting typical
dwellings and making sample checks.

Fair rents were introduced by annual steps beginning in the financial year
1972–3. Rents below the fair rent level were increased by up to £1 from
October 1972 and by 50p from the following October, and it was intended
that they would be redetermined every three years. The impact of the Act
depended very much upon where tenants lived. In 1971 rents varied
enormously from £2.17 for a post-1964 three bedroom house in Barnsley to
£5.00 in Newmarket, with the average being £2.25.

The government believed that the introduction of fair rents in the public
sector was a move in the right direction, Mr Peter Walker (1971) stating:
that:

> the real injustice of the Labour party's system of historic cost rents was
> that local authorities which had the biggest need to provide new houses
> would, by necessity, put the biggest rent burden on the tenants. It was an
> unfair way of fixing rents. . . . Under my system the worse the condition of
> the house, the lower the rent.

It was thought that under the Act, local authorities would have a profit
incentive to build on a much larger scale than hitherto, and they would

> no longer be forced to put up rates every year in order to keep families
> who can well afford proper rents in houses for which they pay artificially
> low rents.
>
> (Rogaly, 1971)

As Ministry of Housing statistics showed, 75 per cent of council tenants paid
less than 10 per cent of family earnings in rent, compared with payments of
at least 20 per cent in the private rented sector. But the principal of
extending fair rents was not without considerable criticism. Mr Anthony
Crosland (1971d) argued that:

> the practical implications of the new method of rent fixing are totally
> muddled and at the same time highly authoritarian . . . it was muddled
> because fair rents . . . were fundamentally intended for a market situation.
> Local authorities . . . have certain social responsibilities, which the private
> landlord does not have, to rehouse people from clearance areas and those
> on waiting lists.

More forcibly, Merrett (1975) asserted that:

> the only meaningful interpretation [of a fair rent] is one which would
> encourage private capitalists to supply on a continuing basis a sufficient
> number of dwellings to shelter the whole of the working class who are not
> council tenants or owner occupiers, which the class could pay for, but

which would not give the capitalists a rate of return on capital higher than the average obtainable in other forms of investment. This 'fair rent', then, is a concept which has meaning only in a capitalist society.

The determination of 5.5 million fair rents within nine months of the Act was an enormous task. It had taken five years to register 200 000 fair rents in the private sector, and inevitably there were inconsistencies and muddle in fixing council rents—a muddle which would have been tolerated if tenants had the democratic right of appeal to the Rent Scrutiny Board.

Between 1935 and 1972 local authorities had been free to set their own rent levels, provided that rents were 'reasonable' (to both tenants and ratepayers), and although there were great dissimilarities between rents paid for similar accommodation in different areas they were fixed by elected representatives. Under the 1972 Act local authorities lost their freedom and autonomy to set rents for their area, and they became simply rent collectors for Whitehall.

Rent Rebates

Every authority was under a duty to consider tenants' views on the rent assessment and to grant a rebate to any who could not afford the fair rent. Local authorities were required to commence the rebate scheme not later than October 1972. A tenant was assessed as having a 'needs allowance' for himself and his wife of £13.50, and £2.50 for each child. When this was the same as his gross income, he would pay 40 per cent of the rent on his dwelling. If his income was more than the needs allowance, he paid 40 per cent of his rent plus 17p for every pound his income exceeded his allowance. If his income was less, he paid 40 per cent of his rent minus 25p for every pound it fell below the allowance. Some families paid no rents at all.

The rebate scheme reduced the rent income obtainable by local authorities, but the government considered a 100 per cent Exchequer subsidy for rebates was wrong in principle, called in question the financial independence of local authorities and failed to reflect their responsibilities. Local authorities therefore had to meet from the rates sums amounting to 10 per cent of the deficit. The Act provided for special publicity to ensure that tenants knew their rights. These, if exerted, would in some cases mean that tenants would not pay rent at all—for example a man earning £12 per week, having a wife and two children and renting a £3 house. But if his take home pay rose to £30 he would have to pay the full rent being ineligible for a rebate. In effect all the subsidies relating to buildings were being replaced by subsidies related to the means of individual tenants. The aim was to save about £300 million per annum.

Mr Peter Walker was sure that the new rebate scheme was 'a very important reform'. It would wipe out the anomaly in which 60 per cent of local authorities operated some rebate scheme and 40 per cent none. Security of tenure would be greatly increased, he believed, because the reason for insecurity in the past had been the inability to meet the rent, and this would be particularly beneficial to tenants in low wage areas. Rogaly (1971) thought that the rent rebate scheme might become

> a new social service, possibly equal in . . . scope to the Supplementary Benefits Commission . . . the rebates will take care of the poor, and they will be at such a level that the really needy will be better-off.

The Concentration of Exchequer Subsidies

A new slum clearance subsidy was proposed which was to meet for the first 15 years at least 75 per cent of the loss to the general rate fund incurred through slum clearance whatever the use—housing or otherwise—chosen for the cleared land. It was payable towards losses arising from 1971 to 1972 onwards. By the early 1970s slum clearance was at a rate of just under 70 000 dwellings per annum. It was hoped that by giving subsidies without specifying what was to be done with the land the annual clearance rate would exceed 100 000.

Although the slum clearance programme was formidable and socially desirable, it meant trebling the rate at which slum dwellers had to be rehoused, ensuring that demolition and housebuilding were in unison, and relocating employment in areas of new housing.

As council rents could no longer be altered to correspond to the state of the Housing Revenue Account or the authority's building programme, authorities with historically high costs and continuing building programmes would clearly have deficits. A new rising cost subsidy was therefore introduced and was particularly relevant to housing stress areas. It was payable to authorities for the credit of their housing revenue account when reckonable expenditure falling on the account for any financial year exceeded the expenditure for the preceding year. After 1974–5 it was intended that the subsidy would settle down at 75 per cent of the increased cost. Conversely councils which had surpluses had to pay them to the Department of the Environment but could receive an amount back depending on the subsidies received during the year.

Criticisms of the 1972 Act

Except for the slum clearance and rising cost subsidies, all other subsidies were to be phased out, and it was estimated that the Act would save £200 million (at 1971 prices) annually. Local authorities were thus being made to discharge their housing responsibilities increasingly on a commercial basis— housing becoming less and less a social service.

But before discussing the effects of the 1972 Act, it is necessary to dispel the belief that the vast majority of council tenants were in any way subsidised. As many as 4 million out of 5.5 million tenants were already paying profit rents in 1971 (the exceptions being those families who claimed rebates because of their circumstances). The remaining 1.5 million tenants, occupying mainly post-1960 housing, received by far the greatest proportion of their subsidy from their fellow council tenants under the system of historic rent pooling.

The government may have hoped that fair rents would have made mortgage repayments seem comparatively attractive, encouraging higher wage tenants to become owner-occupiers elsewhere. But Rogaly (1971) suggested that:

> it may turn out that the proportion of really rich council tenants is low, and that the number granted rebates is very high, so that the net effect will be that a vast new machine will have been created in order to winkle out a numerically insignificant proportion of people who are taking advantage.

Socially, the arguments against turning council estates into one class ghettoes had been understood since Bevan was the Minister responsible for housing, but in the 1950s–60s owner-occupation had increased substantially, resulting in an over-representation of the lower income groups in public sector housing. The rebate system was thus applicable to a high proportion of tenants, with a consequent increase in bureaucracy. But many tenants eligible for rebates preferred not to apply for what they may have regarded as charity. In March 1972 rent rebate schemes covered just under 70 per cent of all council houses, yet only 10 per cent of eligible tenants took up the rebate—form filling being a further deterring factor. The low take up of rebates could easily have caused serious family hardship. That is why the

> principle should [have been] to set rents at a level which people could pay without a means test and without a rebate.
>
> (Crosland, 1971d)

This principal, which had generally been the basis of local authority rent policy since 1919, had been discarded.

The Act càn be particularly criticised for attempting to curb the subsidisation of local authority housing without making any reference to owner-occupation, the latter being subsidised by the option mortgage scheme or tax allowances on mortgage interest (which increase with the size of income and mortgage). The Act seemed to be clearly regressive, council tenants receiving general subsidies of £592 million in 1972–3 (£478 million as Exchequer grants and £114 million from rates) and owner-occupiers getting £803 million in subsidy or tax relief. Meacher (1972) predicted that whereas tax relief to an owner-occupier would rise from an average of £60 to £68 per annum, 1972–6, the total subsidy to a local authority tenant would fall from an average of £75 per annum to £33 per annum having a major redistribution affect in favour of the owner-occupier. But the latter prediction was inaccurate, largely because of the rapid increase in the price of land particularly for council building in the inner cities; in London, for example the average cost of land for a council house was £300 in 1953, but was £6000 in 1973 (the house costing £20 000). Yet the owner-occupier on average received more assistance than the council tenant throughout the period in question, and unlike the tenant was not subjected to a 'means test'.

The Act did not induce public sector housebuilding as table 5.2 shows but it may have given it an advantage over private housebuilding during inflation as it accounted for an increasing proportion of total completions in 1972–4.

Table 5.2   Housing Completions, Great Britain, 1971–4

Year	Public sector (000s)	(%)	Total (000s)
1971	158.9	(45)	350.5
1972	122.8	(39)	319.1
1973	107.5	(45)	293.6
1974	128.6	(48)	268.8

Source: Department of the Environment, *Housing and Construction Statistics*

1974–79

On resuming office in 1974, the Labour government was faced with a declining public housing sector in absolute terms. The number of completions had fallen almost to a post-war low, and investment in the sector had dropped by 60 per cent (1968–73). Meanwhile council houses had been increasingly sold off, the number of sales in England and Wales rising from 6231 in 1970 to 45 058 by 1972. Local authority housing waiting lists were growing, particularly in the major cities, for example in London from 192 000 to 201 000 (1973–4). Under the 1972 Act, higher rents were to be paid by 2.5 million council tenants in April 1974, and a further 2.5 million were liable for an increase on 1 October, although local authorities in England and Wales had made an overall profit of £20 million on housing in 1973.

One of the first measures which the new government introduced was a freeze on rents until the end of 1974 (later extended to March 1975), and Labour's election pledge to repeal the 1972 Act was fulfilled by the Housing Rent and Subsidies Act of 1975. By this, local authorities no longer had to charge fair rents; Rent Scrutiny Boards were abolished and local authorities again had the legal right to decide council rents; the 'no profit rule' was restored to council housing—though local authorities could maintain a 'reasonable working balance' in their Housing Revenue Accounts, but the national rent rebate scheme for poorer tenants—introduced by the 1972 Act—was retained.

'Reasonable rents' were introduced (a level of rent not too low to impose a burden on tax and rate payers, and not too high to provide a profit), and the system of statutory rent increases was abolished. The government introduced a guideline which limited each local authority from increasing rents by more than an average of 60p per week per annum from 1975 to 1976. Although not statutorily enforced, the average unrebated rent increased approximately in accordance with the guideline after April 1975, and in real terms rents remained fairly stable—in contrast to their rapid increase 1971-4 (table 5.3).

Table 5.3 Council Rents, England and Wales, 1970–7

From:	*Average unrebated rent*	*In real terms (relative to retail prices)*
March 1970	£2.23	100
April 1971	£2.48	100
April 1972	£2.75	104
May 1973	£3.44	118
January 1974	£3.75	120
April 1975	£4.16	103
April 1976	£4.77	100
April 1977	£5.52	98

Source: Department of the Environment, *Housing and Construction Statistics*

At a time of high rates of inflation and interest, the 1975 Act increased subsidies in order to hold back rents and increase housebuilding. Local authority Housing Revenue Accounts were to receive from 1975/76 injections of: a 'basic element'—a subsidy fixed in cash terms; a 'new capital cost element'—equal to 66 per cent of loan charges incurred on new capital expenditure; and a 'supplementary financing element'—equal to 33 per cent of any increase in loan charges on capital expenditure undertaken before 1975/76. But in certain high cost areas, local authorities would still incur deficits on their Housing Revenue Accounts unless they greatly increased rate revenue or rents, or reduced capital expenditure. Therefore a 'special element' was introduced in 1975/76 (meeting a £21 deficit per dwelling by 1976/77), and a 'high cost element' was introduced in 1976/77 (meeting up to 75 per cent of the deficit above £21 per dwelling and 50 per cent of the deficit below that sum). Table 5.4 shows that although subsidies increased from 1975/76, the rate fund contributions declined—shifting the burden of support from the ratepayer to the Exchequer. The 1975 Act sustained local

Table 5.4   General Subsidies to Council Housing, Capital Expenditure and Public Sector Housebuilding

	1972/73	*1973/74*	*1974/75*	*1975/76*	*1976/77*	*1977/78*
Total subsidies (£ million)	592	722	1188	1236	1320	1283
Exchequer subsidies	*478*	*558*	*913*	*962*	*1110*	*1073*
Rate fund contributions	*114*	*164*	*275*	*274*	*210*	*210*
Capital expenditure (£ million)	1844	2029	2324	2317	2115	1781
	1972	*1973*	*1974*	*1975*	*1976*	*1977*
Public sector housing completions (000s)	122.8	107.5	128.6	162.3	163.0	162.5

Source: The Government's Expenditure Plans, 1978/79 to 1981/82 (Cmnd 7049, Jan. 1978); Department of the Environment, Housing and Construction Statistics

authority housing investment (despite unprecedented inflation and interest rates) until 1977/78 when the effects of public spending cuts and underspending by Conservative local authorities had their effect. Table 5.4 shows that although investment fell substantially 1975/76–1977/78, public sector housebuilding was sustained at an annual rate higher than under the Conservatives during 1972–4.

Although increased rents were kept in line with the increase in retail prices, the *Financial Times* (21 June 1975) showed that the amount the average tenant paid as a percentage of household income fell from 17.5 per cent in 1968 (when the average income per household was £21.12 per week) to 10.2 per cent in 1975 (when the average income was £54.80). Whereas Exchequer subsidies to the Housing Revenue Account had increased from 27.8 to 54 per cent from 1967/68 to 1975/76, the share of rental payments decreased from 55.3 per cent to 27 per cent over the same period. In 1976 it was announced that by 1978/79 Exchequer subsidies and rate contributions would be lowered by £310 million—necessitating rent increases of about £2.50 per week with the aim of making tenants pay over 50 per cent of the cost or 'breakeven' rent. It became part of the Labour Party's thinking that incomes rather than retail prices should influence rent levels, *Labour's Programme* (1976) stating:

> Where existing rents are broadly based upon pooled historic costs, rents should not go up faster than the proportionate increase in the tenant's income

—a superficially generous intention, but one marking a radical change in philosophy.

In the late 1970s council housing became a victim of public expenditure cuts. The number of public sector house starts in Great Britain fell from 173 800 in 1975 to 80 100 in 1979, and improvements fell from a peak of almost 193 300 dwellings in 1973 to only 52 250 in 1979 (figure 5.1). In addition many councils slashed their repairs and maintenance expenditure causing delays in getting repairs done, and frustration to tenants. Council housebuilding in 1979 was at its lowest since the 1930s. Although the Treasury had allocated £2480 million for local authority housebuilding (1978/79), £650 million of this sum was not taken up since Conservative councils were reluctant to expand the public sector housing stock. In 1979 the incoming Conservative government cut Exchequer grants by £300 million (1979/80), and then many Labour councils were faced with cuts of 40 per cent with drastic effects upon their housebuilding programmes.

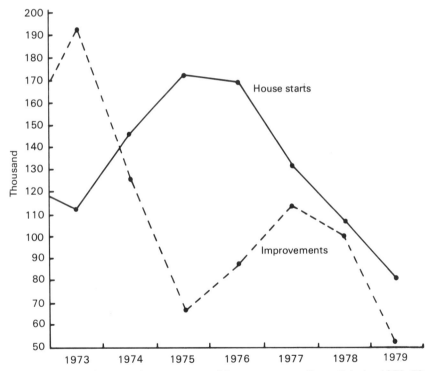

Figure 5.1 Public sector house starts and improvements, Great Britain, 1973–79.

The Housing Finance Review

In 1975/76 the average subsidy to council tenants was £195, and house purchasers received an average of £185 in the form of tax relief on mortgage interest and option mortgage subsidy. But whereas house purchasers received increased assistance as their incomes rose (chapter 2), tenants on average received more if their incomes were small. In 1974, Mr Anthony Crosland (Secretary of State for the Environment) realised that housing subsidies had failed the tests of resource effectiveness and equity, and set up a committee to review housing finance. From this emerged (18 months behind schedule) the Green Paper, *Housing Policy* (1977). The main questions which the review was designed to answer were:

(1) *How much housing do we need and how can resources be used to supply it?*

(2) *How much should individuals pay for their housing?* Although subsidies were necessary they should not be indiscriminate or limitless.

The Green Paper stated that:

general housing assistance should be retained, but should be distributed more fairly and more evenly—

but it dismissed all means of doing this as it risked a drastic and disruptive effect on household budgets. Instead, it proposed that council rents should rise with earnings, but only in the rising cost and subsidised authorities. This is in marked contrast with owner-occupation, where the greatest tax relief goes to those with the most expensive housing and highest income (table 5.5). The Green Paper largely ignored the evidence that there was a growing concentration of poorer households in the public sector, with 55 per cent of tenants being eligible for means tested rent rebates and a growing number receiving supplementary benefits.

Table 5.5   **Housing Subsidies and Tax Relief, 1974/75**

| | Local authority sector | | | Owner-occupiers |
	Subsidy	*Rebate*	*Total*	*Tax relief and option mortgage subsidy*
Under £1000	£120	£46	£166	£59
£2500–£2999	£147	—	£147	£101
Over £5000	£154	—	£154	£275

Source: Green Paper, *Housing Policy* (1977)

(3) *What are the wider social implications of the way housing is organised?* The local authority sector contains one in three households in Britain. It is a community asset and it ought to offer the possibility of a choice between renting and owning to households during their life cycle. Local authorities should be able to use their surpluses to expand (like the permanent building societies). In no sense should the sector resemble the

public sector in the United States, where 'welfare housing' is provided for only one in thirty households (the poor, the old, the otherwise disadvantaged). But there is a danger that this might happen. Mr Crosland (1975) was particularly concerned with the growing polarisation between owner-occupiers and council tenants:

> a deep divide has opened between the two; a division which threatens to become as deep and as fundamental as the other major divide in our society between classes.

After considering the above questions, the housing finance review largely upheld the *status quo* in the owner-occupied sector, but the Green Paper proposed some major changes in the public sector in the areas of resource effectiveness and subsidisation.

The Green Paper's innovation of Housing Investment Programmes (HIPs) was a major change in the system of allocating Exchequer funds to local authorities. HIPs are determined by the government measuring national demand (by adding together local demand), and this demand is used as a basis for local authority bids for capital expenditure—the total amount available being restricted by the Treasury's cash limits within the public sector's total borrowing requirement. The new system means that funds are to be allocated generally according to a formula combining a national index of housing stress with the spending records of authorities—subsidies ceasing to be fixed amounts per dwelling. Local authorities have to justify their programmes according to the shortages and needs not catered for in the private sector. The Green Paper thus made public housing a 'residual' rather than a 'normal' tenure, thereby undermining all the principles on which the social ownership of housing is based. Moreover, government funds to local authorities are no longer dependent upon them building council houses—they could instead finance the private sector (through mortgages and improvement grants) and housing associations.

The extent of subsidisation in the public sector is influenced by two intrinsic advantages which local authority housing has over owner-occupation. The first is that past investments are held at their fixed historic cost which averaged £3000 per dwelling in 1976 (although 75 per cent of council houses were built post-war), and the Exchequer subsidy on interest charges declines in real terms. The existing stock therefore offers cheap housing to the end of the century or beyond. In contrast, the cost of owner-occupied housing and interest payments generally increase by virtue of revaluation and exchange. Even without a subsidy the average breakeven rent—given pooled interest costs and making allowance for management and maintenance—would have been £11 per week in 1976, and with a subsidy of say 33 per cent (equal to the standard relief rate for owner-occupiers) on just the interest charge the rent would have been £8.50–£9.0. The second advantage is that within a local authority area cross subsidisation can take place—

'surplus' rents from areas of older or cheaper housing can offset 'deficit' rents from areas of newer and more costly housing. Although inflation puts an increased strain on cost pooling especially as a higher proportion of the housing stock becomes modern, over time the financial self-sufficiency of local authority housing will reassert itself as it is generally free from the process of revaluation and exchange. The Green Paper was opposed to inter-authority cross subsidisation as it would have breached the 'no profit rule'. Areas with rising costs would therefore have to meet these by raising rents in line with incomes and seeking additional subsidies—although there is no automatic entitlement. Even 'falling cost' and 'stable cost' authorities may be in no better position, as the former may need to sell-off their older houses to prevent making profits, and the latter may need to trim their capital expenditure as it might be difficult to justify on the basis of local need or housing stress. Rising cost authorities who need to build large numbers of houses will be under greater government scrutiny than ever before.

The introduction of this new system of subsidisation with its effects upon rents occurred at a time when the income tax threshold was at a low level. Because of generous tax allowances on mortgage interest, and the foregoing of Schedule A and capital gains tax— all benefitting owner-occupiers (chapter 2)—the tax base was eroded. The rate of income tax in general was consequently high with the burden falling on tenants in particular. Nevitt (1978) stated that:

> This makes it more difficult for tenants to pay the cost rent of their dwellings and subsidies to this sector have increased with tax burdens; this has in turn raised central government taxes and local rates, making it still more difficult for individuals to pay for their housing. Once a circular system has been generated it is very difficult to break into it and inhibit the feed back effects. However taxes now fall on even the poorest working families and it might be possible to lower taxes and simultaneously increase rents.

Although at the time of writing it is uncertain how net personal taxation will change in the near future—to what extent reductions in income tax will be offset by higher indirect tax—it is certain that council rents will rise quite substantially following the implementation of the Green Paper's recommendations. According to the Centre for Environmental Studies (1978) reduced government subsidies to local authorities will mean that tenants will have to pay an extra £190 million in rent by 1988 assuming that contributions from the Exchequer will decrease and rate contributions are unchanged. In February 1980 Mr Michael Heseltine, Secretary of State for the Environment, announced a 33.4 per cent cut of up to £1000 million in the total housing allocation which necessitated an average rent increase for council tenants of 60p in October 1980, bringing the average increase to £2.10 per week for the year. Although council rents had not been keeping pace with incomes, the rise in rents in 1980 was well ahead of the annual increase in earnings, and its effect on inflation and industrial relations was bound to be unfavourable. With further cuts in public expenditure, it is probable that by 1984, the average council rent will have risen to £21 per week (at 1980 prices), a threefold increase from 1980.

The Reform of Local Government Housing

Local authority housing can be reformed in two major but conflicting ways. The first way is to strengthen it and to encourage its expansion for general needs. The second is to weaken it and promote its contraction to little more than a welfare facility.

To many people council housing is not only an 'undesirable' tenure in an economic sense, but is unattractive socially and psychologically. This was a view opposed by Mr Anthony Crosland (1971e):

There is still . . . a taint attached to living in a council house—a whiff of the welfare, of subsidisation, of huge uniform estates, and generally of second class citizenship. . . . For myself I reject the view that municipal housing should be purely a welfare service or a safety net for people who cannot be housed in the private sector. I believe it must be the main provider of housing for all those who wish to rent. . . . Local authorities must now take responsibility for meeting the total need for rented accommodation from whatever source it comes.

Mr Crosland believed that the private rented sector should not be encouraged to perform this function:

private landlordism is not an appropriate form of house-ownership in an advanced society . . . the [private] landlord wields a degree of power over his tenant's life which is unacceptable in a democratic society.

But Mr Crosland accepted that the status of council tenure needed to be raised and suggested a number of improvements. These consisted of more choice of local authority accommodation to suit the different needs of tenants; more community services such as shops, pubs, community centres, play areas and libraries; a greater variety of estates, General Improvement Areas and Housing Action Areas; more security of tenure at least on a par with the private rented sector under the Rent Act of 1968; and more tenant participation eventually leading to management by tenants or co-operative ownership.

But throughout the 1970s council housing did not become more generally available, nor were tenants granted greater security. In 1979 five major charities (Shelter, Help the Aged, Campaign for the Single Homeless, National Council for One-Parent Families, and SHAC-the London Housing Aid Centre) called for an end of all restrictions on people applying for council houses, and for a change in the regulations affecting the allocation (or lack of allocation) of housing to the elderly, single parents, single people, migrants and people without residential qualifications—some local authorities not housing single people under 40–50, and some not housing pensioners unless they were single.

In the last days of the 1974–9 Labour government a Housing Bill was presented intended to introduce a 'Tenants' Charter'. It would have incorporated some of the proposals made by Mr Anthony Crosland seven years earlier. The Bill's proposals included security of tenure equivalent to that in the private rented sector; the right of tenant participation (although local authorities would select tenant representatives); a national tenant mobility scheme whereby a certain proportion of dwellings would be set aside for applicants without residential qualifications; home repair grants and improvement grants for tenants; and the right to take in lodgers. The Secretary of State would have been given powers to fix grant levels for improvement, decide how many homes a council should allocate for mobility schemes, and to buy houses for improvement and to resell them after improvement on the open market (a £5000 subsidy per dwelling being available from the Treasury for this purpose). The Bill however made no reference to housing single persons or disadvantaged households.

To strengthen the public sector, it might be necessary to introduce an alternative form of finance than that prescribed by the 1977 Green Paper. Kilroy (1978) proposed a system of national rent pooling based on cross-subsidisation between authorities. Kilroy argued that if cross-subsidisation is permitted within an authority, why should it not be applied across the whole of the public housing sector? Local authority boundaries had changed under the Local Government Act of 1972 and in many cases increased rent disparities between authorities. The system would be acceptable to most authorities if their housebuilding and improvement programmes were financed on a revolving fund basis taking into account the different 'life cycles' of local authority housing.

Kilroy explained that:

National rent pooling would not involve some 'national average rent'; rents would vary according to the value of the dwelling ... [and] ... subsidies would be paid each year in the form of interest relief on local authorities' aggregated outstanding housing debt at a rate in line with the [prevailing basic] rate of tax relief to which mortgagors are automatically entitled.

The method of apportioning the subsidy between authorities would involve:

balancing each authority's loan charges expenditure against its means to pay according to a 'target income' formula, which would increase according to changes in the overall value of that authority's housing stock. Each authority would be required to raise sufficient 'mortgage element' in its rents to meet this target income. Where this was less than its actual loan charges, the national pool would cover the deficit; where more, the surplus would be paid into the pool.

There would be no pooling and subsidisation of management and maintenance costs as this would 'cushion' inefficient authorities.

The above proposals would preserve the freedom of local authorities to set rents, as target incomes would be assessed in relation to the aggregate gross rateable value of the local housing stock. It would be unlikely that rents would rise to a higher level than under the Green Paper, and perhaps more importantly:

> pooling would remove the need for making cuts in capital programmes to replace surpluses otherwise retained by the authorities with falling costs.

—thereby assisting housebuilding and rehabilitation.

Abandoned Council Houses

Housing finance also needs to be reformed to avoid an increase in the number of empty council houses or the need to demolish 'unlettable' blocks. Despite long waiting lists, many urban authorities, such as the Inner London boroughs, have rendered unusuable and boarded up empty council dwellings; Liverpool is either selling off or giving away properties such as the infamous 'piggeries'; and other authorities such as Glasgow are pulling down blocks built in the 1950s.

Although empty council housing accounted for less than 4 per cent of the total stock in the late 1970s, it was highly concentrated in the inner urban areas and was severely vandalised. Donnison (1979) suggested that the main reason for the abandonment of these areas was that the younger and more prosperous tenants have moved out to the suburbs or beyond; that the growth of service industries in the inner areas has not compensated for the loss of manufacturing jobs; that because of housing improvement in the private sector, the standard of the worst council housing has fallen below that of the better private rented housing; and that within the public sector the 'fortunate, the well organised and the articulate' have gradually gained possession of the better housing—normally with little or no increase in rent. Whilst the demand curve for council housing slopes downwards as distance from the centre of an urban area increases, the supply price generally remains constant with distance. Therefore, among higher income tenants, there is a great incentive to abandon the inner areas.

Donnison proposed that in the public sector, there should be a reassessment of rents and valuation for rating purposes on the basis of matching 'shelter costs' with tenants' preferences. This would involve charging higher rents and rates in the more popular estates (with increased rent and rate rebates and child allowances for the poorer tenants). Consequently—

there would probably be a smaller outflow of the more demanding and 'respectable' tenants from estates low on the ladders of esteem.

Additionally it would be necessary—

to create better opportunities for work and for earning for the people in deprived and unpopular neighbourhoods—

presumably so that they would be able to pay increasingly unrebated rents and rates towards the cost of maintenance and repairs. But, by implication, the crux of Donnison's main proposal is that higher surpluses could be realised on housing in the more popular estates and these could be used to increase the cross-subsidisation of currently less popular housing in some of the inner urban areas—reducing the possibility of it becoming 'unlettable' or having to be demolished.

A further way of strengthening the public sector is by means of municipalisation (chapter 4). By curtailing the disappearance of rented accommodation currently in the private sector, it would preserve the stock of housing available for letting, and because of its diversity offer a wider choice of housing to council tenants.

With a change from a Labour to a Conservative government in May 1979, the emphasis was placed not on strengthening the role of local authority housing but on reducing its importance. The selling-off of council houses again became a major plank in the Conservative's housing policy.

Sale of Council Houses

Local authorities were empowered to sell council houses to sitting tenants by the Conservatives under section 104 of the Housing Act of 1957, and under Circular 54/70 which allowed sales either at full market value with no conditions attached, or at 20 per cent below provided that (a) the tenant offer the dwelling back to the council if he wished to sell within five years of acquisition, *or* (b) if the authority did not wish to re-acquire the property, he could sell it in the open market but at a price no higher than he paid for it plus the value of any improvements. Table 5.6 shows that council house sales were particularly high during the Conservative period of office, 1970–4, and low during the middle 1970s when the Labour government was able to control sales. Whereas Mrs Margaret Thatcher, as Shadow Environmental Minister before the October 1974 General Election, pledged that local authority tenants of three years standing would be able to buy their council houses at one-third less than market value (instead of the prevailing 20 per cent discount), Labour's Circular 70/74 was cautious about council sales and stressed that:

The first duty of a local authority is to ensure an adequate supply of rented dwellings. In areas where there are substantial needs to meet for rented dwellings, as in the large cities, the Secretaries of State consider that it is generally wrong for local authorities to sell council houses.

The increase of sales in the late 1970s was mainly due to the Conservatives regaining control of many urban local authorities in 1977–8.

The arguments which have been presented in favour of selling council houses include the following:

(1) By 1974–5 council housing costs—especially in the major cities— seemed to be spiralling out of control, for example new housing was costing the London Borough of Camden £50 800 per unit, which would have necessitated a cost rent of £120 per week in contrast to the actual rent charged of £10–£15 per week; in Islington flats were being developed at £23 000 requiring a cost rent of £45 per week compared with £8.50 being charged; in Hackney flats costing £27 200 with a cost rent of £49 per week were let at £5.85, and in Kensington and Chelsea (where there were relatively few new houses) average cost rents were £52 per week compared with average fair rents of £11. With such costs of development and discrepancies between cost rents and rents paid, many people have argued that council houses (costing on average £1200 per annum in subsidies by the late 1970s) should be sold or even given away.

(2) It was argued that it would be cheaper to provide a housebuyer with a nominal grant (of say £1000) and a 25 year mortgage than to build a council house which would attract a £1200 subsidy in the first year and maintenance costs and loan charges in the future.

(3) Although tenants received accommodation at considerably below market rents and in many cases below cost rents, it was not in their long term interest to be tenants. Mr Peter Walker (1978) explained that over the period 1950–78 whereas a council tenant might have paid say £4750 in rent, not have owned his dwelling, and would have to incur increased rents in the

Table 5.6 Local Authority Dwellings Sold for Owner-Occupation, England and Wales, 1970–8

1970	6 231
1971	16 851
1972	45 058
1973	33 720
1974	4 153
1975	2 089
1976	4 582
1977	12 019
1978	28 540

Source: Department of the Environment, *Housing and Construction Statistics*

future—an owner-occupier who bought a house for say £2000 in 1950 would have paid £2750 (after tax relief) on a 25 year mortgage ((plus repair and maintenance costs) and would have a realisable asset of at least £12 000 with no further mortgage repayments. To end this division between council tenants and owner-occupiers, Mr Walker proposed that tenants of 30 years or more standing should be given their dwellings, tenants of 15 years would pay mortgage repayments for 15 years, and tenants of five years would pay repayments for 25 years. This would save £500 million of subsidies which could either lead to a reduction in taxation and rates or a diversion of revenue for other purposes.

(4) The sale of council houses would satisfy the increasing desire for home ownership as real incomes rise.

(5) Since many council tenants cannot raise a sufficient mortgage from a building society for the purchase of a private sector house, therefore the availability of a local authority mortgage to buy a council house provides a choice between renting and buying.

(6) Council sales might eventually ease the pressure on the owner-occupied market and help to stabilise house prices.

(7) Owner-occupation would offer a household greater security of tenure than council housing—even though security is being increased in the latter sector.

(8) Owner-occupation of former council housing might reduce the degree of vandalism to property.

(9) Donnison (1979) argued that although in many areas of scarcity, council housing should not be sold as there will always be a need for publicly owned subsidised housing, elsewhere—

> sales may help to keep the whole stock of council property in houseproud use, and retain people—particularly the children of present tenants—in neighbourhoods which they might otherwise desert altogether.

But most of the above arguments can be easily refuted:

(1) Arguments in favour of selling council housing are often based on extreme examples (such as in inner London) of the subsidised cost of a new council house. The fact that local authorities are able to spread out these costs over the whole of their stock is ignored. The system of 'pooled historic costs' enables the surplus of rents from older houses to be used to keep rents on newer houses (built when capital costs and interest rates were high) down to within the means of lower income households who either do not wish or cannot afford to buy a house of their own. Even though the cost of developing housing in the inner areas, of for example London, may seem excessive, the average price of land for a local authority two bedroom flat may be as high as £12 000, equivalent to as much as one-third of the cost of the dwelling. If sites could be acquired more cheaply— either by a more

'realistic' method of valuation where appropriate, or by the local authority acquiring land in the outer urban areas—the total cost of development would diminish, for example in inner London the average cost of building a new council dwelling was about £28 000 in 1975, compared with £21 050 in outer London (and £15 000 just beyond the Green Belt). But even if it is desirable to sponsor overspill housing (taking into account the need to house many essential workers in inner London), most outer London boroughs have used their planning powers to oppose decentralisation.

(2) The argument that by selling-off council houses, local authorities can contribute towards a major cut in public expenditure (to the advantage of the tax and rate payer) is extremely fallacious. Although debt charges (totalling £1948 million in 1978), management and maintenance costs exceed rent in the first 10–15 years of the life of a council dwelling, for the next 40–50 years the rent is normally greater than outgoings—especially during inflation when the rent subsidy gets less and less in real terms. But if council dwellings are sold, although in the first few years mortgage repayments would exceed rent (and there would be savings to the authority in management and maintenance), in the long term mortgage repayments would fall in real terms and be considerably less than rent revenue. Ratepayers would also need to contribute to the cost incurred by councils in advertising, offering bonuses to sales staff, appointing sales directors and in commissioning estate agents—all of whom may be thought necessary if a council's sales programme is to succeed.

Taxpayers also would lose as mortgage interest relief would be greater than rent subsidy, and the former would increase every time a dwelling is resold (normally every seven years on average).

Shelter (1979b) estimated that £3000 per house would be the net total loss over 40 years to public spending from selling the average council dwelling, and if the annual disposal reached 250 000 dwellings per annum (the Conservatives' target), then £3000 million could be lost (1979–84). The Department of the Environment (1979) reporting to the Labour government estimated that losses would be between £2735 and £8535 per home.

But the stripping of a public asset by a local authority—with the net cost borne by rate and tax payers—may be followed after a few years by former council properties (bought at a discount at public expense) being sold privately at a profit free of tax. Disposal might not necessarily be due to the owner wishing to make a capital gain, but due to him being unable to continue with mortgage repayments and maintain a property which he was persuaded (probably by intensive advertising) to buy.

(3) Mr Peter Walker's proposal of giving away council property to tenants of long standing and selling-off the remainder with mortgages of different lengths (ostensibly to the benefit of ratepayers and tenants) has provoked much criticism. McIntosh, Augaton and Kilroy (1978) argued that

Mr Walker (in stating that local authority housing was running at a loss) included in his calculations the cost of rent rebates and supplementary benefits (which presumably would still have to be paid to low income tenants if they were able to buy their homes). But if income support is not taken into account, rent revenue less management and maintenance costs would have amounted to £827 million in 1977/78 leaving £1100 million of debt to be met by subsidies—an amount approximately equal to tax relief to owner mortgagors. It was also argued that Mr Walker ignored the cost of repairs which owners would have to incur on top of mortgage repayments (which they would incur as part of rent if they were tenants), and the cost of tax relief on mortgage interest which could rise as housing changes hands.

(4) It is doubtful whether the sale of council houses would satisfy the increasing desire of households to become owner-occupiers. Only high income tenants (those who earned more than £6000 per annum in 1979) would be able to afford to buy their homes as prices would still be high (especially in the inner cities) despite discounts. Based on a 15 year, 100 per cent local authority mortgage, and assuming an interest rate of 10.75 per cent, a typical council house would cost a buyer £61 per month initially if the rate of discount was 50 per cent, rising to £97 per month at a discount of 20 per cent. With these outgoings, the vast majority of the 6 million council tenants (who earned less than £4000 per annum) would remain tenants.

(5) Instead of council mortgages being granted to tenants in order to deplete the local authority housing stock, public funds could be injected into the building societies (or building societies could set aside a greater proportion of their funds) to enable council tenants to buy properties in the private sector (chapter 2). This could save ratepayers a substantial sum, for example a council house valued at £25 000 would be offered to a tenant at a discount of £7500 (assuming a 30 per cent rate). If a subsidy of less than this were granted the tenant could buy privately (with a council mortgage if necessary), and release his council house for a family in need. This, together with other means of assisting first-time buyers, would be a more cost-effective way of widening the choice between buying and renting, and it would keep the public sector intact for the benefit of a high proportion of households wanting to rent. But a doctrinaire antipathy towards council housing seemingly stands in the way of an economic allocation of resources.

(6) If public funds were not injected into the building society movement, the increase in demand for mortgages as a result of council house sales, could push up mortgage rates to unprecedented levels to the disadvantage particularly of young first-time buyers.

(7) Donnison's view that council houses should be sold off to retain people in their familiar neighbourhoods, ignores the fact that some authorities may sell to applicants from outside of the community. But more probably, as it would only be the better houses which were saleable (notably

two storey dwellings with gardens), they would continue to be occupied by the same families whether they were council properties or privately owned. Yet if sold, the buyers would probably be families with children growing up, whilst families with young children and low incomes would be increasingly confined to less desirable and often high rise property. There would also be a consequent increase in rents in the inner areas since the selling-off of older and surplus-yielding housing in the suburbs would reduce the degree of cross subsidisation. Sales would also reduce the possibility of tenants being transferred from inner area flats to suburban houses if the latter were sold off and became no longer available. But allocation would generally become inflexible. When council tenants die, buy private houses or move elsewhere, their dwellings normally become available for new tenants—as many as one half of all new tenants are housed in this way. But if the properties are sold and then become vacant these houses can no longer be used for allocation.

By the late 1970s there were 1.5 million households on council waiting lists. In the major cities very few of these people can expect to be housed by local authorities in the forseeable future. In Greater London in 1976 there were 192 000 households on waiting lists but only 19 000 of this number were provided with council housing, the local authorities having a prior duty to rehouse tenants from clearance schemes. Under the Housing (Homeless Persons) Act of 1977 this responsibility has been extended to the registered homeless. The selling-off of council houses frustrates the ability of major housing authorities to satisfy these needs.

The Pace of Council House Sales

On becoming the majority party in the Greater London Council (GLC) in 1977 the Conservatives planned to offer 218 000 tenants the chance to buy their homes. Kilroy (1977) calculated that the cost to the ratepayers of selling-off an initial 50 000 dwellings would amount to £80 million. By 1978 the GLC had a 1000 empty dwellings (losing £510 000 in lost rents and rates) which it hoped to sell. Houses costing between £35 000 and £39 000 and flats costing £26 800–£37 500 could only be sold for £19 500 and £10 000 respectively. In 1977–8 the GLC had sold 7000 of its total stock of 225 000 dwellings, many sales being in the open market, and it was in the open market that the GLC planned to make a loss of £10–£15 million. Mrs Gladys Dimson (1978) Labour spokesman on housing commented:

> These figures show up the sales policy as the policy of the lunatic asylum. ... If the homes were rented to tenants and people in need ... after 15 years we could recoup the money and eventually ... make a profit. .... Once these properties have been sold on the open market they will change hands in a few years' time at enormous profit.

In the London borough of Wandsworth, every available council house was put on the market for sale, not just to sitting tenants but to anyone even if they were not a resident of the borough—despite there being a waiting list of over 7000 households by 1979. Houses were often sold up-market at prices of up to £36 000. In 1979 some Surrey and Essex authorities were planning to sell 80 per cent of their stock, although buyers were not immediately forthcoming.

Outside of the South East, sales were concentrated in Birmingham (second only to the GLC as the largest seller of council housing in Britain), Nottingham, Bradford, Leeds, Derby, Leicester, Bolton and Tameside. In Liverpool, the Liberal controlled city council offered 80 000 houses for sale and many were virtually given away—for example dwellings in three 15 storey blocks were being sold at £1 each and 2000 other dwellings were being sold for 10p each. This, in the view of the local Labour Party, did little to help the 16 000 households on the waiting list, and it meant even longer waits, and discrimination against those remaining council tenants, who, due to the loss of surplus yielding housing, inevitably have to incur higher rents. But Liverpool at least has a major rehabilitation programme making full use of compulsory purchase, and the council were building houses for leasehold sale at prices £2000 lower than they would have been in the private market. Many large urban authorities, for example Merseyside, Newcastle, Edinburgh and Cardiff sold very few properties, and Glasgow sold none (up to 1979). In Manchester council houses sold in the period 1971–8 were being bought back generally at £6000 more than they were initially sold for, the council preferring to incur a £6000 loss than to spend £13 000 building new houses. In 1977 authorities throughout England were re-acquiring houses at a cost of £1 million per month—perhaps a foretaste of the future. But council house sales were far greater in number, reaching a total of 18 000 in 1978.

Conclusion

In March 1979, Mr Peter Shore, Secretary of State for the Environment, announced curbs on the sale of council houses. These restrictions applied to sales of newly completed dwellings; sales of empty houses; tenants' rights to take out options to buy their houses in the future, and sales to tenants of under three years' standing. Restrictions were not imposed on sales to tenants of three or more years' standing; the building of houses by local authorities for sale, and equity sharing schemes.

The return of a Conservative government in May 1979 resulted in a major change in policy. Restrictions on council house sales were largely discontinued, and tenants were given the statutory right to buy the freehold of their house or a 125-year leasehold of their flat by the Housing Act of 1980. To counter the possibility that a council might delay or impede a sale, the Secretary of State has the right to intervene and complete the sale. Discounts of 33 per cent were offered to tenants of three years' standing, rising to 50 per cent to those of 20 or more years' standing. Council mortgages of 100 per cent have become available, and if the property is resold within five years, the capital gain is shared between the owner and the local authority (other sections of the Act gave council tenants greater security of tenure, the right to take in lodgers, and to get improvement grants on the same basis as owner-occupiers). Although Mr Michael Heseltine (1979b), Secretary of State for the Environment stated that the legislation

> lays the foundations for one of the most important social revolutions of this century,

Mr Gerald Kaufmann (1979), MP, former Department of Environment Minister, said the measures

> will not provide a single new home and will deprive many homeless people or families living in tower blocks from getting suitable accommodation.

The government disagreed with Labour's claim that the loss on sales would average £5000 per house (with discounts of only 16–17 per cent), a £50 million loss on every 10 000 houses sold. The Department of the Environment (1980) suggested that profits could reach £9218 on each house sold, reversing earlier official claims.

In general, short-term economies in public spending will only make it more difficult for councils to reduce homelessness, reduce their waiting and transfer lists, and limit rent increases to the rate of increase in wages. But changes in the political control of local authorities produced resistance to the government's policy of encouraging house sales, for example in the local government elections of May 1979, Labour recaptured Coventry, Sandwell, South Tyneside, Tameside and Wolverhampton from the Conservatives, and in May 1980 gained Birmingham, Bolton, Bradford, Kirklees, Oldham, Rochdale and Walsall. Labour also won control of many non-metropolitan districts (1979–80), most notably Derby, Leicester, Nottingham, Oxford and Preston. Manchester, already Labour controlled, declared its intention not to sell until forced to by law. Other large authorities such as Sheffield, West Midlands, Sunderland and Hull, together with many smaller councils, similarly banned sales, and even the GLC had to hold back 96 000 dwellings because they were being transferred to mainly Labour-controlled London boroughs. Shelter (1979c) claimed that 60 per cent of all local authorities were opposed to unrestricted council house sales, and that this included 30 per cent of Conservative councils. It is not surprising that the Labour Party Conference of 1979 endorsed the National Executive Committee's statement condemning the Conservative policy of selling council houses, and carried a motion that the next Labour government would repeal the 1980 Act.

Public sector housebuilding remains at a low level. As Mr Neil McIntosh (1979a) Director of Shelter was reported to have said:

> This disastrous slump—and not the sale of council houses—must be the Tories top housing priority. ... What sense can this abysmal level [of housebuilding] make to the millions waiting for a council house, the 50 000 families becoming homeless each year, or the 200 000 construction workers who are unemployed.

In concentrating on providing for the 'needy'—the poor, elderly or disabled—and in abolishing Parker Morris standards the government is turning the clock back to the 1930s when council housing was only built as a 'welfare' provision. But higher rents and reduced subsidies impose an increased burden on council tenants. Even in 1978, 44 per cent of all local authority and new town tenants in England and Wales were dependent upon means tested assistance—either as rent rebates or supplementary benefits—and a further 9 per cent were eligible but did not claim.

6 The Voluntary Housing Movement, Tenant Co-operatives and Equity Sharing

The Voluntary Movement

Voluntary housing has a long history. It has taken many forms over the last century and a half, but since the 1960s the movement has been mainly composed of four types of organisations: housing associations, co-owner-ship societies, cost rent housing societies and self build societies. Their functions differ widely.

Housing Associations

Although housing associations account for only just over 2 per cent of the total stock of dwellings, they became increasingly important in the 1970s. The number of housing starts and completions in this sub-sector nearly trebled 1973–7 to 11 and 7 per cent of the national total respectively, and the number of renovations approved for grants increased almost fourfold to 29 per cent of the total (table 6.1), but with the housebuilding slump in 1978–79 activity generally diminished.

Table 6.1   Housing Association Dwellings, Great Britain, 1973–9

	1973	1975	1976	1977	1979
New dwellings started	11 137	19 610	29 223	28 219	15 556
New dwellings completed	8 852	14 703	15 760	25 090	22 676
Renovations approved	5 051	5 278	13 868	19 772	21 658

Source: Department of the Environment, *Housing and Construction Statistics*

Housing associations originate from 1830 when the Labourer's Friendly Society was formed. The society built very few houses but these were better than most low income dwellings at the time and had proper drainage. But throughout the rest of the century poor people failed to attract financial

139

backing therefore charitable trusts were formed and attempted to show that private enterprise could provide decent housing for the working classes. Bodies such as the Guinness Trust, the Peabody Donation Fund, the Joseph Rowntree Trust and the Sutton Dwellings Trust, formed in the nineteenth century, are still active today in supplying general family housing. Nowadays funds come less from charity than from local and central government, and since 1964 registered associations have been eligible for loans and grants from the Housing Corporation for the purchase, rehabilitation and conversion of old houses or building of new dwellings. Until the early 1970s, housing associations were able to charge cost rents to cover the cost of construction and maintenance. But realistic cost rents were becoming too high for low income tenants, reaching £30–£40 per week for an average association dwelling. The Housing Finance Act of 1972 therefore brought all housing associations into the fair rent system, but Section 5 of the Rent Act of 1968 continued to exempt housing associations from the Act's provisions on security of tenure, although tenants of unregistered associations gained security in 1974. Most association tenants therefore not only had to pay higher rents than council tenants (council rents remaining below the fair rent level throughout most of the 1970s), but lacked the security of most private tenants.

Associations provide accommodation for special groups such as single parent families, the elderly, former mental patients and discharged prisoners who fail to qualify for local authority housing. Many associations are technically still charities under the Charities Act of 1960 and can therefore supplement funds by voluntary donation. Associations are non-profit making bodies run by voluntary committees, and sometimes they have an advantage over local authorities in that they can rehabilitate a few houses at a time or build small infill schemes which contrast with large council estate development.

By 1979 there were about 2700 housing associations in the United Kingdom. Most were small and lacked expertise. Under 20 per cent employed full time staff. Only 30 owned more than a 1000 dwellings and as few as 10 owned more than 4000 (these included the London and Quadrant Housing Trust, the Notting Hill Housing Trust, the Paddington Housing Trust and the Liverpool Improved Houses Association). But because the associations are usually small they can build up a close relationship with tenants—often closer than local authorities are able to do.

Associations often exert a considerable influence in low income and stress areas such as North Kensington, where in the mid-1970s housing associations owned the same number of houses (approximately 4000) as the London borough of Kensington and Chelsea, and the Greater London Council combined. Associations fill a useful role in urban areas, if local government, often for political reasons, is opposed to meeting housing need by municipal housing development or rehabilitation.

Co-ownership Societies

Housing society co-ownership schemes provide a 'half way house' between renting a property and buying one with a mortgage. The residents collectively own the dwellings and receive either tax relief or a direct housing subsidy under the option mortgage scheme. Since 1964 loans have been available from the Housing Corporation, but they were only paid to 'parent societies' (normally consisting of architects, surveyors, solicitors or accountants) set up for the purpose of acquiring the land, obtaining planning permission, designing the housing, organising the building and finally finding co-owners to live in the dwellings. Very rarely do the members of the parent society become residents. The development may take three to five years to complete and during this time the parent society charges fees for its services. On completion the Housing Corporation insists that the parents sign a management agreement which assigns responsibility for general management, the allocation of vacant dwellings, and all financial matters to managing agents. The members of the parent society then resign and a committee is elected from among the co-owners—its degree of responsibility for the scheme being dependent upon the management agreement.

Apart from receiving finance from the Housing Corporation, housing societies obtain 40 year mortgages from building societies. Membership of a housing society (in the 1970s) was by means of a £5 share, and this conferred the right to live in one of the societies houses or flats. The mortgage is granted to the housing society, and the society is responsible for repayments. These are made by the co-owners paying a monthly sum equal to capital repayment and interest plus management, maintenance, landscaping and insurance outgoings.

Co-ownership schemes are mainly intended for middle income households and most schemes operate outside stress areas. Some societies benefit those who would not qualify for a building society mortgage, for example low income households; those who could get a 20–25 year mortgage but who would get noticeably better and more spacious accommodation in a more desirable area if they were financed by a 40 year mortgage; single women and the elderly. Residents help in the day to day running of the property and its surrounds, and after five years if they want to move they might realise up to 90 per cent of the increase in the value of their dwelling—that is some of the capital which has been repaid plus a sum representing any increase in the 'co-ownership value'. If the owner lives in the property for more than 40 years, it is assumed that he will subsequently live there at no cost except for management and maintenance expenses. In the short term however co-ownership offers few if any advantages over a tenancy. By the late 1970s there were over 1000 housing societies in the United Kingdom running co-ownership schemes and owning over 40 000 dwellings. But rapidly increasing building costs in the 1970s (units costing £14 000–£20 000 by

1974) made the development of co-ownership housing less and less practicable.

Cost Rent Societies

Cost rent housing societies do not receive sponsorship from the Housing Corporation. Flats are developed and let (mainly to middle income families) by architects and other professionals who draw fees for their services. This form of housing became increasingly unattractive as building costs, and consequently rents, escalated in the 1970s.

Self Build Societies

Self build societies are fairly rare. Housing is constructed by their members (usually skilled building workers) who receive loans from the Housing Corporation for the purchase of materials. The houses may cost only 60 per cent of the price of equivalent houses sold in the open market. On completion members obtain individual mortgages to repay their short term finance, and subsequently become owner-occupiers. Since 1945 only about 10 000 houses have been built in this (or a similar way) by a thousand groups.

Public Policy towards the Voluntary Housing Movement

Under the Housing Acts of 1885 and 1890, public authorities became the main suppliers of housing for the needy and largely usurped the role of the charities and self-help organisations. This responsibility of government was further confirmed by the Housing and Town Planning Act of 1919, and financial facilities and subsidies were extended to the voluntary movement. In 1935, the National Federation of Housing Societies (NFHS) was formed as a co-ordinating body to take over from the Garden Cities and Town Planning Association (established by Ebenezer Howard in 1899) the central functions of the 75 societies affiliated to it, and to promote and advise new societies—responsibilities acknowledged by the Housing Act of 1936.

In 1936, 100 societies were registered with the NFHS and there were a further 126 unregistered societies. By 1939 the number of registered societies had grown to 150 and by 1950 the number had reached 409 despite local authorities having the major responsibility for post-war housing. The Conservatives favoured extending voluntary housing when they were in office in the 1950s—a policy not opposed by the Labour Party. The government extended the role of the housing associations in an attempt to increase the pace of rehabilitation. This was enabled by the Housing Act of 1957 which allowed associations to obtain loans for house purchase and conversion from building societies, local authorities and other public lending bodies. Like private owners they could now apply for improvement grants for property to be converted into rented dwellings after consultation with the appropriate local authority. Housebuilding was encouraged by the Housing Act of 1961 which provided cost-rent societies with £25 million of loans—the scheme being administered by the NFHS. Some 7000 dwellings were consequently built. It was hoped that private capital would likewise be injected into voluntary housing, but philanthropists were not as forthcoming as they were in the nineteenth century.

The Milner Holland Report (1965) not only showed that owner-occupied, private rented and local authority housing was failing to meet the needs of people with low incomes particularly in the inner urban areas, but that non-profit housing associations could not make an effective contribution to need until the fiscal and legal provisions governing their activity were rationalised—notably their tax liability.

Until 1964, the words 'housing association' and 'housing society' were synonymous, and the NFHS as well as many of its registered associations used the word 'society'. The statutory definition of 'housing association' in the Housing Act of 1957 had been a broad one covering associations, societies and bodies of trustees or companies. But after the setting up of the Housing Corporation by the Conservatives' Housing Act of 1964, associations and societies became clearly defined and had separate functions (as described at the beginning of this chapter). The Housing Corporation was to encourage the expansion of housing society co-ownership and cost-rent schemes and to arrange 100 per cent mortgages for the former. In 1968 option mortgage schemes were introduced by the Labour government, offering low income co-owners a subsidy instead of tax relief on mortgage interest (chapter 2). By 1968 there were 527 co-ownership societies—in contrast to 471 cost-rent societies, members of the latter having to cover interest payments on society finance with rent which was not eligible for tax relief or subsidy. But co-ownership schemes attracted predominantly middle income households, and it became difficult for the Housing Corporation to find low-cost co-ownership schemes to sponsor. This sufficiently concerned the Minister of Housing, Mr Anthony Greenwood that he consequently made an Order prohibiting the corporation from lending to societies developing housing at a cost in excess of £7000 a unit. With the price of land escalating in the early 1970s, and the paternalistic attitude of many society management agents, new co-ownership schemes generally became both unviable and unattractive.

The Weaknesses of Co-ownership

The advantages of co-ownership to households unable or unwilling to raise a 20–25 year mortgage for house purchase are obvious. But co-ownership schemes in the 1970s were not free from severe criticism:

(1) The members of parent societies allocated professional work to themselves, their fees becoming expenses of the co-ownership societies. They were simultaneously clients (being members of parent societies) and professional consultants (receiving fees). It was clear that although co-ownership societies were non-profit making they were far from being philanthropic.

(2) The Housing Corporation put little trust in co-owners even after they became shareholders and were responsible for the society's mortgage. The corporation gave substantial power to the parent societies and did not regard them as 'servants' of the shareholders.

(3) After the parent societies were dissolved, ex-members often became managing agents. When the co-owner committees were formed they often found that the more important responsibilities had been signed away from them and were still in the hands of the 'parents' but in another guise.

(4) Many co-owners became disappointed when they became aware of how little control they had over their home environment, especially those who were paying over £100 per month. Managing agents generally regarded co-owners as tenants and restricted participation to the minimum.

(5) It was questionable whether co-owners were better off than tenants. Under the Housing Finance Act of 1972, co-owners (unlike most unfurnished tenants) did not qualify for rent allowances or rebates, nor did they pay fair rents—fixed for three years—but fluctuating payments as mortgage interest rates changed. Neither did co-owners selling their houses always benefit. If inflation had pulled the price of a house up for example from £10 000 to £25 000, the co-owner might only have been able to realise say £3000 (after five years), a sum based on the increase in general housebuilding costs (excluding the cost of land).

Because of these disadvantages, co-ownership became less attractive than owner-occupation, especially when the latter became increasingly important as an inflation-proof asset in the 1970s.

The 1970s

The voluntary movement became increasingly synonymous with housing associations—a trend encouraged by the Conservative government in 1970–4. Under Part IV of the Housing Act of 1972, housing associations became eligible for subsidies from the Exchequer. On new construction, the government gave subsidies on a sliding scale to cover the gap between income from rent and 'reckonable expenditure' which included running costs and capital expenditure, and on conversion subsidies of £5 per week payable for 20 years. Associations could borrow from the Housing Corporation under Section 77 of the act and obtain mortgages from local authorities up to 100 per cent of the cost of acquiring property including loan costs. In return for the mortgage, associations were usually required to take a number of families from local authority housing lists.

Subsidisation was becoming increasingly necessary as cost-rents were rising very rapidly. A house suitable for letting as flats might have cost £30 000 and a further £20 000 might have been necessary to have converted it. Even on a long council mortgage, cost rents of £20 per week may have been necessary to cover construction and maintenance costs. The government therefore gave help only if the housing association charged fair rents under the 1972 Act rather than cost rents. As in the private rented sector, fair rents were based on the property and what it would fetch in its area and condition in a free market less any 'scarcity value'. Rents were determined by the Rent Officer, and rent allowances were available from the local authority if households were unable to afford the rent.

Government support for housing associations was emphasised by the White Paper, *Widening the Choice: The Next Steps in Housing* (1973). It proposed:

> to widen the range and choice of rented accommodation by the expansion of the voluntary housing movement .... The voluntary housing movement can and should play a bigger part in eliminating the worst housing conditions and widening housing choice for everyone.

A further White Paper, *Better Homes, The Next Priorities* (1973) proposed that Housing Action Areas (HAAs) should be declared in areas of housing stress and that housing associations (helped by the Housing Corporation and National Building Agency) should play a major role in acquiring, improving and managing properties in those areas. It was hoped that housing associations and local authorities would work closely together to provide accommodation to replace the dwindling supply of private rented housing.

In the 10 years to 1973, housing associations had been especially concerned with rehabilitation, particularly conversions, in the inner cities, rehabilitation being far cheaper than redevelopment (chapter 8). In London the Notting Hill Housing Trust bought up properties with sitting tenants who were then rehoused in already rehabilitated dwellings, and the process started all over again. By the early 1970s the trust was producing one conversion per working day. Another association, the London and Quadrant Housing Trust (the largest in the United Kingdom) had converted and improved 3000 houses in the 1960s–70s but concentrated on taking tenants referred to it by the welfare machinery—mainly families with children and the elderly. By 1973 housing associations were nationally producing 15 000 new dwellings per annum and were providing approximately a quarter of a million dwellings—about 1.3 per cent of the total housing stock of Great Britain. But associations had not fully grasped the opportunities offered for the improvement and conversion of existing accommodation by the Housing Act of 1969, and by 1973 they accounted for only 1 per cent of total improvements and conversions—less than a decade earlier.

With soaring house prices in 1971–3, housing associations were increasingly catering for general housing need—as many would-be buyers could neither afford a mortgage nor (in 1973) obtain one when interest rates fell but mortgage rationing was introduced. Council housing was also difficult to obtain. Waiting lists were long and it was not possible to add people to the list if they already had accommodation—however unsatisfactory. Homelessness was increasing especially in London, and local authorities were building fewer houses.

Although housing associations did not add appreciably to the housing stock—concentrating on buying up existing properties—they often came between existing residents and speculators, and provided a degree of security and improved conditions. They may have done little to reduce homelessness but they did prevent it from increasing. But the increase in housing association activity was not immune from public constraint, or criticism. The Greater London Council (GLC)—committed in 1973 to municipalisation—strictly rationed the aid it was allocating to housing associations. Although £20 million had been committed for the financial year 1973/74, further aid was only granted to schemes costing less than £50 000 and where there was a resulting 100 per cent housing gain. Little or no acquisition consequently took place in the stress areas of inner London. Mr Iltyd Harrington, Deputy Leader of the GLC (1973) stated that the Labour majority in County hall were not opposed to housing associations but were faced with a financial problem, and that:

> Until such time as the Housing Corporation can help . . . we will have to limit assistance to those schemes which give most direct assistance to the council, and in those areas where nominations would be most valuable. That is where there is acute housing shortage.

But in 1973 it was doubtful whether local authorities were ready to embark upon extensive municipalisation programmes, yet housing associations—despite being well equipped administratively—were being inhibited from acquiring a great deal of property on the market at that time. Their role was increasingly being questioned. The National and Local Government Officers Association (NALGO) (1974) doubted whether housing associations could provide action on the scale required, and it was feared that they might—in competition with local authorities—bid up house prices. NALGO believed that local authorities were in a better position than the associations to provide scarce housing management skills.

In 1974 housebuilding slumped to its lowest level since the early 1950s, and more people were homeless or on housing waiting lists than ever before. It was recognised that local authorities could not by themselves deal with the problem of housing need. The voluntary housing movement was therefore strengthened. Although introduced by the incoming Labour government, the Housing Act of 1974 had been substantially drafted by its Conservative predecessors, and generally enjoyed bi-partisan support. It was intended to encourage the expansion of housing associations under public supervision. The Housing Corporation's powers of lending and control were greatly extended. Previously the corporation had sponsored only co-ownership and cost-rent societies. Neither was an accessible form of tenure or popular during the inflation of the early 1970s. Under the 1974 Act the corporation's main function was to promote housing associations and to intervene in their activities where it appeared that they were being mismanaged. The registration of housing associations was introduced, administered by the Housing Corporation—associations having to be non-profit bodies and registered as charities or under the Industrial and Provident Societies Act of 1965. Only registered associations were able to receive loans and grants from public funds—mainly under a new subsidy system, a major element of which was the Housing Association Grant (HAG). The HAG was to be paid on completion of a housing association scheme and allowed the association to pay back 75–80 per cent of the loans it had received from the Housing Corporation and local authority to finance the scheme. The annual loan charges on the remaining debt (together with management and maintenance costs) should then be recovered from rent income, but if there was a shortfall this could be offset by a Revenue Deficit Grant (RDG). The Housing Corporation was also granted powers to provide dwellings for letting by means of construction, acquisition (by compulsory purchase if necessary), conversion and improvement, and it could borrow up to £750 million for this purpose.

Within the first year of the corporation obtaining these extended powers, it approved finance for 37 000 houses, over twice the number approved in 1973–4 and nearly 40 per cent of total approvals since it was founded ten years earlier. Loan approvals in 1974–5 amounted to 14.4 per cent of the total number of housing starts in Great Britain or 24.2 per cent of the total starts in the public sector. The corporation however was slow in using its compulsory purchase powers, the first time being in 1978 when it acquired a block of 11 privately owned houses in Paddington, and subsequently sold the properties to the Paddington Churches Housing Association. Compulsory purchase required the approval of the local council (in the above example the Westminster City Council) and confirmation by the Department of the Environment.

Additional finance became available to the Housing Corporation in 1977. It set up a private company (under the 1974 Act) to borrow £25 million (for seven years at the market rate of interest) from the City to help housing associations adversely affected by public expenditure cuts in 1976. The Housing Corporation's Finance Company had 40 per cent of its shares held by the Housing Corporation and 60 per cent held by the NFHA, the Guinness Trust, the Sutton Trust, the Notting Hill Housing Trust, the Paddington Churches Housing Association and the London and Quadrant Housing Trust. The loan was facilitated by Morgan Greenfell (merchant bankers), approved by the Department of the Environment and secured with a mortgage on properties in schemes sponsored by the Housing Corporation. This intermeshing of public and private finance could lead to further injections of private investment into public sector housing, since there would be a guaranteed return irrespective of the rent policy of the government of the day.

Encouraged by the government and the Housing Corporation, housing associations therefore rapidly increased their activity (table 6.1). The type of activity was largely determined by *Circular 170/74* which emphasised that housing associations should play an important role in: relieving housing stress or homelessness by their operations in General Improvement Areas and Housing Action Areas; provide housing for those with special needs such as the single and elderly; design schemes to maintain the stock of rented accommodation in areas where there were severe shortages; acquire properties from private landlords who were failing in their duty towards their tenants or property, and make provision for key workers. The increased role of housing associations in the late 1970s was reflected by increases in public expenditure on housing associations (table 6.2).

Table 6.2   Public Expenditure on Housing Associations, Great Britain, 1973–8

	1973/4	*1974/5*	*1975/6*	*1976/7*	*1977/8*
Capital grants by central government	—	—	146	374	472
Loans by Housing Corporation (net)	68	146	105	44	2
Loans by local authorities (net)	112	110	124	6	1
	180	256	375	424	475

Source: *The Government's Expenditure Plans, 1978/79 to 1981/82* (Cmnd. 7049)
Note: Capital grants by central government were mainly Housing Association Grants (HAGs) used by associations to repay loans received from the Housing Corporation.

Both Conservative and Labour governments have given support to the activities of housing associations. They felt that with the virtual demise of the private landlord, an alternative form of rented tenure was necessary. But the Conservatives also regarded housing associations as an alternative to council housing, for example in the London borough of Kensington and Chelsea, and in Brighton, and allocated resources increasingly in favour of housing associations. The party had for long preferred backing charity rather than a state policy of supplying good housing for everyone in need, but until the late1970s it failed to take into account that the associations were themselves heavily subsidised by the state and were relatively unaccountable to the public. The Conservatives might have thought that with the disappearance of private rented accommodation, housing associations offered people a choice of accommodation (as Conservative philosophy also prescribes in education and medicine). But the party hoped that the powers of the Housing Corporation would be diminished, so that its role would be mainly to register new associations rather than to control in detail every association scheme. The Conservatives also hoped that housing associations would be given greater freedom to fix their own rents and in principle supported the sale of association properties to sitting tenants. Housing associations also appealed to a section of the Labour Party, because associations often had more enlightened management than many local authorities, there were flexible allocation policies, there was an element of tenant freedom and control, and a number of neo-utopian socialists (usually students) became involved in housing associations. But Labour did not see housing associations as a substitute for local authority housing. *Labour's Programme 1976* stressed that:

> the main role of Housing Associations must be to complement the efforts of local authorities and not to compete against them for scarce land and housing resources.

Whichever party is in power nationally or locally, associations are very dependent upon local authority co-operation and assistance. Many schemes are jointly run and many homes go to applicants on the council's waiting lists. But in view of the Conservative's philosophy of selling off council houses, and the Labour government's reduced expenditure on local authority housing in the late 1970s, housing associations must be examined closely to ascertain whether they do provide an acceptable alternative to council housing.

The Advantages and Disadvantages of Housing Associations and the Housing Corporation

To a limited extent housing associations perform a useful function. They can house certain groups which are normally unhoused by local authorities, such as single people, unmarried mothers, discharged mental patients and released prisoners. But this may be a defect of local authority housing policy rather than an intrinsic feature of housing associations—although local authorities must obviously have a prior responsibility for housing families with young children and the elderly.

Housing associations also provide temporary accommodation when local authorities are involved in large scale municipalisation and rehabilitation, and associations may be better suited than local authorities to rehabilitate individual properties in a terrace, councils preferring to acquire whole blocks for clearance or rehabilitation. The NFHA believes that given financial help, housing associations could do considerably more, and as fewer and fewer large council estates are built they will need to extend their activities to nurseries and youth clubs. Associations are now the major agents of urban renewal and some are already managing General Improvement Areas and Housing Action Areas.

But housing associations have been severely criticised:

(1) Their rents were often higher than council rents for similar accommodation, in spite of subsidies being received from local authorities and the Housing Corporation (and tax relief from the Exchequer if they were charities). The Housing Rent and Subsidies Act of 1975 reintroduced 'reasonable rents' to local authority housing—rents which struck a balance between the interests of the tenants and ratepayers, and which were based on pooled historic costs. With the extension of housing association activity, an increasing proportion of low income tenants were discriminated against as they had to pay fair rather than (lower) reasonable rents.

(2) Standards of accommodation were often poor, and much improvement or conversion was shoddy—Parker Morris Standards not having to be applied (in contrast to council housing). Building work was often done by the 'lump' rather than by local authority direct labour organisations.

(3) Although receiving generous subsidies, housing associations were not publicly accountable. They either channelled public funds into private hands, or where this did not happen they used the funds inefficiently. It was therefore questionable whether they should have been given control over public funds on such a scale. They are essentially a form of private landlordism, and when financial commitments cease (normally after 30 years) association property can be sold to private developers.

(4) In return for subsidies, housing associations have been obliged to accept nominations from local authority waiting lists. But allocation rules were not published and tenants were carefully screened—implying that some form of discrimination took place. Would-be tenants were generally vulnerable to the prejudices of association managers.

(5) Unlike local authorities, associations did not have compulsory purchase powers, or the powers to declare General Improvement or Housing Action Areas.

(6) Tenants were not protected by the Rent Acts and it was not uncommon for there to be evictions in circumstances of hardship and injustice. Petty rules were often imposed upon them by management—self

appointed bodies which often operated secretly. Local authorities were rarely represented on management boards, despite handing over vast sums of money. There was little or no participation by tenants in management, and housing associations were often paternalistic—run by the middle classes for the less well off. Although management boards might have got a reputation for public service—often providing housing ostensibly to improve the moral as well as the material wellbeing of tenants—they also got their hands on a great deal of public money. Many of the associations were charitable trusts, were often set up as tax-avoidance devices and benefitted from tax relief. Unlike council tenants, housing association tenants were often spread out and could not easily form themselves into tenant associations, put pressure on local councillors or obtain publicity for their case in the local press which tended to focus on controversy involving local authorities.

(7) A housing association was sometimes used to rehouse a sitting tenant in order to give vacant possession (and an increased value property) to an owner or estate agent connected with the association.

(8) Associations have been used by 'professionals' to obtain substantial fees for services rendered. These normal profits appear as costs in the accounts of housing associations rendering them technically non-profit making.

(9) In general, housing associations have been very inefficient. Association entrepreneurs were for example surveyors passing through a phase in their career or people connected with a charity or church. They would usually have had only a temporary or part-time interest in the association. Liquidity crises were frequent as the associations had to continually apply for funds afresh. The staff were often of a good quality, but the turnover rate was high because of limited security. Most associations suffered from the diseconomies of small scale operations.

Some of the larger and older housing associations were free from many of the above weaknesses. Local authorities could have more effectively done the work of the remainder. But the housing association movement continues to grow. Although associations are non-profit making and are philanthropic ideologically, the same applies to the building societies, and like them associations are expanding financial institutions, often insensitive and often inflexible.

The Housing Corporation had been largely instrumental in the increase of housing association activity. By the end of 1978 the corporation had lent about £1000 million to 2700 housing associations, £370 million in 1978 alone. In 1978 it had promoted 22 000 new housing association completions and 20 024 renovations. But the corporation recognised its weaknesses. The management and control of its accounts needed improving—the corporation making a deficit of £6 million in 1978, and it was criticised by the House of Commons Public Accounts Committee for exercising insufficient control over the associations it finances. The House of Commons (1979) recommended that financial penalties should be imposed on associations which delay or fail to submit annual accounts, and it criticised the management committees of associations for not being better trained, and using housing associations for personal gain. Hencke (1979) reported that Sir Lou Sherman, the corporation's chairman wanted new legislation to remove people who had dual interests such as estate agents and property developers from sitting on the boards of housing associations, and to abolish management consultancy agents from handling development, allocating accommodation, and collecting rent from association tenants. In the meantime the Housing Corporation, responding to the Public Accounts Committee report, began scrutinising the accounts and administration of more than 750 of Britain's largest housing associations.

Conservative support for the voluntary housing movement waned in the 1980s. The Housing Act of 1980 granted housing association tenants the right to buy their homes off their landlords, and mortgages were to be made available by the Housing Corporation (housing associations registered as charities under the Charities Act of 1960 were also given the right to sell, although tenants were not given the right to buy, an exclusion affecting half of all association households. The government also cut the budget of the Housing Corporation from £368 to £305 million (1979/80–1980/81) with adverse effects on housebuilding and rehabilitation.

Tenant Co-operatives

In reaction to the general run down in council housing, and the imperfections in the voluntary housing movement, a number of tenant co-operative schemes have been promoted. The government formed a Working Party on Tenant Co-operatives in December 1974. In its interim report, the working party showed that there was currently little interest in self-management due to the belief that local authorities wanted to transfer the cost of management and maintenance to the tenants in an attempt to reduce public expenditure. But in its final report, the working party concluded that increased tenant involvement was desirable and that local authorities and housing associations should encourage the setting up of co-operatives.

Partly in response to this report, local authorities considered setting up management co-operatives in which tenants would become 'sub-landlords' with the responsibility for all maintenance and repairs. Although the Department of the Environment's *Circular 8/76* aimed by this process to 'bring additional personal resources into housing', the idea of co-operatives has been unpopular among tenants. It is argued that co-operatives would be socially divisive creating first and second class citizens if introduced on part of an estate; that local authorities may cut down on repairs generally to the disadvantage of weaker households and those in substandard estates; that little work could be offered to direct labour organisations as tenants would only be able to afford the 'lump'; that estates would have to compete with each other for limited resources; and that if a co-operative is set up in new or vacant housing the selection of tenants would be discriminatory as permitted under *Circular 8/76*. There was a suspicion that co-operatives would be set up by Conservative local authorities wishing to shed their housing responsibilities, and co-operatives might be attractive to tenants disadvantaged by poor local authority housing management and maintenance.

The second form of co-operative, a non-equity or par value organisation—where tenants collectively own or lease property but do not have an individual stake in the equity—has been adopted mainly by housing associations (which are often responsible for management), and funded by either local authorities or the Housing Corporation.

The progress of tenant co-operatives in Britain has been very slow in marked contrast with other European countries notably Denmark, Norway, Sweden and West Germany (by 1976 there were only nine tenant co-operatives in Britain). The Co-operative Housing Agency was therefore set up by the government in 1976 to encourage the formation of co-operatives—considered by the Minister of Housing, Mr Reginald Freeson to be one of the most challenging and important tasks in housing scene. But in December 1978, the Minister decided to close the agency—£28 million (75 per cent of its allocation for 1977/78) not being spent. In London only £8 million of its allocation of £36 million for 1976/77 and 1977/78 had been taken up. The agency had been prevented from adding to its staff in the second half of 1978 and it faced delays in helping would-be co-operatives with their applications to the Housing Corporation for funds. Its 'pressure group' function had evidently been frustrated by its controlling and sponsoring activities, and its responsibilities were transferred to the Housing Corporation. Nevertheless by the end of 1978, 161 co-operative groups had been formed representing a total membership of 8400, and there were 17 local authorities and 31 housing associations assisting in the development of co-operative housing.

Although the Conservatives, in their 1979 manifesto did not specifically pledge support for tenant co-operatives, they did state that they would encourage tenants' participation in management and maintenance. In view of the party's proposals to sell-off council houses, and raise rents and lower subsidies (chapter 5), it is unlikely that they would oppose the further formation of co-operatives if it meant that fewer public resources (especially local authority staff) would be required to manage and maintain council estates.

Equity Sharing

In an attempt to compensate for the slowing down of the growth of co-ownership—partly due to inflation—the Housing Corporation adopted equity sharing in 1977 as an alternative form of hybrid tenure. Equity sharing now takes three forms:

(1) community leasehold—partly financed by a Housing Corporation loan and partly by a building society mortgage secured on a long lease, with the occupier incurring a mixture of rent and mortgage repayment,

(2) leasehold schemes for the elderly—partly financed by the Housing Corporation and partly by a lump sum provided by the occupier who also pays rent, and

(3) the main form of sharing involving the partial transfer of council housing—financed by a mortgage, with the occupier incurring both a local authority rent and a mortgage repayment.

It was pioneered by Birmingham City Council in the early 1970s, and by January 1978 there were 20 schemes in operation throughout Britain accounting for 585 dwellings. In areas where housing is mainly council owned with a very small proportion of owner-occupied property, equity sharing may be particularly attractive to incoming middle income households as normally neither council housing nor owner-occupied property would be available or at the right price. The London docklands is such an area. In its *Strategic Plan*, the London Docklands Joint Committee (1977) suggested that whereas 50 per cent of households in East London could afford equity sharing, only 15–20 per cent could afford owner-occupation as first-time buyers. The joint committee explained the characteristics of equity sharing as follows:

> Equity sharing involves a housing authority—including a recognised housing association or society—paying some proportion of the price of a dwelling with the occupier owning the remainder of the dwelling and taking out a mortgage on it. In addition to mortgage repayments, the occupier would pay a proportion of the normal rent corresponding to the proportion of the property owned by the authority. Should the occupier wish to move, the house would be sold at the prevailing market value and the occupier would receive his proportion of the proceeds. As a simplified example, a £14 000 house taken by a 50 per cent equity shareholder would require a mortgage of £7000. The sale value after five years might be £18 000, and the occupier's share of the proceeds would be £9000.

The proportion of the occupier's equity could in practice vary from as little as 25 to 75 per cent depending on the household's finances, and at any time the occupier could convert equity sharing into either a full public sector tenancy or full ownership.

The Conservative government's version of equity sharing—shared ownership—was introduced in July 1979, and was intended (very optimistically) to appeal (together with the sale of council and new town development corporation houses) to up to six million tenants.

The advantages of equity sharing are straightforward. It offers househunters an opportunity to obtain accommodation in an area where other tenures are unavailable or unsuitable; local authorities are able to keep a degree of control over the allocation of housing and house prices; it is a means of creating a more socially balanced community, and once established it is possible that the balance can be maintained as each equity shared property must be offered back to the housing authority when the occupier wishes to move. The disadvantages are that, like co-operative schemes, equity sharing may not appeal to (or be within the means of) the lower income groups—those in most need, and these groups may come under increased pressure if competition for a limited supply of inner city housing becomes more severe. Some local authorities may use shared ownership as a means of diminishing their responsibility for public housing by off-loading a percentage of the cost of providing dwellings to a building society—which then imposes a debt on the tenant. Shared ownership could thus become an indirect and gradual way of selling-off council housing with all the disadvantages that result (chapter 5), yet even Conservative-controlled authorities were apprehensive about tenants being given the right to buy a share of their council homes in view of the restricted availability of mortgage finance. A further and very notable disadvantage is that when households eventually wish to acquire the remaining equity of the property the purchase price is based on the prevailing market value and not the initial value, forcing many equity sharers either to sell-up, or to carry on paying rent with the chance of full home-ownership increasingly receding.

7 The Housebuilding Industry

The housebuilding industry is exceptionally fragmented. Although there were about 80 000 firms in the construction industry in the late 1970s, there were less than 100 housebuilding firms employing a 1000 or more workers, and although the largest constructed up to 20 000 dwellings per annum, the typical medium firm built little more than a 1000 houses each year. But 95 per cent of Britain's builders are small, family-run concerns employing less than 50 workers. They operate locally and work on minor contracts. They are often solely involved in small scale infilling. Many do little more than collect together skilled craftsmen at the right time and employ labour-only subcontractors. In 1975 the Department of the Environment estimated that there were at least 220 000 self-employed construction workers (about a quarter of the labour force of the industry), most of whom were employed on the 'lump'. The 'lump' is a system in which the worker is notionally self-employed, work being subcontracted on a labour-only basis. Some of the workers are skilled, but many are unskilled and receive little training because of their status. The result is often shoddy building and skimped work. They work on piecework, in appalling safety and health conditions and receive neither basic wages nor security of employment. Tax avoidance was substantial throughout most of the 1970s, workers being paid lump sums rather than tax deducted earnings. Capital expenditure per housebuilding worker is less than half that in manufacturing industry.

In the private sector, the housebuilding industry is mainly speculative, and in the 1970s about a half of all speculative housebuilding was undertaken by firms employing less than 100 workers. Houses are mainly built in expectation of being sold during or shortly after construction. The industry—especially because of the preponderance of small firms—is greatly affected by changes in government economic policy. At times of low interest rates with easy mortgage and credit availability the number of housing starts usually increases rapidly. The poorest years for starts are when there is a tight fiscal and monetary policy. In boom years (for example 1971–2) prices initially agreed between the developer and the prospective buyer are revised upwards—the buyer being 'gazumpted'. During deflation some builders have to cut their profits and accept a lower price than they anticipated, while others became bankrupt as their minimum selling prices remain above the maximum bid prices of potential buyers.

The Housebuilding Cycle

The cyclical nature of housebuilding has been evident over the last century but was particularly pronounced in the 1960s and 1970s (figure 7.1). Following a period of continual growth in the 1950s, the private house-building industry thereafter faced a period of instability. There were peaks in the number of housing starts in 1964, 1967, 1972 and 1976, but these were followed in quick succession by troughs in 1966, 1970, 1974 and 1979. The public sector declined severely from the 1950s to the mid-1960s (due to the lack of support given by the Conservative government), but this was followed by peaks in 1967 and 1975 with troughs in 1973 and 1979

Table 7.1 Houses Started and Completed, Great Britain, 1950–79

Year	Starts (000s)			Completions (000s)		
	Public sector	Private sector	Total	Public sector	Private sector	Total
1950	184.4	19.8	204.6	170.8	27.4	198.2
1955	185.3	127.5	312.8	203.9	113.5	317.4
1960	126.3	182.8	309.1	129.2	168.6	297.8
1961	122.9	189.4	312.3	118.6	177.5	296.1
1962	137.7	186.0	323.7	130.6	174.8	305.4
1963	168.6	199.4	368.0	124.0	177.9	298.9
1964	178.6	247.5	426.1	155.6	218.1	373.7
1965	181.4	211.1	392.5	168.5	213.8	382.3
1966	185.9	193.4	379.3	180.1	205.4	385.5
1967	213.9	233.6	447.6	203.9	200.4	404.4
1968	194.3	200.1	394.4	191.7	222.0	413.7
1969	176.6	166.8	343.5	185.1	181.7	366.8
1970	154.1	165.1	319.2	180.1	170.3	350.4
1971	136.6	207.3	343.9	158.9	191.6	350.5
1972	123.0	227.4	350.4	122.8	196.3	319.1
1973	112.8	214.9	327.7	107.5	186.1	293.6
1974	146.7	105.3	252.1	128.6	140.1	268.8
1975	173.8	149.1	322.9	162.3	150.8	313.0
1976	170.8	154.7	325.4	163.0	152.2	315.2
1977	132.1	134.8	266.9	162.5	140.3	302.7
1978	107.2	157.0	264.2	130.6	148.7	279.4
1979	80.1	140.1	220.2	102.0	132.9	234.9

Sources: Ministry of Housing and Local Government; Scottish Development Department; Department of the Environment, *Housing and Construction Statistics*

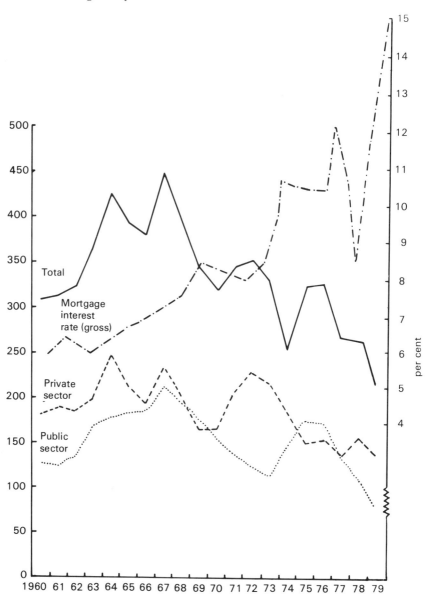

Figure 7.1 The housebuilding cycle, Great Britain, 1960–79.

(table 7.1). Despite quite marked increases and decreases in housebuilding in the 1960s and 1970s, the overall trend has been downwards since 1967. Housebuilding slumped from a record total of 447 600 starts in 1967 to 220 200 in 1979 (the lowest since the early 1950s)—a decrease of 51 per cent. In December 1979 the Building Economic Development Council predicted a further decline in the early 1980s.

The Cycle, 1969–79

After the post-war peak year of 1967, the total number of starts declined by 28 per cent 1967–70 to a lower level than at any time since 1961, and many of Britain's building firms went bankrupt in the winter of 1969. But in 1971–2 the industry partly recovered, assisted by low interest rates and mortgage availability. The house price boom (which mainly occurred within the existing stock of housing as the percentage annual addition to the stock is minute) stimulated housebuilding in the private sector, the number of starts rising by 38 per cent in 1970-2. Rapidly increasing house prices were also associated with speculation in the market for housing land. But public sector housebuilding continued to decline. Local authorities found it difficult to get contractors to do the work and were quoted grossly inflated tender prices (the local authority house tender price index increased by 38 per cent in 1972–3 compared with the general rate of inflation of about 9 per cent). Either the contractors made vast profits when they were willing to do the work, or local authorities expanded their direct works departments. Contractors voiced little objection to competition from direct labour as there was a high level of demand from all directions. However local authorities were unable to make good the reduction in public sector house-building, especially in the context of a shift of emphasis in government policy from demolition and clearance to rehabilitation and area improvement (chapter 8). In retrospect, it was clearly evident that the structure of the housebuilding industry was inadequate to its tasks. Mr Anthony Crosland (1973), Shadow Secretary of State for the Environment stated:

> Both in the public and private sector, needs are being met too slowly. . . . While we cannot lay down a precise national target, we can certainly make the broad judgement that total housing investment . . . should be substantially increased. How? The biggest constraint lies in the capacity of the construction industry, which is quite inadequate to meet a generally higher level of demand and especially local authority demand; councils cannot even get firms to tender in many parts of the country. The cause lies partly in the perennial crisis created by the 'lump', partly by the damaging effects of stop-go building society lending, partly in a chronic in-efficiency.

By 1973 the boom was over and recession set in. Private sector house-building fell rapidly (by 50 per cent in 1973–4). The conurbations were particularly badly hit as public sector housebuilding reached a low level (112 800 starts in 1973). Although there was a minor recovery in 1975–6, from 1973 throughout the rest of the 1970s the construction industry faced a crisis of unprecedented proportions. Such a slump in housebuilding and employment had not occurred in peacetime since before the First World War. The slump had the following characteristics:

(1) *Reduced output*   In the period 1972–9 the total number of housing starts fell by 37 per cent (with a 39 per cent reduction in the private sector).

(2) *Reduced employment*   In the same period unemployment in the industry increased from approximately 60 000 to 250 000. Many workers (especially the skilled) left the industry. According to the Department of the Environment, 287 000 jobs were lost in 1973–6, reaching 320 000 by 1979. The number exceeded 400 000 if those associated with construction such as architects were included.

(3) *Under capacity*   The industry suffered from severe under capacity. According to the National Federation of Building Trades Employers (1977) only 6 per cent of firms were operating at full capacity, and as many as 24 per cent of firms were operating at less than half capacity.

(4) *Bankruptcy*   Since the industry is characterised by a vast number of small firms, many falter when demand sags. Most firms depend upon short-term bank credit during building, and when interest rates increase and a slump occurs, banks cut finance to builders and it is difficult for firms to repay outstanding loans/overdrafts. In 1973 construction output amounted to 12.5 per cent of the Gross National Product, but the industry had 20 per cent of the bankruptcies and liquidations among firms and 13 000 firms disappeared in 1973–6, with resulting disruption to work underway.

(5) *Reduced productive efficiency*   This resulted when output fell more rapidly than employment. Firms often stretched-out workloads by extending completion times.

(6) *Recurring restrictions on building society lending*   The big decrease in private housebuilding in 1977 was largely due to the shortage of building society funds and high interest rates on mortgages, the year being the second worst since 1951 for this sector. In March 1978 the government imposed a £610 million monthly limit on building society lending and a limit of £640 million from July. Although these measures were intended to curb the demand for owner-occupied housing and hence slow down the increase in prices, they also deterred housebuilding and consequently inflated the price of new houses.

Building society lending was further restricted in 1978 after the government raised the rate of interest on national savings to a higher level than that paid by building societies to their subscribers. The resulting drying up of funds lowered the level of potential demand for new housing causing further depression in the housebuilding industry. Again, reductions in output raised the price of new houses perhaps by as much as £400–£500 per dwelling.

The slump in the construction industry differed from slumps in other industries. Most large and medium construction firms continued to make substantial profits, and record levels were obtained by the largest firms. Much of these profits were used to play the money markets and Stock Exchange rather than reinvested in the industry. The fall in demand had been largely at the expense of the labour force and small builder. Nevertheless the contractors lobbied the government to increase demand not least in the public sector, and voiced their opposition to direct labour organisations now that the market had shrunk. The government responded by increasing demand whenever possible. The Budget of March 1974 allocated £150 million more to local authorities to support new building projects already in the pipeline and current housebuilding. Also £500 million was made available as a loan to building societies (at a rate of £100 million per month, April–August 1974) to ease the prevailing mortgage famine. But private sector housebuilding did not recover immediately as building societies instead of increasing mortgage lending replenished their reserves. Demand consequently remained slack, and in June 1974 there were 30 000 unsold houses on the market. Again, the Budget of October 1977 added £400 million to public sector construction expenditure (in addition to the extra £100 million which had been allocated to rehabilitation by the July Budget), and the government's housing Green Paper of 1977 preserved the *status quo* with regard to income tax relief on mortgage interest thereby ensuring that the demand for owner-occupied houses remained buoyant even if not fully satisfied. Government policy towards the problems of the construction industry was in part similar to that advocated by Mr Anthony Crosland (1973). He believed that:

> the cure must lie in legislating against the 'lump', controlling building society lending, and injecting some competitive public enterprise through the expansion of direct labour departments (perhaps regionally organised) which would build for sale as well as for rent.

The Labour government (1974–9) was in favour of decasualisation and job security in the industry, and made several attempts to stabilise building society lending (chapter 2) apart from the measures outlined above. It was also in favour of expanding direct labour organisations (DLOs). But unlike some other industries (and firms) such as aerospace, shipbuilding and BL (British Leyland), the construction industry was not restructured. The viability of the industry hinged entirely on the level of demand.

The Contractors' Response to the Housebuilding Cycle

In the private sector   Low overheads and fixed costs; the ability of firms to live off past profits (even by the late 1970s many firms were drawing on profits made during the boom of 1971–2); ample scope for tax avoidance (contractors were paid at various stages of a project but declared profits only on completion); and the switching of work from housing to offices and hotels, or from private to public sector housebuilding (1973–6) all enabled most medium and large firms to survive the crisis of the 1970s.

Many firms were stronger in the mid-1970s than before due to mergers and takeovers which had occurred during the previous boom years. The taking-over firm could move into the most profitable markets previously denied them.

A ripple effect occurred throughout the industry as contractors having failed to secure work in one area (perhaps due to competition from DLOs) looked elsewhere for opportunities, for example large firms moved into modernisation and improvement for local authorities—an area which they once ignored. This in turn caused medium firms to look for work previously done by small firms. Most private firms were of course opposed to DLOs, as it was probably direct labour which created the ripple in the first place, and at the same time reduced the scope for encroachment into new areas.

Although diversification provided protection against a downturn in the housing cycle, it nevertheless did not offset the debilitating effects upon the industry and exacerbated difficulties in recovery. New house construction is fundamentally related to confidence (as well as to the availability of finance and existing house prices). If this is lacking, the industry will continue to be dominated by small, inefficient and vulnerable firms and a sizeable part of the labour force of the industry will be employed on the 'lump'.

In the public sector   From the 1940s to the present, council houses were largely built when it suited the private housebuilding industry. The kind and form of council dwellings were often shaped by the needs of the construction industry as dictated by profit. In the 1950s large contractors became increasingly involved in development as mass production enabled them to develop new technology. Only the large firms could afford to incur the costs of new machinery and special kinds of technology, small contractors using traditional methods of building being squeezed out. The result was tower blocks—a form of housing much more costly than two storey houses made of bricks and mortar. Firms were paid subsidies to build high, despite the accommodation being unpopular among tenants. In many cases densities were not increased but decreased to below that of the houses which were replaced. By the mid-1960s nearly 25 per cent of all new council dwellings were flats in tower blocks of five or more stories. But in the early 1970s during the private sector property boom, the contractors pulled out of local authority housing and moved to private sector housebuilding or the development of offices, hotels and shops. The new technology (developed in public housing with government subsidies) was now being utilised for commercial development.

During the boom, the switch to more profitable commercial work was also the result of firms being reluctant to be tied to fixed contracts when they faced rocketting costs of labour and materials (the wages of 'lump' workers being uncontrolled by Incomes Policies), and firms found that official cost yardsticks were hopelessly inadequate given inflation. Only local authorities with DLOs were able to maintain their housebuilding programmes, but even they were short of architects, planners and quantity surveyors due to inflated demand. Local authorities also found that craftsmen and bricks were in short supply on switching from the industrialised building methods of the 1960s to medium and low rise development in the 1970s. But the Conservative government failed to support the expansion of direct labour activity—quite the reverse. The government took a:

> doctrinaire, dogmatic blow against the local authority direct labour organisations, the only publicly owned part of the construction industry ... the government forbade councils from using their own direct labour organisations to build houses for sale [yet] the councils [were] hamstrung by the 'cost yardsticks' set down for council houses ... and by the lack of building land.
>
> (Linton, 1973)

During the slump, the Labour government was sympathetic to direct labour involvement, but direct labour faced many difficulties in its relations with private contractors and some Conservative local authorities. Due to a low level of private sector demand, private firms again sought local authority contracts, but work was now being let in small contracts for example modernisation, improvement and infill housing projects. Work went mainly to medium firms, causing bankruptcies among the previous specialists—the smaller firms. Firms on the verge of bankruptcy skimped work and 'cut corners', and direct labour was required to remedy the effects. After the swing to the Conservatives in the 1976 local government elections, many local authorities, for example the Greater London Council, attempted to cut their DLOs ostensibly to improve the 'efficiency' of small firms.

Skimped work, poor safety standards, atrocious working conditions, wage cutting, delays and structural defects in buildings were all results of private firms putting in low tender bids in order to secure contracts in the face of competition from direct labour. But final prices were often much higher assuming that the firm survived long enough to complete the work. DLOs were put in a difficult position by cut-price tendering. They were not able to compete on equal terms, since unlike private firms, they were not cross-subsidised from more profitable activity in other areas. It is unrealistic, on the basis of tender prices, to compare the efficiency of private firms with direct labour.

In the late 1970s the traditional work of DLOs (for example repairs and maintenance of council houses) was increasingly put out to tender due to increases in the scale of activity, a trend notable in Conservative controlled authorities. Direct labour was also under threat as public sector housebuilding fell to its lowest level since the Second World War, Conservative local authorities reserving the depleted number of contracts for private firms. DLOs were thus attacked by private contractors and by their political supporters. They were accused of inefficiency and of being a source of unfair competition.

Housebuilding, House Prices and Land Costs

Land may be withheld from the market if landowners believe that the future price of land is going to rise more quickly than other prices. Builders holding land banks will similarly withhold sites from development, but other builders without land banks will be faced with higher costs of site acquisition due to competition within the industry to acquire land. Even though house prices may be consequently pushed up, builders at best may only realise normal profits and at worst incur losses—the whole price increase benefitting the landowner due to the inelasticity of the supply of land. Increased land prices thus provide little or no incentive for builders to expand output.

Since land is heterogeneous there are very great differences in site values. As a proportion of the average price of owner-occupied houses they ranged for example from as much as 38.7 per cent in the Southern region to 11.4 per cent in Scotland in 1973 (table 7.2), and from 23.2 per cent in the Southern region to 13.8 per cent in Northern Ireland in 1977. In the United Kingdom there was a decrease in the proportion from 27.7 per cent to 19.7 per cent (1973–7) reflecting the slump in housebuilding and the consequent demand for sites. Local authority site acquisition costs as a proportion of the value of newly constructed dwellings tended to be lower.

During the boom period 1969–73, site values in the United Kingdom increased by 136 per cent, ranging from 193 per cent in Southern region to 28 per cent in Scotland. But in the slump, with house prices rising at a slower rate than inflation and housebuilding costs, site values increased by only 13 per cent nationally (1973–7) and in some regions such as the Southern region, London and the South East, and South West decreased (although in Scotland and Northern Ireland there were remarkable increases). The general way in which site values changed during the boom and slump underlines the relationship between a buoyant or stagnant housing market and land values, and suggests that land prices are largely residual.

Table 7.2 Housing Site Values, United Kingdom, 1969–77

Region	1969		1973			1977		
	Average value of sites (£)	Site values as a proportion of house price (%)	Average value of sites (£)	Site values as a proportion of house price (%)	Change in average site values 1969–1973 (%)	Average value of sites (£)	Site values as a proportion of house price (%)	Change in average site values 1973–1977 (%)
London and the South East	1816	28.9	4952	37.5	+173	3597	21.5	–27
Southern	1485	26.8	4346	38.7	+193	2694	23.2	–38
South Western*	NA	NA	2517	27.5	—	2149	17.3	–14
Midlands	990	22.0	2348	28.9	+137	2556	20.6	+9
Eastern	1013	22.0	1556	33.8	+54	2882	20.8	+85
North Western	761	17.3	1922	24.4	+153	2399	18.8	+25
North Eastern	650	15.5	1177	17.0	+81	2127	17.5	+81
Wales*	NA	NA	1333	18.3	—	1794	14.3	+35
Scotland	653	12.6	839	11.4	+28	2173	14.9	+159
Northern Ireland	639	14.9	902	16.1	+41	2254	13.8	+150
United Kingdom	1022	21.2	2417	27.7	+136	2738	19.7	+13

Source: Co-operative Permanent Building Society, and Nationwide Building Society, *Occasional Bulletin*
* In 1969 the South Western region and Wales were combined as the Western region, separate data for the former areas not being available.

There had been a broad correlation between house prices, building and land costs until the late 1960s, but between 1969 and 1973 the price of a house plot increased by an average of 136 per cent. The rapid increase in new house prices throughout this period (for example by 25 per cent between July 1971 and July 1972) increased the prices bid for building land—sometimes by as much as 100 per cent in six months.

The land shortage (which together with inflated demand had escalated site prices) may have been partly due to delays in developing land for which planning permission for housing development had been obtained. It was suggested by Mr Ernie Mooney (1972), MP, that the five year limit on planning permission for housing development should be cut to one year, and that if housebuilding was not started in that period, the local authority should impose a fine or 'contingency fee' until development got underway, and Mr Peter Walker (Secretary of State for the Environment) warned that compulsory purchase would be used to acquire hoarded land especially where contiguous plots could be obtained to help builders. The White Paper, *Widening the Choice: The Next Steps in Housing* (1973) threatened land hoarders with a tax, and proposed that land must be developed within either four years after outline planning permission was granted, or three years after detailed consent was given. New guidlines were proposed for the treatment of planning permission in respect of housing, and it was recognised that some rethinking was necessary on green belt land. It was acknowledged that more housing land should be released by local authorities and other public bodies. The government announced its intention in December 1973 to implement these proposals, but the slump had already set in, rendering the proposals less relevant, and in the spring General Election the Conservative government was defeated and the incoming Labour government had another solution to the problem.

By the late 1970s, in addition to private landowners, some local authorities had become major land hoarders. Serviced housing land with planning permission attached was often not released for development, even in places where there was a considerable housing need such as the inner urban areas. Most sites needed for development had to be acquired by builders from other builders who had sold up or gone bankrupt during the slump. There was a danger that the shortage of available sites could have reduced private sector housebuilding to 100 000 dwellings or less by the early 1980s, and that the building industry could have been reduced to a rump in the private sector, building only 'up-market' houses for the wealthy.

The shortage and slowness of planning consents further inflated land prices at a time of a rapid increase in house prices. It was estimated that on average it took six months to obtain planning permission while about one in six applications was refused, and that the average time between appeal and decision was nine months if decided by the Inspectorate or one year if decided ministerially (Pennance, 1974). Mainly to hasten this process, the Dobry Report of 1975 recommended major changes in procedure. It was recognised that the development process had become increasingly hamstrung by delays at the planning application stage.

In an attempt to resolve the problem of land scarcity and the rising cost of acquisition, the Labour government (1966–70) established the Land Commission under the Land Commission Act of 1967. The Act was intended to ensure that the burden of the cost of land for essential purposes (especially housing) was reduced, and that suitable land was available at the right time for the implementation of local plans. The Commission, in order to achieve these aims, was equipped with ordinary powers of compulsory purchase and could use the normal machinery for appeals and public inquiry. Land could be purchased at the market value and sold at the best possible price, and a Crownhold would be granted subject to restrictions with the future development value reserved for the Commission. Alternatively, in the case of land for essential housing development Concessionary Crownhold could be created and sites would subsequently be sold at sub-market prices. The Commission also had powers to assess and collect a 40 per cent levy on net development value to ensure that part of increased value of land (resulting from development demand) returned to the community. But by 1970, the Commission had purchased only 2800 acres (1120 ha) (although a further 9000 acres [3600ha] were in the pipeline) and only about 400 acres (160 ha) had been sold and not all of this land was for housing. A major criticism of the Act was that it may have contributed to the further escalation of land prices. Landowners reduced the supply of development land by withholding it from the market as they may not have wished to incur the levy, or that they may have anticipated that the Act would be repealed if it proved to be unworkable, or that they may have foreseen that there would be a change from a Labour to a Conservative government—the Conservatives pledging that they would wind up the Commission and abolish the levy. Some of the biggest withholders of land were local authorities, which (often for political reasons) obstructed the Land Commission's proposed development by failing to grant planning permission. Local authorities could not have been expected to have been fully co-operative with the Land Commission as they received neither a share of levy revenue nor a portion of the return on established Crownhold.

After the defeat of the Labour government by the Conservatives in 1970, the Land Commission Act was repealed and development land reverted to the free market. No central organisation was reconstituted for the purpose of acquiring land. The problem of local authorities withholding land remained and was recognised by Mr Graham Page, Minister for Local Government and Development (1971), who, in moving the second reading of the Bill to dissolve the Land Commission, declared that:

> the solution must lie with local authorities themselves. They must be prepared to release sufficient quantities of land . . . To release it parsimoniously acre by acre in the wake of demand only creates artificial scarcity and fancy prices.

The National and Local Government Officers Association (1973) proposed that in order to ensure a readily available supply of land for development a public land bank should be created in preparation for the public ownership of all development land. It should be run by a public land agency which would release land direct to local authorities for building or, together with local authorities, to private builders—but at a profit.

With the return of a Labour government in 1974, steps were taken immediately to deal with the problems of land scarcity and development value. Based on *Labour's Programme for Britain* (1972) and the *White Paper Land* (1974), the Community Land Act of 1975 required that ultimately all development land should be acquired by local authorities at current use value, and the Development Land Tax Act of 1976 introduced a tax, which was to rise ultimately to 100 per cent of realised development value. Owner-occupied properties of up to 1 acre (0.45 ha) and single house plots producing under 10 000 ft^2 (929 m^2) were included among the exemptions from the community land scheme. Land acquired by local authorities (either by agreement or compulsorily) was leased at market values to developers, 99 year leases being established with 60-year-old rebuilding clauses. Alternatively acquired sites were developed by the local authorities or jointly by the local authorities and private developers. Housing development was given top priority. The Act was intended to ensure that the development value of land was largely gained by the community as a whole. The Exchequer initially received 40 per cent of the surplus on land transactions, the local authority 30 per cent and the remaining 30 per cent was shared among other councils. In 1978, the local authority's share increased to 40 per cent at the expense of the Exchequer.

The community land scheme was welcomed by the Royal Town Planning Institute, the Town and Country Planning Association and probably most urban local authorities (before the swing from Labour to Conservative in the local government elections of 1976 and 1977). It was thought that the cost of acquiring land for the development of housing and essential services would be less in real terms, benefitting the community as a whole and not least the owner-occupier ratepayer. It was also thought that the scheme could become a 'builders' charter'. Free from the need to accumulate land banks and identify profitable projects, developers and contractors would be able to enter into a viable partnership with the community. The Chief Executive of a major building firm was quoted by Powell (1975) as saying:

> The idea of local government taking over all building land and allocating it

with planning permission to builders is not necessarily a bad one in theory, particularly for the big builder.It will be taxpayers' money which pays for the land right up to the stage when the builder can start work; consequently it could remove a lot of capital risks and interest charges incurred in our business today.

But the community land scheme adversely affected builders if they had accummulated land banks. The retention of a substantial proportion of development value was necessary to recompense builders for development risk, but most of this was liable to development land tax.

The operation of the Community Land Act was tragically similar to that of the Land Commission Act. Over the three and a half years to May 1979, the English local authorities acquired about 3600 acres (1458 ha) of development land and of this sold only 700 acres (284 ha), producing a deficit of over £52 million (this is in contrast to the anticipated net surplus of over £300 million per annum in the country as a whole). Although public expenditure was severely curbed in the late 1970s (like deflation followed the Land Commission Act from 1967 to 1969), local authorities failed to take up the money allocated to them for the scheme, therefore allocations under the White Paper, *The Government Expenditure Plans, 1978/79 to 1981/82* (1978) were reduced from £83 to £54 million (1979–80), and for each of the subsequent two years cut from £102 to £64 million. At a local level the apparent lack of interest in the community land scheme may have been attributable to Conservative control of many of the urban authorities, the party being opposed to the 1975 Act. Many counties such as Buckingham-shire, Suffolk and Wiltshire acquired no land at all. Many councils were unable rather than unwilling to move into a new entrepreneurial field. The scheme required an extra 12 750–14 000 staff (with a third or more being members of the land professions). Without this full complement of additional staff local authorities were unable to operate the scheme as intended and could not fully utilise the financial resources which were available.

By 1979, these weaknesses of the community land scheme were recognised. The scheme particularly was ineffectual in the inner urban areas where site values reached their peak. Local authorities were thus often inhibited from acquiring land for housing development. At the 1979 General Election, the Labour Party's manifesto therefore stated that it would 'ensure that land is valued very much more closely to its present use value'. This would imply that land which was derelict or 'abandoned' would not be valued as though it was for example industrial (if that is what was shown on the development plan). It would be valued at a much lower rate perhaps approximating to agricultural use value, that would be at say £2000 per acre (£4940 per ha) instead of £40 000 per acre (£98 800 per ha) on the edge of an urban area. Under the Community Land Act, local authorities could then assemble building land considerably more cheaply than before, and reap larger surpluses if the land was then sold to private developers. At the same election, the Conservatives pledged that they would amend development land tax and repeal the Community Land Act, reverting to an almost unfettered free market—a repeat of their policy aim in 1970.

Soon after winning the General Election, one of the first steps of Conservatives in dismantling the community land scheme was to reduce the rate of development land tax. The Budget of June 1979 cut the tax from 80 and 66.66 per cent to a single rate of 60 per cent, and raised the threshold from £10 000 to £50 000—a prelude to the repeal of the 1975 Act, by the Local Government, Planning and Land Act of 1980.

Material, Labour and Finance Costs

Since 1945 housebuilding material prices have risen more quickly than the retail price index and the prices of materials bought by manufacturing industry generally, for example building material prices doubled while manufacturing material prices rose by 60 per cent, 1963–73. To some extent the increased price of imported materials following devaluation in 1967 and the downward floating of Sterling after 1971 had an inflating affect on aggregate building material costs, although domestic inflation was a more important contributory factor.

Due to the existence of the 'lump' and labour-only subcontracting among many skilled craftsman it is difficult to obtain accurate data on wage costs in the housebuilding industry. But recorded labour costs have increased at about the same rate as those in industry generally—although hours worked tend to be higher and more variable in relation to the level of output. There has been comparatively little opportunity for wage costs per unit of output to fall as only small changes in production methods have occurred. It is probable that productivity has increased much more slowly than in industry as a whole. Rising material and labour costs have had little effect on house prices. If house prices are rising rapidly (because of inflated demand) rising costs can be passed on, but if not developers will either reduce the quality of the houses or cut back on output.

Housebuilding depends very largely upon the ability of firms and potential house purchasers to raise finance. Builders have to borrow to cover construction costs and can only repay credit when they have sold the houses. When interest rates are low and credit is easy, housebuilding proceeds at a steady to rapid rate. Demand is usually buoyant as mortgage interest rates are also low and mortgages readily available. But increased interest rates often coupled with credit squeezes raise builders' costs and reduce their ability to undertake development. Simultaneously, demand is deflated as mortgage interest rates rise and mortgages become difficult to obtain. There is thus a very strong relationship between the upturns and downturns of housing starts and the number of advances for new houses (figure 7.2). The economics of housebuilding is principally demand determined. The way in which the government influences demand is thus crucial to both builders and house purchasers.

Conclusion

Housebuilding is closely linked to the general economic situation. During periods of 'go' in the general stop-go cycle, the number of housing starts usually increases, but during the 'stop' or deflation stage, the number of starts usually diminish. Public sector housing programmes have several times been cut by reduced government expenditure, but because of the complexity of the housebuilding process there are inevitably time-lags before the falling off of activity—housing not being a good economic regulator. Conversely, government induced expansion may have been often too little and too late.

From 1973 throughout the 1970s the housebuilding industry went through a crisis of unprecedented dimensions. A quarter of a million building workers became unemployed and output fell to its lowest level since the immediate post-war period, but the profits of the large contractors reached record heights. Housebuilding is the only industry in which increases in demand are seen as the sole remedy to all problems. This emphasis on demand (rather than on efficiency) reflected the fact that profits were made out of the contracting system at a time when there was a major downturn in demand from the private sector. But if this system ensured profitability it did so at the expense of the quality and cost of building work and of the labour force. Local authorities needed to employ architects, quantity surveyors, solicitors and barristers to service the contracting system and a vast bureaucratic machine was required to deal with tendering. That the contracting system brought with it the advantages of competition was clearly a myth.

In the late 1970s it seemed that the crisis would continue and that the housebuilding industry would remain largely dependent upon the contracting system. In 1977 the Labour Party published *Building Britain's Future* which proposed a greater degree of state control and the setting up of a state-owned construction corporation (perhaps by nationalising one or two of the largest construction firms). However these proposals were not included in the party's manifesto. The privately owned construction industry and the Conservatives spent £500 000 in rebutting the arguments for nationalisation, and contractors heightened their attack on DLOs believing them to be synonymous with 'back door' nationalisation. As DLOs show that the contracting system is unnecessary, and since they are controlled by publicly elected bodies, they are obviously seen within the context of nationalisation. In its 1979 election manifesto, the Labour Party pledged that it would expand DLOs and ensure that they were efficiently run as separate municipal enterprises, and were publicly accountable for their performance. The Conservatives planned a diminution of their role.

In mid–1979, more than 200 000 were employed on direct labour schemes at an annual cost of £1405 million. Many Conservative-controlled authorities, immediately after the party won the General Election, set about dismantling the DLOs, for example the Greater London Council (GLC) was reported in June 1979 to be planning to close down its direct labour department involving 860 redundancies. The GLC alleged that the main reason for the DLO's estimated loss of £5.6 million was due to its failure to compete effectively with private contractors. But Mullin (1979) revealed that according to a GLC report:

> the use of private sub-contractors was one of the main causes of the loss. It also blamed poor management and the GLC's own decision to run down the direct labour workforce over the previous two years.

It is ironic that the GLC's DLO has from time to time saved ratepayers considerable expense. In 1977, GLC auditors confirmed that the council's maintenance and repairs direct labour department had undertaken its work at a cost of £8 million a year less than the lowest outside tender received, and it was probably only the existence of the council's DLO that deterred private contractors from putting in exorbitantly high tenders. One wonders how many DLOs will be sacrificed on the altar of 'efficiency' either for the 'offence' of being unable to compete on unequal terms with private contractors or because of a doctrinaire support for a market rather than a mixed economy.

The Conservative government, as part of its philosophy of minimising public expenditure and ostensibly supporting private industry, decided to impose severe restrictions on the DLOs. The Local Government, Planning and Land Act of 1980 puts an obligation on local authorities to put out for tender all except the smallest jobs, rather than negotiate terms with their own DLOs; it required the DLOs to adopt accounting procedures which showed a profit or loss in each of their activities; and it warned DLOs that if they were 'consistently unsuccessful' they would be wound up. It would be false to regard this approach as being mainly concerned with efficiency. The intended diminution of direct labour is consistent with the Conservatives' doctrinaire opposition to council house building except at an abysmally low rate (see chapter 5) and its desire to return to a free market economy. It is not surprising that while the Conservatives place great emphasis on competition the above Act cuts out Labour's proposal to permit DLOs to tender on the open market beyond their own local authority boundaries. But Conservative monetarism did not help private industry. With the increase in MLR to 17 per cent in November 1979 (followed by mortgage rates rising to 15 per cent), and with local authorities cutting housing expenditure by 5.6 per cent (1979/80–1980/81), private building firms also entered the 1980s in a state of despondency, the construction industry suffering from a slump worse than that of the late 1970s.

8 Housing Rehabilitation

History of Housing Rehabilitation Policy to 1969

The substantial increase in population in the first half of the nineteenth century, the growth in the proportion of the population living in urban areas and the almost complete absence of controls over building and public health resulted in unprecedented congestion and squalor. Within the new industrial towns of the coalfields and in much of London the rationale of housing development was to get as many dwellings as possible on to a site at the least cost and as close as possible to places of work. From the 1840s there was a partial movement away from laissez-faire attitudes concerning the urban environment, but except away for some public sector infilling and development by charitable bodies, housing within the inner areas remained largely neglected up until the Second World War. By the Public Health Act of 1936, local authorities were however empowered to compulsorily purchase 'working class' houses which were unfit and to rehabilitate them so that they would have a further life of 20 years, but as no subsidies were given for this task the Act produced few results. Additional powers given to local authorities to enforce the repair or improvement of unfit houses (with default powers to undertake the work and recover the expense) similarly had little impact.

Throughout the 1950s and most of the 1960s there was very little rehabilitation. In the immediate post-war period there was official opposition to improvement or 'patching-up' as the process was then termed. The White Paper, *Capital Investment in 1948* (1947) and the Ministry of Health Circular 40/48 both attempted to restrict rehabilitation as resources were to be steered towards local authority housing development and the redevelopment of blitzed city centres. Yet within a year, the Housing Act of 1949 offered improvement grants to private owners and subsidies to local authorities in an attempt to make rehabilitation attractive or at least feasible. In part this was seen to be necessary as rent control reduced the ability of both private and public landlords to maintain or improve their tenancies. Grants were available to private persons up to half of the cost of improvement or conversion where the estimated cost of the work was between £100 and £600. Three-quarters of the cost of the grant was paid by the central government. Local authorities received commensurate assistance for the refurbishing of their own properties. But very little improvement (whether by local authorities, owner-occupiers or private landlords) resulted, the Ministry of Housing and Local Government (1955) reporting that between 1949 and 1954 only 5463 dwellings had been improved and only 624 new dwellings were produced by grant-aided conversions.

Local authorities were still constrained by central government policy which firmly placed improvement in a secondary role behind housebuilding—the Ministry of Health Circular 90/49 recommending that resources could be more effectively used in providing new houses than in patching-up older houses which would remain unsatisfactory in many respects. Many local authorities, moreover, were prejudiced against allocating grants for private improvements and used their discretionary powers to the full. To prevent any use of public money for private profit improvement grants were offered subject to a complex web of conditions:

(i)   that the new dwelling would comply with the required standard;

(ii) that the new dwelling would have a future life of not less than 30 years;

(iii) that the applicant had an interest in the property for that period; and

(iv) that the local authority would fix the maximum rent which could be charged for the dwelling which in general would equal 6 per cent of the cost of improvement to the landlord.

These onerous (though possibly fair) conditions and the bureaucratic delays to which they gave rise, resulted in private property owners being reluctant to take advantage of the grant facility.

The change from a Labour to a Conservative government in 1951 brought about a shift of emphasis from public to private housing. Not only did the completion of new houses rise by 63 per cent from about 200 000 in 1951 to 326 000 in 1953 (of which 56 000 were for private owners—the number of private completions achieving parity with public completions by the late 1950s), but the improvement grant scheme was made more flexible in an attempt to attract private landlords and owner-occupiers. The government appreciated that if resources were to be available for private house building, rehabilitation would be a way of partly offsetting the necessary rundown in local authority housebuilding. The proposals of the White Paper, *Housing— The Next Step* (1953) were largely implemented by the Housing Repairs and Rents Act of 1954 and were intended to increase the pace of housing improvement. The top limits on the cost of work eligible for an improvement grant (£100–£600) were removed (though the local authority limit remained at £400); the maximum grant was fixed at £400; the minimum life of an improved dwelling (in approved cases) was lowered from 30 to 15 years; and permitted rent increases were raised to allow a landlord to charge an additional rent of 8 per cent of the cost to him of the improvement.

Although in 1954 the number of grant-aided improvements and conversions showed a 100 per cent increase over previous years there was a small take-up of grants as conditions were still unfavourable. A high element of repair work was required prior to grant-aided improvements, and as there were still limitations imposed on additional rents chargeable, landlords had little incentive to improve their properties. It was not surprising that 90 per cent of improvement grants were awarded to owner-occupiers in the mid-1950s. The Housing Act of 1957 which enabled housing associations to qualify for improvement grants had very little impact upon the pace of rehabilitation. The 1950s was clearly not a period of rehabilitation—from 1949 to 1958 only 159 869 dwellings in England and Wales were rehabilitated with improvement grants.

By the late 1950s the slow pace of improvement was officially recognised. The Housing Purchase and Housing Act of 1959 enabled rents to be increased by 12.5 per cent of the landlord's cost of improvement or up to the rent of similar dwellings in the area where property did not contain controlled tenants. Standard grants were introduced which could be claimed as a right. These were available in specific amounts for the installation of the standard amenities—bath/shower, wash hand-basin, hot water supply, W.C. and a food store—the total grant available was £155. The Housing Act of 1961 brought houses containing controlled tenants under the Rent Act of 1957 into line with all others by permitting rent increases of 12.5 per cent of the landlord's cost of improvement. It was further recognised that there was a disincentive to improve a house if other houses within the same street or area remained in an unfit condition or at least severely dilapidated. The Housing Act of 1964 was designed to improve areas of poor housing. Local authorities were empowered to declare 'improvement areas' if dwellings lacked the standard amenities and where at least half of the dwellings could be brought up to the approved standard and be expected to last 15 years or more. Local authorities could require landlords to improve their tenancies in these areas with the consent of their tenants. Local authorities could also apply these powers of compulsion outside of the improvement areas. The use of improvement grants was encouraged by a relaxation of conditions of allocation. Standard grants could be used to offset part of the cost of installing some of the standard amenities (but only where it was not practicable to provide all five at reasonable expense), the period over which the grant conditions applied was reduced from 10 to three years, the maximum grant for converting houses of three or more storeys was raised from £400 to £500 per unit, and the rent limit was increased for improved dwellings not subject to controlled tenancies.

Although between 1958 and 1968, 1 147 875 dwellings were improved with discretionary and standard grants (a sixfold increase over the previous ten year period), the pace of rehabilitation in relation to the number of poor houses remained very slow. From 130 832 grants being awarded in 1960 (the highest number up to that date) the number fell to 108 938 in 1969 (figure 8.1). The economic incentive for landlords to use improvement grants was insufficient. Despite a gradual relaxation in the conditions of grant provision and the slight increase in the permitted rate of return, landlords remained reluctant to undertake improvement. Local authorities were also unwilling to undertake modernisation programmes especially where this would have required the acquisition of properties. The lack of a government subsidy coupled with low rent levels proved to be major constraints.

Coming into office in 1964 the Labour Government had (according to the Party's election manifesto of the same year) a housebuilding target of half a

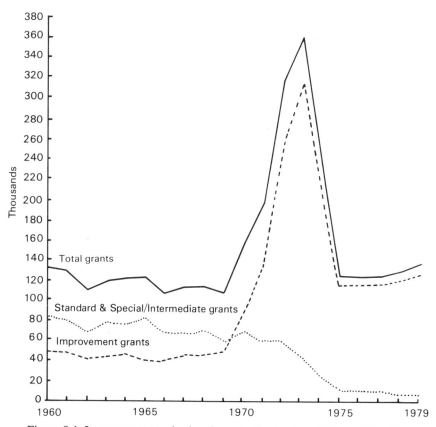

Figure 8.1 Improvement and related grants, England and Wales, 1960–78.

million dwellings per annum. In 1965 the White Paper, *The Housing Programme, 1965–1969,* confirmed this target and proclaimed that the post-war emphasis on new house building (rather than on improvement) was to continue. But devaluation in 1967 and the accompanying disinflationary measures made the Government revise its housebuilding programme—in January 1968 the public sector's target being reduced by 16 500 per annum. The number of houses built in the public sector consequently declined by 9.2 per cent from 203 918 in 1967 to 185 090 in 1969 and the total number of houses built—after reaching a peak of 404 356 in 1967—fell by 9.3 per cent to 366 793 in 1969.

The decrease in housebuilding occurred at the same time as it was acknowledged that the number of unfit houses was much greater than previously thought. The *Housing Condition Survey* (1967) revised the number of unfit houses in England and Wales up by 125 per cent from 0.8 million to 1.8 million and it showed that 2.3 million lacked one or more of the basic amenities (780 000 dwellings without a bath/shower and 1.5 million without an inside W.C. or wash basin) and that 3.7 million dwellings—although not unfit—required over £125 million to be spent on essential repairs. Out of a total housing stock of 15.7 million the proportion of poor dwellings was not inconsiderable.

The decline in housebuilding and the recognition of the extent of the problem of poor housing inevitably resulted in a shift of emphasis to rehabilitation. Local authority housing programmes needed to be changed. The White Paper, *Old Houses into New Homes* (1968) therefore proposed that:

> within a total of public investment in housing at about the level it [had] reached a greater share should go to the improvement of older houses.

There were obvious relative cost advantages of rehabilitation as opposed to redevelopment. Needleman (1965) proposed that usually the best way to improve the minimum standard of housing with the available resources was to concentrate upon rehabilitation up until at least the 1980s, a conclusion also reached by Stone (1970). Hillman (1969) indicated the comparative cost advantage of rehabilitation. It would cost, for example, £600 million per annum to construct 200 000 local authority houses, but only £115 million per annum (half paid through rates and taxation) to improve 230 000 homes (realistic annual costings in 1969 for the early 1970s).

The Housing Act of 1969

Stemming from the 1968 White Paper, the Housing Act of 1969 was intended to hasten substantially the pace of rehabilitation. The Minister of Housing and Local Government, Mr Anthony Greenwood (1969a) clearly stated that a major goal of the provisions of the Act was to raise the standard of living of those residing in areas of bad housing which had the potential for improvement:

> The idea of continuing to live year after year without basic amenities . . . is totally unacceptable at this period in our history. Older people may have got used to a settled way of life, and in many cases it would be wrong to disturb them, but we should do everything we can to see that children are brought up in better than substandard conditions.

Improvement was to be encouraged by increased grants and a relaxation of the conditions attached to them. For private housing, standard grants were to be raised from £155 to £200 to assist in the provision of the standard amenities. Discretionary grants were also increased—from £400 to £1000—to enable such work as essential repairs, dampproofing and rewiring to be done in addition to the installation of the standard amenities. Discretionary grants could also be used for conversions—up to £1000 per dwelling being available for a conversion into two flats or up to £1200 per dwelling for conversion into three or more flats. In all cases the grants would have to be matched pound for pound by the applicant's authorised expenditure and the discretionary grant would be conditional on improvement up to a 12 point standard.

The government contribution towards the improvement of local authority and housing association properties was £1000 per dwelling if improvements alone were to be done and £1250 per dwelling if acquisition was necessary in addition. The grants were calculated at 50 per cent of the cost of improvement and acquisition. The intention was to provide local authorities with the equivalent assistance for the purchase of houses for improvement as they received from the subsidy for building new houses under the Housing Subsidies Act of 1967. The Housing Act of 1971 adjusted the amount of the improvement subsidy available to private owners, local authorities and housing associations. Discretionary grants paid by local authorities to private owner-occupiers and landlords in Development and Intermediate Areas were increased to 75 per cent of the approved expense of improvement works, but the government's share of the cost of improving local authority housing fell to 3/8 of the cost, the local authority having to meet the remaining 5/8 (75 per cent and 25 per cent in development and intermediate areas). Where local authorities acquired properties for conversion or improvement, their acquisition costs were included in the approved expense for improvement contributions, together with the costs of works, and were subject to higher cost limits. Housing associations could receive either cash grants in the same way as private owners or contributions in the same way as local authorities, but, outside of Development or Intermediate Areas, the proportion of government contribution was higher than that to local authorities, one half instead of 3/8 of the total approved cost.

It is important to note that as a result of inflation, the discretionary grant of £1000 in 1969 was in real terms worth only £500 as compared with 1949 when improvement grants (up to a maximum of £300) were first introduced. The real increase in the grant over these years was thus about 67 per cent rather than approximately 233 per cent—the absolute increase. But the principal incentive for improvement may not have been the size of the grant but that it did not have to be repaid.

Further encouragement was given to improvement by the rent provisions of the Housing Act of 1969. If grant-aided improvements were carried out in the case of regulated tenancies then the rent could rise to a new fair rent level as certified by the Rent Officer (under the provisions of the Rent Act of 1968), with the increase phased over three equal annual stages. Where improvements to controlled tenancies reached the qualifying standard, the local authority would issue a qualification certificate. Upon receipt of the certificate a landlord could apply to the Rent Officer who would determine a fair rent. Increases in rent would have to be phased over five years. If the property was rated at over £90 in London or over £60 elsewhere the increases could start in January 1971; and lower-rated properties—once improved—were eligible for rent increases from July 1971. In the case of furnished tenancies, the Rent Officer could supply and give guidance on the completion of application forms which could be submitted to the Rent Tribunal, which might then fix a rent limit and grant security of tenure to a tenant for a maximum of six months. If a property was empty when improvement or conversion took place and was then let unfurnished, the Rent Officer was required to establish a fair rent.

General Improvement Areas

The 1969 Act re-enforced the idea of area improvement introduced by the 1964 Act, and placed great emphasis on the declaration of General Improvement areas (GIAs)—areas which in scale could vary widely from small and compact areas of say 300 houses up to larger areas of between 500 and 800 houses.

Local authorities were invited to consider which mainly-residential areas could be upgraded; to subsequently declare GIAs and to concentrate their activities on the improvement of those areas. Prior to the declaration of a GIA, it would be desirable if a large element of corporate planning could be established, combining partially the activities of the local housing, planning and environmental health departments which had to be integrated into a total policy of urban renewal. The local authority needed to refer to a report concerning the physical potential of the area, its planning future and the general attitude of residents towards improvements. At the outset both the Labour and Conservative parties in Parliament had agreed that the benefits of area improvement should be enjoyed by the residents of the chosen areas.

This fundamental condition was incorporated into Circular 64/69 accompanying the Act stating:

> it is much to be hoped that from the beginning of their enquiries local authorities will make it absolutely clear that what is under consideration is a programme of action designed to raise the standards of comfort and amenity for the residents.

An important aim of area improvement was to realise the potential of housing so far as was feasible and with this aim a local authority might have insisted on issuing full improvement grants rather than standard grants. This would have been justified according to Mr Anthony Greenwood (1969b) who stated that:

> if the standard grant was available as of right the local authority would be in a very weak position in its discussions with the owners. What we are trying to do here is to put the local authority in a stronger position, so that the owners of property in the area will not simply be able to fall back on the very minimum requirements. The local authority will be able to set out to persuade them to achieve a higher standard of improvement than would otherwise be the case.

But the 1969 Act already contained the condition—even for the allocation of standard grants—that after an improvement a dwelling would be required to be in good repair, having regard to its age, character and locality. The public interest in a GIA might have been adequately protected by this requirement without any 'persuasive' powers being granted to local authorities, powers which may have deterred many owners (especially owner-occupiers) from improving their properties at all.

The Act envisaged that housing associations would make a very useful contribution to rehabilitation by buying houses which came on to the market within the GIAs and improving or converting them under arrangement with the local authority.

Under the 1969 Act local authorities received reserve powers enabling them to acquire property compulsorily especially if owners threatened the success of a whole scheme by failing to take up improvement grants. Yet it was emphasised that encouragement and voluntary action should be the underlying principle. Local authorities would provide improvement and conversion plans and would seek cooperation from builders. Acquisition by agreement or compulsory purchase would only be used at the last resort—the latter requiring the approval of the Department of the Environment.

But the improvement of housing was not sufficient. The improvement of the residential environment was also important. Government grants of one half the cost of environmental improvement were to be available up to a limit of £50 per house in the area. The Act enabled local authorities to improve amenities and to acquire land for this purpose. Improvement works specified in the circulars included tree planting, the grassing or paving over of open space, the provision of play spaces, parking facilities and garages and the repairing and renewing of fences. In addition an area might be improved by the exclusion of through traffic, pedestrianisation of highways, the repair of road surfaces and the renewal or re-siting of street lighting. The importance of area improvement was clearly recognised by the Denington Committee which had been set up to examine the standards for slum clearance and the improvement and repair of the housing stock. Its report, *Our Older Homes: A Call for Action* (1966) argued that a dwelling is not satisfactory unless it stands in a satisfactory environment and when improving a dwelling, the local authority should also attempt to improve the environment.

It was consequently acknowledged by the 1969 Act that the resources and effort devoted to rehabilitation would produce a better return if they were directed to whole areas rather than to individual and dispersed dwellings. It was also important that continuity was seen to be an essential element on which improvement policy was based, therefore a GIA should not be an area which was subject to major structural change or redevelopment in the forseeable future.

The Political View of Rehabilitation

The 1969 Act, it was agreed in Parliament, would increase the supply of minimum standard private accommodation. While preferring the municipalisation of all private rented property, Anthony Greenwood (1969a) argued that in his view the management and financial problems involved were prohibitive and that landlords would only maintain their property if they derived a profit on the capital they invested. The government regarded the maintenance of the private rented sector as necessary rather than desirable, as an expediency rather than a goal. Provisions were thus made in the Act to permit an improved property to be changed from a controlled to a regulated tenancy.

The Conservatives saw the Act as a stimulant to the private market. Placing greater reliance on the market system than on public intervention, the Conservatives have continually argued that the private rented sector declined as a consequence of rent control. They predicted that the Act by diminishing the number of controlled tenancies would reduce the pace of this decline. This prediction was supported by the argument that within a relatively free market the private tenant would be the most mobile of all households.

Because of their belief in a 'property-owning democracy', the Conservatives viewed the Act with its grant concession as a means of achieving one of their principal housing goals—an increase in the proportion of owner-occupiers. The Conservatives considered that about 50 per cent of the housing stock being owner-occupied was too low a proportion. A Conservative shadow minister, Mr Peter Walker (1969) further believed that:

> it is the owner-occupier who takes the greatest pride and care in the maintenance of his home. It is the owner-occupier who makes the major improvements so as to provide the modern amenities of a bathroom and a kitchen. It is the owner-occupier who takes the most positive interest in the decisions affecting the entire community.

The Conservatives therefore regarded the Act as a means of both preserving privately rented housing by reducing rent control and encouraging an increase in owner-occupation through improvement grants.

Following the Conservative victory at the general election, Mr Peter Walker (1970), then Secretary of State for the Environment reiterated the emphasis which the previous government had placed on improvement:

> New houses are not enough. We need many more new houses, but it should be remembered that whilst new homes take a matter of months to build, it takes much longer to build a community. . . . We have established communities, with their local churches, their local schools, their local pubs and their local football teams, where the inhabitants are friends and neighbours of each other. It is important that where possible, instead of using the bulldozer we retain the community and improve the whole quality of the housing and its environment.

To help realise these objectives the Circulars to the Act had referred previously to the great stress laid by the Minister in Parliament on the obligation of local authorities both to advise the residents of the planning proposals for their area and to be receptive to the ideas and attitudes of the inhabitants themselves. Public participation would necessitate that the improvement proposals for the area were sufficiently detailed to be intelligible, but adequately flexible to permit modification in response to popular feeling. By means of public meetings and personal visits to households, local authorities were to make every effort to secure the confidence of residents and gain their co-operation. Local authorities should also encourage the formation of residents associations which would focus attention on the problems of rehabilitation and provide a further channel of communication. In areas of housing stress local authorities were faced with further obligations.

The Social View of Rehabilitation

It became increasingly acknowledged that a major weakness of planning—not least in the context of housing—was that it failed to take social considerations sufficiently into account. Cherry (1970) pointed out that the planner has been continually pre-occupied with the physical condition of housing and the environment. Only recently has it been realised that residents are the most important aspect of this environment. The 1969 Act was seen by the government not only as a means of implementing its housing programme but as an important element in its social policy. Mr Richard Crossman (1969), as Secretary of State for Social Services, stated that 'improvement was safer than building new houses because it created fewer social problems' a passive but nevertheless valid recognition of the social value of rehabilitation.

The sociological importance of good housing cannot be overstated. The relationship between poor housing and man's opportunities in society have been demonstrated frequently. The home environment in which a child spends its early life can have a profound effect upon his educational attainment and social adjustment. Circular 64/69 acknowledged the social as well as the economic aspects of improvement, and recognised that although:

> in some instances there may be little economic justification for improvement [there would be] an overwhelming social case where the installation of one or more standard amenities would help to make life tolerable for a family living in a house with a comparatively short estimated life.

Yet in general the Act was mainly concerned with encouraging the use of discretionary grants as a means of realising a property's full potential—an extended life of at least thirty years. Comprehensive improvement up to the 12 point standard rather than patching-up was seen as a preferable way of attempting to meet the accommodation needs of households who would otherwise be living in substandard dwellings.

The social benefits of rehabilitation are not just confined to the sum of household satisfaction resulting from the improvement of individual homes. There is in addition the benefits—often intangible—of the preservation of the local community. Following research undertaken in East London, Young and Willmott (1957) argued that the community feeling which existed in areas of bad housing should be retained by accommodating the existing residents in the same redevelopment scheme: The research showed that:

> the sense of loyalty to each other amongst the inhabitants of a place like Bethnal Green is not due to buildings. It is due far more to ties of kinship and friendship which connect the people of one household to the people of another. In such a district, community spirit does not have to be fostered, it is already there. If the authorities regard that spirit as a social asset worth preserving, they will not uproot more people, but build the new houses around the social groups to which they already belong.

It was becoming accepted that people generally wish to live in the same neighbourhood as others of the same socio-economic group. There are many explanations for social agglomeration. First, as Anderson (1962) noted, people in a specific socio-economic group may prefer to interact with others in the same group rather than among people in other groups. It is probable, that *ceteris paribus*, the greater the proportion of a group living in the same area, the greater the advantages to that group. Second, social agglomeration can be explained using the concept of social space. If the household has a preference to interact with others in the same socio-economic group its neighbourhood space will be smallest in area if it locates in the same neighbourhood as others in the same group. Buttimer (1969) noted that research has shown that there are:

> thresholds in space beyond which certain groups cannot travel without experiencing frustration, tensions and feelings of anomie.

Each household would wish not to cross this threshold within its daily or local movement (that is, its neighbourhood space). Only by locating in the same area as others in the same socio-economic group can it achieve this. Third, people in different socio-economic groups have different consumption characteristics. Households will be able to minimise their cost of shopping journeys by living in the same neighbourhood as others in the same group. Similarly, if people locate in the same local authority area as others in the same group they may get the public services they prefer. These explanations justify the preservation of existing neighbourhoods, not least the areas of low-income housing.

Redevelopment in the 1950s and 1960s usually involved the provision of lower density housing than that which it replaced. It may also have involved the insensitive relocation of low income communities and severe planning blight between the announcement and completion of a plan. The distress suffered by the residents of slum clearance areas has provoked opposition to redevelopment schemes. Improvement policy was seen as a means of avoiding these problems; Mr Anthony Greenwood (1969a) launching the Housing Bill stated that:

> it is remarkable how much attraction many older areas have for their inhabitants. They are familiar, and their friends live there. Slum clearance means disruption, scattering or beginning again. This is not a plea to slow down slum clearance, far from it, it is a plea that whenever possible we should step in well before slum clearance is necessary—10 or 20 years before—and give suitable areas a longer span of life.

Circular 65/69 to the Act ended by acknowledging that:

> there are a limited number of areas, mainly in large cities, where the problems of physical decay are combined with problems of overcrowding and multiple occupation and other severe and intractable problems. They have been called twilight areas and coincide in some areas with what have been called in another context areas of multiple deprivation. The social

reasons for taking action in such areas may be imperative even if the economic prospects are doubtful.

The Circular suggested that in order that improvement should take place in such areas it might be necessary to make more use of compulsory purchase than would be usual in for example most general improvement areas. The references in the above Circulars both to the need for public participation and the social reasons for taking action in twilight areas further stresses the intention of the legislation that it was the needs of existing residents which had to be primarily considered.

Some Effects of the Housing Act of 1969

The 1969 Act was a major factor in restoring many properties which otherwise would have remained in poor condition or have been demolished. Between 1969 and 1973 the number of improvement grants approved increased by 230 per cent from 108 938 to a record 360 954 in England and Wales (figure 8.1). Discretionary grant expenditure over the same period increased from almost £40 million per annum to over £300 million. By 1973 house building in Great Britain had fallen to 294 000 completions from 319 000 in 1972—rehabilitation now being on a greater scale. Even as early as 1971 the *House Condition Survey* showed the extent of improvement (table 8.1). The number of unfit dwellings had been reduced by 31.0 per cent from 1.80 million in 1967 to 1.24 million while 2.87 million still lacked one or more basic amenities; the highest proportion of unfit housing, 51.8 per cent being rented from private owners. By the end of 1973 less than 2.5

Table 8.1 House Condition Survey, England and Wales, 1971, Stock of Dwellings Lacking Basic Amenities

Condition	Thousand dwellings	%
Unfit dwellings	1 244	7.3
All dwellings not unfit	15 856	92.7
Total dwellings	17 100	100.00
Lack of basic amenities		
Dwellings lacking		
w.c. inside dwelling	2 032	11.9
fixed bath in a bathroom	1 630	9.5
wash basin	2 043	11.9
sink	84	0.5
hot and cold water at 3 points	2 374	13.9
one or more of these amenities	2 866	16.8
Dwellings with all these amenities	14 234	83.2

Source: National House Condition Survey, 1971

million dwellings lacked basic amenities. At the 1973 rate of rehabilitation it would have taken probably only a decade to rectify this deficiency. Some regions witnessed a faster rate of improvement than others. In the North East virtually every pre-war local authority house was modernised, in the period 1970–2, and by 1972 the Assisted Areas were allocating about half of the national total of grants received by owner-occupiers and local authorities. Progress was also being made with the declaration of GIAs. By September 1973, 733 GIAs had been set up in England and Wales comprising 223 000 dwellings—of which approximately 50 000 had been approved for improvement grants. But there are many side effects of improvement. Mr Anthony Crosland (1971a), then Shadow Minister for the Environment, argued that:

> Improvement grants [although] highly successful in improving the housing stock, [also] operate regressively. They are overwhelmingly taken up by better off owner-occupiers and speculative property developers, who receive not only the amount of grant, but also the appreciation in the capital value of the house.

The economic rationale for development with the aid of discretionary grants can be illustrated by the following developer's 'balance sheet' (quoted by Kilroy 1972) in respect of a private conversion of two houses into 22 flats in North Kensington:

	£
Cost of houses	43 000
Conversion costs	100 000
Fees and interest charges	17 500
Total outlay	160 500
22 grants of £1200	26 400
Sale price of £8000 per unit	176 000
Total receipts	202 400
Profit	41 900

Not only would there have been a return of over 25 per cent to the developer but nearly two-thirds of that return would have been provided by improvement grants. Although this particular scheme did not go ahead as the developers failed to get vacant possession, a large number of other similar developments were undertaken where the improvement grants accounted for a substantial proportion of profits. In many cases because of the inelasticity of supply, grants were added completely to the capital value of the house or the profit of the speculator. Resultant house prices would for the most part be beyond the reach of the former tenants. Yet housing associations could provide dwellings of comparable quality to privately rehabilitated properties and generally each unit would not be sold much in excess of £5000. Similar improved private flats would fetch £8000 to £10 000 reflecting the extent of the profit to be realised.

Within GIAs these trends and comparisons were especially pronounced, Babbage (1973) argued that:

> by declaring a general improvement area in an area of housing stress . . . the local authority may just as well have been putting a flag on the developer's office wall map to show where he might operate with the best return on investment.

Improvement grants also enabled private landlords to raise rents and thus increase the capital-value of their investments. At first they were reluctant to take up improvement grants because many tenants could neither afford nor wish to pay higher rents. This was particularly evident in the case of controlled tenancies—only 4000 dwellings being improved to the standard of repair and maintenance from 1969 to October 1971. The White Paper, *Fair Deal for Housing* (1971) explained that this was because:

> the landlord of a controlled dwelling who wishes to improve it has to undergo a daunting procedure before obtaining the right to charge a fair rent; and must wait four years after the improvements have been made before the rent can be obtained in full.

The subsequent Housing Finance Act of 1972 enabled improvement work to proceed as soon as the landlord obtained approval for a grant. As soon as the improvement works were carried out, the landlord would then be able to charge a rent increase—its annual rate being 12.5 per cent of the amount (net of grant) spent on improvement. A further rent increase up to the fair rent level (if not yet reached) would then be permitted—after the dwelling had been certified as being up to the qualification standard of repair and amenity—the increase being spread over a two year period. The 1972 Act probably had some effect on the rapidly increasing number of improvement grants taken up in 1972 and 1973, but this should not be over emphasised.

Although it was the intention of the Labour government in 1969 that tenants would benefit from housing improvement with landlords being rewarded by getting fair rents, few small landlords could afford improvement despite the relaxation in conditions. Landlords had to match grants pound for pound, and taking into account allowances, it was forecast that average rents would increase by only 35p per week in 1972 and by 25p in 1973. Landlords would therefore either look forward to vacant possession or would sell to larger landlords who would increase the capital value of their newly acquired property if it became vacant. Comparatively low rent tenancies would be converted into high rent furnished luxury flats or maisonettes. New higher income tenants could afford the furnished rents at the market level without recourse to the Rent Tribunal and the authorised eviction which such action frequently provoked. Both for the purpose of development for sale and for the creation of 'up market' tenancies, owners usually felt it necessary to displace their tenants. Results of social research by the Department of the Environment (1975) have shown that over 60 per cent of households were displaced from properties owned by landlords in receipt of grants for improvement or conversion. Although many of the affected tenancies were furnished, housing young transient occupiers, many contained families who had made their homes over many years in the less expensive furnished accommodation typical of a high proportion of lettings in stress areas. Babbage (1973) described how 'winkling' was a common method used to encourage tenants to quit:

> Offers of as much as £5000 were made to tenants to give up their statutory tenancy. The greatest worry was the larger proportion of cases where, particularly with older people, an offer of a few hundred pounds was made. To the poorer family it seemed a large sum and they were tempted to move out only to find it insufficient to assist them in finding another home. In some cases winkling was combined with an agreement that the landlord would 'evict' the tenant on the presumption he would then have to be rehoused by the local authority as 'homeless'.

Harassment was a further process used to displace tenants. It was probable that the degree of alleged harassment—when compared to that affecting non-grant properties—was much greater in the case of properties which were either already or later to be the subject of discretionary grant application. Although prosecution was often inhibited by inadequate evidence there was usually enough of it to link allegations of malpractice to the owner's desire for vacant possession.

Inevitably the displaced low-income tenants would seek homes in an ever-shrinking pool of privately rented accommodation. Many of these households shifted to the already overcrowded furnished areas. Here they joined those destined to become eventually homeless. But some became immediately homeless. It fell to the local authority social services:

> to find temporary accommodation (usually at high cost in hotels and boarding houses) and then to the housing department permanently to rehouse them. . . . How absurd that the same hand which dangles the carrot should then pay the bill for bed and board and lose a dwelling at the expense of the waiting list, at the expense of conversion schemes which showed no housing gain and very often, a housing loss (Babbage, 1973).

The then Secretary of State for the Environment, Mr Peter Walker (1972) became aware of this dual and conflicting responsibility of local authorities—the statutory duty (or so it was believed) to provide improvement grants on the one hand and the duty to house the homeless on the other. But he did not accept that tenants should be displaced immediately an owner acquired a grant:

> I recognise that certain tenants in rented properties have been told they have to go because of improvement grants. . . . In their ignorance they have gone. So I am writing to all local authorities to ask them in future where they approve an improvement grant for tenanted property that they should inform the tenants of their basic legal rights.

It can be questioned however whether tenants faced with eviction, and perhaps subjected to the pressures of 'winkling' or harassment would be prepared to claim their legal rights to the full, especially when the end result might not just be security of tenure but a large increase in rent—not withstanding the availability of rent allowances for unfurnished accommodation.

The large increase in property values between 1971 and 1973—which in the inner areas of large cities resulted mainly from the demand of the speculative developer—jeopardised the plans of local authorities and housing associations. Rents and repayments on improved properties would have been greatly in excess of the ability to pay of those in need. Higher grants were clearly required to reduce the amount of expenditure which had to be recouped from tenants.

Whereas the need to eliminate rapidly rising commuter travel costs provided the motive, improvement grants partly provided the means for middle and higher income households to acquire and renovate poor housing within the transitional zone. Developers attempted to satisfy this demand, but not without far-reaching repercussions. Mr Anthony Crosland (1971a) as Shadow Minister for the Environment, argued that:

> The manic rise in prices fosters a speculative investment demand for houses . . . creates a hideous two-nation pattern of housing . . . through the middle class takeover of previously working class areas.

Improvement grants intended to benefit the residents of areas of substandard housing were manifestly not benefitting those residents. They were adding to the profit of developers, increasing the capital value of the properties of often non-resident landlords and helping to provide new homes for former commuters. Simultaneously communities were being destroyed as quickly as if major clearance schemes had been undertaken— many former residents doubling-up in increasingly multi-occupied dwellings, becoming homeless or moving elsewhere, often without trace. Within the GIAs—particularly in areas of high stress—these trends were magnified, improvement grants causing:

> massive socio-economic change [and] leaving a juxtaposition of affluence and squalor with the extremes of the social index in neighbouring

properties, only some of which are improved [it is evident that] the professional and managerial classes are keen to move into an area being socially and environmentally upgraded and are happy to live next door to a working class family in the expectation that 'they will eventually move away' (Babbage, 1973).

A body of opinion evolved in the 1970s which either ignored the social effects of the 1969 Act or actually welcomed them.

The 'bricks and mortar' approach, applied before official research had indicated the social implications of rehabilitation, doubtless prompted the Minister of Housing and Construction, Mr Julian Amery (1972a) to state that 'the name of the game is improvement'. he referred (1972b) to the distribution of improvement grants nationally (75 per cent to owner-occupiers and 25 per cent to private landlords/developers), thus under-estimating the real effects of improvement especially within the inner areas of cities where the distribution of grants was the reverse of the national pattern.

The *Estates Gazette* (1972) similarly saw improvement mainly in physical terms:

One of the great assets bequeathed by Victorian enterprise is a large stock of solid buildings. Many of these have another century of worthwhile life in them, and by adaption, conversion and modernisation—or in other words by improvement—they can make an extremely valuable contribution to the total number of homes available. . . . Certainly a proportion of the grants may be considered by some to be misdirected, but this may be a cheap price to pay for an overall increase in the available housing stock.

The journal implied that even if improvement benefitted initially the middle classes:

the cumulative process of filtration would benefit all sectors of the community. Every addition to the housing stock provides an extra home for someone, somewhere.

Yet, as was discussed above, this process is very imperfect and it is questionable whether it works at all within the transitional zone where both rehabilitation and redevelopment usually result in lower density and more expensive housing.

In theoretical terms an argument can be presented for the assimilation of socio-economic groups within the same areas of housing, indeed this was a basis of public housing policy in Britain in the years just after the Second World War. In Bevan's Housing Act of 1949 all reference to the working classes was omitted because it was believed that housing should be an indivisible subject. Any attempt in the 1980s to restructure housing policy on the class basis which existed before this Act should be vigorously opposed. It is equally important that it is recognised than in-migration by the professional and managerial groups could reinvigorate both the economic and social structure of the transitional areas. The cause for concern was not that improvement grants may have been associated with the creation of more balanced communities, or that sometimes houses were bought by the wealthy after low-income households had moved out to overspill housing, but that certain areas may have been taken-over by the higher income groups—with the poorer classes being displaced. In many parts of Inner London, this take-over was particularly evident—gentrification resulting in the displacement of existing, mainly low income residents, and the conversion of private rented accommodation into owner-occupied properties or luxury flats (Balchin, 1979).

Proposals for Reform 1972–4

The consequences of the 1969 Act became increasingly identified—but at first not openly admitted by the government. Mr Julian Amery (1972b) thought that:

the landlords of the country are doing a very good job [and] it is very difficult to judge which developers should qualify for improvement grants and which should not.

Yet within the Conservative Party there was growing recognition of the social consequences of grant approval. Mr David Hunt (1972) Young Conservative national chairman thought it necessary to:

impose strict conditions on the availability of improvement grants to ensure that they are repaid if the property is resold after five years.

In a report on rehabilitation, Shelter (1972) asked the questions:

does improvement have to happen as it does? Should families be made homeless in the name of home improvement? Should the Government give tacit approval to the increased pressure upon private tenants?

Shelter thought not, and made the following proposals to safeguard tenants:

(1) All families displaced by improvement should be rehoused by the council or landlord. Since furnished tenants were particularly susceptible to eviction they should be given full security of tenure.

(2) The rent officer or Rent Tribunal should fix the rents of improved properties.

(3) Councils should nominate the tenants of improved properties.

(4) If the improved property is sold (within say 3 years) the grant should be repaid—if need be on a sliding scale.

(5) With regard to Inner London a code of practice should be drawn up by the London Boroughs Association to constrain the activities of speculators.

Shelter advised greater protection for households especially tenants of unfurnished lettings in improving areas. It was necessary, argued Shelter, that those living in improvement areas benefitted from improvement (the intention of the Act). Where compulsory purchase was required for this purpose (and for the acquisition of empty property) 100 per cent grants should be made available. To deter eviction, Shelter proposed that private property left empty pending improvement should be rated at 200 per cent. But the Association of Public Health Inspectors (1972) was concerned with the pace of rehabilitation. In a memorandum to the Department of the Environment it drew attention to the shortage of available builders to undertake improvement work. It proposed that rehabilitation would only be effective in helping to eliminate substandard housing if improvement grants were increased up to 75 per cent throughout the United Kingdom, and that the £200–£300 standard grant were raised and its 50–75 per cent (of cost) limit relaxed. It was also argued that there were too few general improvement areas—comprising only about 2.75 per cent of poor housing in England and Wales, and that the size of a typical GIA (about 300 houses) was too small.

The House Condition Survey (1971) published in 1973 indicated that it would take until 1982 to eliminate all the unfit housing—a prediction based on the rate of improvement over the previous $4\frac{1}{2}$ years. Although the numbers of unfit dwellings and those lacking basic amenities had fallen from 1.8 to 1.2 million, and 3.9 to 2.9 million respectively from 1967 to 1971, one in six households still lacked at least one basic amenity. The government consequently accepted that the improvement grant system should be subject to thorough scrutiny.

In 1972 the House of Commons Expenditure Committee (Environmental and Home Office Sub Committee) on House Improvement Grants was appointed to consider:

(1) Who was receiving grants, how and for what.

(2) The effects of improvement grants on the housing stock, its condition, its ownership and its price.

(3) Whether the legislation was achieving its purpose.

A major supplier of evidence to the Committee, the Royal Town Planning Institute (1973), emphasised that:

the problem of 'gentrification', the movement out of existing tenants and their replacement by groups with higher incomes ... poses important questions about what and who the present legislation is for? Is it intended to upgrade existing areas of sub-standard housing or is it to improve the conditions of the existing residents of these areas? This becomes an urgent problem when those tenants displaced as a result of improvement, by the need for vacant possession by landlords or higher rents, suffer a decline in their housing standards.

The Association of Municipal Corporations (1973) making recommendations, regarded it reasonable and helpful if local authorities were empowered to:

> impose conditions when making improvement grants as to repayment on sale within a defined term of years ... to nominate a tenant to occupy a dwelling improved with a grant (and) to prescribe the type of applicant for a tenancy, or the nature of the letting.

Being disappointed with the low take-up of grants within the GIAs, the Association suggested that local authorities should also be given powers requiring the improvement of houses beyond the limited power they had under section 19 of the Housing Act of 1964; and being concerned that rent increases permitted under the 1972 Act could take place without obligations being imposed on the landlord, proposed that 'certificates of provisional approval' (introduced by the 1969 Act) be reintroduced enabling local authorities to ensure that at least a minimum standard of repair and improvement was carried out before a landlord obtained a rent increase.

The White Paper, *Better Houses—The Next Priorities* (1973) included some of the recommendations of the witnesses to the Select Committee. The White Paper proposed that where improvement grants were awarded to landlords, local authorities should have the right to insist that the dwelling was let for at least seven years, and if a property was sold after improvement (assuming the owner had vacant possession) the grant should be repaid with compound interest to the local authority. It was also proposed that local authorities should have discretion to compel owners to improve their properties (and if they refused the authorities should undertake the work themselves and impose a charge).Local authorities should also be given powers to buy up empty properties using compulsory purchase orders. Perhaps the most important aspect of the White Paper was the proposal to declare Housing Action Areas (HAAs). These would be inner stress areas of about 400–500 houses where developers and large landlords have displaced lower-income tenants, where house prices are rapidly rising and where communities are being broken up and homelessness is increasing. There would be a high proportion of furnished tenants, occupancy rates would be over 1.5 persons per room and multi-occupation would be substantial. There would also be large families, a high proportion of elderly occupants and housing would generally lack basic amenities. Within the HAAs the new powers of the local authorities (specified above) would be exercised to the full but in addition landlords would be prevented from selling their proper-ties to speculators or any private individual without first offering them to the local authority or a housing association. Local authorities would have the responsibility of rehousing tenants evicted as a result of an improvement, and local authorities should also be able to nominate tenants when landlords left rooms empty. GIAs would continue to be declared but specifically within areas free of stress—unlike many which had been declared in the past, often with unsuccessful results. The proposals provoked criticism. From the left it was thought that HAAs would involve another degree of area fragmentation—total community action and neighbourhood renewal being preferred, and from the right it was thought that improvement would slow down as the proposals would deter the activities of developers and specula-tors.

Prior to subsequent legislation, the government considered it necessary to ensure that improvement grants in certain circumstances would not merely be added to developers' profits. Clearly the government was not convinced that if the proposals of the White Paper were implemented developers would cease to convert or improve. Circular 99/73 stated that the refusal of an improvement grant would be justified where its only effect would be to add to the profits flowing from a development scheme which would have proceeded as a commercial venture even without the grant. Since at least 1969, local authorities had discretionary powers but most had been reluc-tant to use them, and in 1973 the Minister for Housing and Construction, Mr Paul Channon became more willing to give permission for compulsory purchase orders realising that this was perhaps the only way to prevent the wholesale eviction of traditional working class communities. The Secretary of State for the Environment Mr Geoffrey Rippon (1973) reiterated official support for rehabilitation declaring that:

> we should now turn away from a policy of massive and widespread redevelopment and give the first priority to providing people with fit, modernised, comfortable houses where they now live ... (their) ... familiar surroundings contain a community structure that has taken generations to build up. It cannot be recreated quickly on remote new estates.

The Housing and Planning Bill of January 1974 seemed a half-hearted attempt to apply the proposals of the White Paper. It accepted that improvement rather than redevelopment was to receive top priority, and HAAs were to be declared specifically for this purpose. The Bill proposed that grants would have to be returned at a compound rate of interest if an improved house within a HAA is sold within seven years (and if located elsewhere within three years); that generally compulsory purchase could be used solely to protect tenants, and that in many cases compulsorily acquired tenancies would be handed over to housing associations and then assisted by funds from the Housing Corporation—the corporation being able to borrow up to £300 million from the government for this purpose. The Bill also proposed that improvement grants should no longer be available for second homes. But many of the recommendations of the White Paper were omitted, especially those applicable to HAAs.

Security of Furnished Tenure and Rehabilitation

In a report on Rent Tribunal cases, Shelter (1973) criticised the increased activity of developers in London's furnished property market. Between 1971 and 1973 the proportion of property companies among landlords which sought to evict households from furnished tenancies increased from 16 to 30 per cent. Shelter found that 36 per cent of property companies and other landlords said that their reason for wanting to evict households from their furnished properties was that they wished to convert or improve the accommodation. The proportion giving this reason for eviction had trebled since 1971 and the number had increased from 12 to 60.

Families accounted for 40 per cent of all cases dealt with by the Tribunals, and over a quarter of tenants were in low paid jobs and 16 per cent were people living on pensions, unemployment benefit or student grants.

Although under the Rent Act of 1958, the Tribunals could have granted security of tenure for up to 6 months, Shelter was concerned that several Tribunals such as Brent and Harrow, and Islington were awarding security for quite shorter periods ranging from on average 2 to 4.1 months. In the 38 Tribunal cases where landlords wanted to evict in order to improve or sell their property it was found that conversions would involve a replacement of tenants by owner-occupiers. Whereas 72 tenants had been given notice to quit properties subject to planning permission, only 54 new leasehold flats were proposed—a reduction of 25 per cent in the number of dwellings.

The Chairman of Shelter hoped that the Rent Act 1974, by granting much greater security of tenure to furnished tenants and by introducing regulated rents (replacing free market rents) would make possible the implementation of:

> systematic programmes for the improvement of older housing in stress areas with the far lower risk that this will simply result in the displacement of low income tenants in favour of well-off owner occupiers (Holmes, 1974).

Rehabilitation Policy Since 1974

A Labour government was returned to office in March 1974. Introducing its new Housing Bill, the Secretary of State for the Environment, Mr Anthony Crosland, (1974) stated:

> I have for long been a passionate opponent of indiscriminate clearance, which I believe has gone too far ... in many areas. I believe that indiscriminate clearance can be appallingly destructive of existing communities and frequently a very expensive solution.

To emphasise the continuing shift of emphasis of public policy the Housing Act of 1974 therefore extended the Housing and Planning Bill of the former government. The Act prevented recipients of improvement grants from selling their properties (or leaving them empty) within five years unless the grant was repaid to the local authority at a compound rate of interest (this contrasted with the three year limit prescribed by the previous Bill). A seven year restriction within the HAAs was also imposed (as the previous Bill had required). Local authorities were empowered to demand the improvement of individual rented properties—a nine month period being imposed on landlords for this purpose. If landlords failed to improve their tenancies, the local authority is able to purchase the properties with a compulsory purchase order if necessary and then to hand the municipalised accommodation back to the original tenants. To alleviate the 'disincentive' effect on owners of the new conditions attached to grant approval, grants and limits of eligible expenses were increased. Improvement grants were raised from £1000 to £1600, or, where a building of three or more storeys was being converted, from £1200 to £1850. These amounts represented 50 per cent of the increased level of eligible expenses—£3200 and £3700 in respect of the above cases. Within the GIAs improvement grants were increased up to £1920 and £2220, and in the HAAs they were raised up to £2400 and £2775. Intermediate grants were introduced replacing standard grants. These were at a higher rate and equal to 60 per cent of eligible expenses up to £700. Repairs or replacement grants were to be made available at 60 per cent of eligible expenses up to a maximum of £800. The principle that improvement grants should give a house a life of at least 30 years was retained. After improvement a dwelling should, if practicable, have all standard amenities and meet a 10 point standard.

Policy towards the GIAs was modified in the light of the problems which had emerged since 1969. Except in some of the larger urban authorities there had been an absence of any systematic attempt to integrate GIA policy with planning in general. Planning staff were very rarely involved with GIAs and little research was undertaken into the relationship between GIAs and for example slum clearance, new housing, local rent levels and employment opportunities. Both the 1973 White Paper, *Better Houses, the Next Priorities*, and the House of Commons Committee on Expenditure expressed dissatisfaction with the rate of progress in declaring GIAs and the rate of improvement within these areas. Circular 13/75 issued under the 1974 Act therefore stressed that confirmation for housing renewal schemes within the GIAs would not be forthcoming unless they are part of a well formulated overall strategy. The same circular advised local authorities to formulate fresh renewal strategies and where appropriate to declare Housing Action Areas as integral parts. In areas of acute stress HAAs would become the principal part of renewal policy. HAAs were seen by Pickup (1974) as:

holding operations, designed to produce a swift amelioration in basic living conditions. . . . In most cases it is hoped that major rehabilitation of the area may turn out to be feasible, perhaps reinforced by its subsequent conversion into a general improvement area.

But other HAAs will have lesser prospects, the object being to make conditions reasonably tolerable towards the end of an area's useful life during which redevelopment will gradually take place.

The 1974 Act soon provoked criticism. Shelter (1974) predicted that landlords without the aid of improvement grants and using their own funds would continue evicting tenants of furnished flats and converting the accommodation into expensive luxury flats.This fear was proved in part groundless as the Rent Act 1974 introduced security of tenure in respect of most furnished lettings, though of course it provided an incentive for some landlords to obtain vacant possession by winkling and harassment. There were also fears that compulsory purchase orders would be used only in the last resort because of the severity of the prevailing economic conditions. It was proposed by the North Islington Housing Rights Project in association with Shelter in 1974 that the government should stress the importance of compulsory purchase orders in the new HAAs especially where properties were in a poor condition; where landlords were known to be negligent; where councils are informed of intended evictions; where housing was offered for sale on the expiry of a tenancy; where overcrowding was acute, and where properties were left empty or under-occupied.

The White Paper, *Public Expenditure to 1978–79* (1975) announced that although expenditure on improvement works was to be reduced from £423 million (in 1974–5) to £297 million (in 1975–6) the emphasis would be on improving the worst housing. The acquisition of property for improvement would therefore increase at the expense of refurbishing existing local authority stock—especially inter-war flats. There was also to be a continuing shift of emphasis away from building new council housing to the rehabilitation of substandard houses. In part this was due to the very high cost of managing and maintaining local authority estates. In 1974 this amounted to about £500 million—much of it being spent on repairs and damage caused by vandalism—a comparatively rare phenomenon in areas of rehabilitation. Yet Shelter (1974) accurately foresaw that local authorities acquiring rundown tenancies would not have enough resources to modernise the properties—the houses remaining empty in consequence. Despite increased local authority waiting lists and increased homelessness, the number of local authority dwellings acquired for improvement but standing empty has rapidly increased—reaching 500 000 in England and Wales in 1975 out of a total of 675 000 empty dwellings.

In the metropolis, the GLC reduced the £26 million it intended spending on improving its own estates and newly acquired property in 1975–6 to £11 million (£1 million less than it spent in 1973–4). There was a concentration of expenditure on improving acquired property which involved helping tenants in the 'greatest need' and avoided the further disruption of community life. But this emphasis was reflected in high opportunity costs. The GLC had to leave over 1000 properties empty on its pre-war estates because of expenditure cuts, and even estates developed in the 1950s were getting increasingly in need of modernisation and were becoming 'ghettoes' with a high proportion of tenants in arrears with their rents.

There was also a sharp decline in the number of improvement grants taken up, a decrease of 65 per cent from the record number of 360 954 in 1973 to 125 823 in 1977 (figure 8.1). Although the recession in the property market, high rates of interest and the financial difficulties of the construction industry were all contributory, it is probable that the more stringent conditions of grant approval introduced by the 1974 Act also had an adverse and possibly major effect upon applications for grants.

In July 1977, the government, to arrest this decline, announced that the maximum cost limits for house improvement grants were to be raised from £3200, of which an owner could receive at best £1600 assistance in the modernisation of his property, to £5000 and £2500 respectively. In GIAs, where applicants qualified for 60 per cent of approved expenditure, grants were increased to £3000; and in HAAs, where the level was 75 per cent (or 90 per cent in special cases), owners were eligible for grants up to £3750 or £4500. In November 1978, a £750 repair grant (available to both owners and tenants) was introduced in respect of pre-1919 properties. These dwellings represented the majority of the 70 000 houses which were falling into disrepair annually. But the government, as if to compensate for this extra commitment, cut the improvement grant outside of the GIAs and HAAs from £2500 to £1500. Both Shelter and the Building Societies Association condemned this reduction, and both wanted the repair grant to apply to all pre-1939 houses lacking basic amenities, and be up to 90 per cent in respect of hardship cases up to a maximum cost-limit of £2500.

Conclusion

At the time of writing one can only be pessimistic about the possibility of improvement grants having a major impact on the condition of housing. Although the number of GIAs and HAAs increased from respectively 964 and 78 in 1975, to 1217 and 384 in 1978, it is doubtful whether they will have little more than a 'cosmetic' effect on housing within the inner urban areas. It might seem that over the long term considerable improvements have been made in the quality of the housing stock. The *House Condition Survey* (1967, 1971, 1976) showed that the number of unfit houses decreased from 1 836 000 in 1967, to 1 244 000 in 1971, and 894 000 in 1976; and the number of dwellings lacking one or more basic amenities fell from 3 943 000, to 2 866 000, and 1 633 000 in the same years—falling again to 1 400 000 in 1977 according to the *National Dwelling and Housing Survey Report* (1978). Yet in total, Shelter (1979d) estimated that there were 3.1 million substandard houses in England and Wales in 1976 which consisted of not only those which were unfit, or lacked basic amenities, but also those which required repairs costing over £1000. Together with an additional 110 000 houses which become substandard as a result of obsolescence, 420 000 dwellings will be needed each year to deal with this backlog—the 135 914 improvements in 1979 being a lamentable contribution. It was particularly regrettable that, according to a Department of the Environment report, improvement in the HAAs was progressing at a disturbingly low rate (Shelter 1979e). It was likewise regrettable that proportionately, more money was being spent on improvement in small provincial towns, where improvement is least necessary, than in the inner urban areas of greatest need (National Home Improvement Council, 1979).

In an attempt to hasten the pace of rehabilitation, the Conservatives, in their Housing Act of 1980, extended the availability of repair grants (with regard to substantial repairs to pre-1919 dwellings); made it easier for low income households (owners and tenants) to obtain grants towards the cost of providing basic amenities—grant aid to be paid for less comprehensive improvement than previously allowed; made the grant system more flexible by giving the Secretary of State powers enabling him to fix, for different cases, eligible expense limits, percentage grant rates and rateable values etc.; abolished the five-year rule, but only in relation to the only or main residence of an owner-occupier; and enabled the Secretary of State to underwrite part of any losses incurred by local authorities acquiring and improving dwellings for resale.

But housing improvement expenditure in real terms is still seriously lagging behind the formation of new slums, and this is at a time when housebuilding is at a considerably lower level than in the late 1960s when the shift of emphasis to rehabilitation occurred. By the late 1970s, one million children lived in bad housing conditions and at least one in five children experienced overcrowding at home, reported Shelter (1979f). Mr Neil McIntosh (1979b), Shelter's director, stated:

In the early 1970s, conditions were getting steadily better and the backlog of bad housing was falling. Now, however . . . the number of people in bad housing may be actually rising. I predict a crisis within the next five years.

Perhaps the only way to avert this crisis is for councils to force owners to comply with compulsory improvement notices or to relinquish their property into social ownership. But Conservative policy generally inhibits the latter approach. The Budget of June 1979 resulted in savage cuts in housing expenditure, especially on public acquisitions. Although municipalisation accounted for less than 10 per cent of the £5000 million allotted to housing it bore 28 per cent of the £300 million cut. Since acquisition is normally followed by improvement, this had a very adverse effect upon the rate of rehabilitation. The Housing Act may also have unfavourable effects. With the relaxation of the five-year rule, gentrification may again become a cause of concern, particularly in London. Grant-aided speculation in the owner-occupied sector may push up house prices beyond the means of even middle income families creating even greater social polarisation in some of our inner urban areas.

9 Conclusions

The Conservative government's first Budget after returning to office in May 1979 was highly regressive in its effects. Higher allowances on income tax and the reduction in the basic rate from 33 to 30 per cent was more than wiped out by the massive rise in value added tax and petrol duty. Almost certainly it was only top earners with incomes over £15 000 per annum who gained in net terms because of the considerable reduction in the top rates of tax. The average wage earner lost out, and the lower paid worker was dramatically worse off. Apart from the redistribution of net money incomes, a high rate of inflation and unemployment further reduced living standards. Although the previous Labour government had reluctantly adopted monetarist policy (with severe effects upon the public and private housing sectors), the Conservatives' Budget of June 1979 applied:

> monetarism with a vengeance. In practice it [was] the most class based and socially divisive budget since the war, ridden with not only the threat of grave social tensions, but also the probable failure of even its basic economic objectives.

> (Mr Stuart Holland, MP, 1979).

In the year which followed, massive cuts in public expenditure debilitated the social services and exacerbated inequalities in society. In housing, social divisiveness was exhibited by existing owner-occupiers continuing to enjoy regressive relief on mortgage interest; would-be first-time housebuyers having to face higher mortgage repayments or to postpone purchase; council tenants having to pay higher rents; and those on council waiting lists and the homeless having to wait longer for new or rehabilitated homes—the selling off of council housing compounding the rate of increase in council rents and reducing the supply of housing to the detriment of the needy. It is against this backcloth (and subsequent economic measures of the same sort) that changes in housing policy are advocated. Many or all of the following recommendations are likely to be presented vociferously in the 1980s.

First, to satisfy the desire for home ownership among a growing proportion of the population, owner-occupation should be extended. Increased assistance should be given to first-time buyers, and the government should discourage building societies from discriminating against inner city housing and older properties. Building societies should be prepared to give block loans to councils for granting mortgages (under guarantee) to applicants who would not otherwise qualify for assistance.

Yet the government would be wrong to respond to the 1975 Conservative Party conference proposal to increase owner-occupation to 80 per cent by the (late) 1980s. There is little evidence that such a level would be desired. In European countries with higher per capita gross domestic products than Britain, the proportion of home ownership in 1974 was for example 44 per cent in France, 39 per cent in West Germany, and 37 per cent in Holland (compared with 53 per cent in Britain). Although other English-speaking countries have higher proportions of home ownership than Britain, the levels have declined recently, for example in Australia from 71 to 68 per cent (1966–76), in New Zealand from 70 to 67 per cent (1967–77), and in Canada from 65 to 59 per cent (1967–76). Because of the lack of choice in Britain, many households may reluctantly have become owner-occupiers. By contrast, others may think that they have a preference for ownership, but in reality they are expressing a preference for a detached or semi-detached house with a garden (and most mortgaged properties happen to be of this type), rather than a flat or terraced house (which constitute the bulk of rented stock).

But house purchase, reluctant or otherwise, should be assisted equitably. It is indefensible that owner-occupiers with the higher incomes and largest mortgages should get the greatest tax relief. At a time when there have been substantial cuts in income tax at the upper levels, it is difficult by any criteria to justify the continuation of regressive assistance to homebuyers.

Secondly, to offer households greater security of tenure and freedom from arbitrary eviction, the loopholes in the Rent Acts of 1974 and 1977 must be closed. Although the Conservative government wishes to strengthen the private rented sector, it must recognise that the demise of the private landlord cannot be checked by shorthold. In order to retain what is left of the stock of private rented accommodation, local programmes of municipalisation must not be impeded by spending cuts or other means.

Thirdly, to prevent a deterioration in the standard of living of council tenants, rents should only increase in line with incomes. It might however be argued that since the net incomes of tenants have risen due to changes in income tax liability (brought in by the June, 1979 Budget) this justifies a proportional increase in rents. But after increases in indirect taxation have been taken into account, the net real income of tenants may have remained static or have decreased. In these circumstances, increased rents would only lower the standard of living of a section of the community already regressively affected by tight monetarist policy.

Although high cost authorities would risk deficits if they related rent increases to changes in tenant income, a system of inter-authority subsidisation could be introduced to offset shortfalls. Deficits or large rent increases could also be avoided if councils refrained from selling off their surplus-yielding housing, and from this source continued cross-subsidising their highest cost stock.

The stock of local authority housing must be maintained or increased and not be sold off indiscriminately. It should be available to meet general housing needs, and not in a diminutive form be retained solely as a welfare provision. It should, together with the owner-occupied sector (and to a much lesser extent the voluntary housing movement), offer the householder a realistic choice between renting and ownership. There should be no stigma attached to being a council tenant, nor should owner-occupation be seen as a privileged form of tenure. A 'property-owning democracy' is only a meaningful concept, if people are given the freedom to choose to opt for it. With a satisfactory alternative, the popular appeal of home ownership would be tested.

Fourthly, to reduce council waiting lists and the amount of homelessness, and to facilitate a greater ease of movement, there must be a substantial increase in housebuilding, particularly in the public sector. The 1977 Green Paper's figure of 300 000 houses a year should be regarded as a bare minimum, and Parker Morris standards should again be applied.

Fifthly, because Britain's housing stock is falling into obsolescence more rapidly than it is being improved, there is a very urgent need for at least a threefold increase in the rate of rehabilitation to provide more than 400 000 improved dwellings a year.

Finally, and of over-riding importance, cuts in public expenditure on housing must be reversed. Without extra spending housebuilding and rehabilitation will remain depressed, unemployment in the construction industry will continue to rise, and more and more people will find it difficult or impossible to satisfy their housing requirements at a price they can afford.

It is probable, however, that few of the above proposals will be implemented in the early 1980s, and Britain will continue to face its worst housing crisis since the Second World War.

References

Aaron, H. J. (1972). *Shelter and Subsidies: Who Benefits from Federal Housing Policies?*, The Brookings Institution, Washington, D.C.

Amery, J. (1972a). Speech to National Housebuilders Registration Council, 1 November 1972

— (1972b). Parliamentary Debates (Hansard) *House of Commons Official Report*, vol. 845, H.M.S.O., London

Anderson, T. R. (1962). Social and Economic Factors Affecting the Location of Residential Neighbourhoods, *Papers and Proceedings of the Regional Science Association*, vol. 9

Association of Municipal Corporations (1973). Memorandum M21, in *House of Commons Tenth Report of the Expenditure Committee, Environmental and Home Office Subcommittee, Session 1972/73*, H.M.S.O., London

Association of Public Health Inspectors (1972). *Memorandum to the Department of the Environment*

Babbage, A. G. (1973). House Improvement in Stress Areas, *Environ. Hlth*, **81**

Balchin, P. N. (1979). *Housing Improvement and Social Inequality*, Saxon House, Farnborough, Hants

Booker, C. and Gray, B. (1974). Bedsitters that cost £50 000 too much. *Observer*, 24 November, 1974

Buttimer, A. (1969), Social Space in Interdisciplinary Perspective, *Geogr. Rev.*, **59**

Central Housing Advisory Committee (1966). *Our Older Homes: A Call for Action* (Denington Report) H.M.S.O., London

Central Statistical Office (1968). House Condition Survey, England and Wales, 1967, *Economic Trends*, May

Centre for Environmental Studies (1978). *CES Rev.*, no. 5

Cherry, G. (1970). *Town Planning in its Social Context*. Leonard Hill, London

Clarke, S. and Ginsburg, N. (1975). The Political Economy of Housing, in *Political Economy and the Housing Question*, Political Economy of Housing Workshop, London

Coates, K. (1975). *The Labour Party and the Struggle for Socialism*, Cambridge University Press, Cambridge

Community Development Project (1976). *Profits against Houses*, C.D.P. Information and Intelligence Unit, London

Crosland, A. (1971a). Housing and Equality, *Guardian*, 15 June 1971

— (1971b). *Towards a Labour Housing Policy*, Fabian Tract 410, Fabian Society, London

204

— (1971c). Twelve Points for a Labour Housing Policy, *Guardian*, 15 December 1971
— (1971d). Parliamentary Debates (Hansard) *House of Commons Official Report*, vol. 826, H.M.S.O., London
— (1971e). A New Deal for Council Tenants, *Guardian*, 16 June 1971
— (1972a). How not to Help Furnished Tenants, *Labour Weekly*, 22 December 1972
— (1972b). Bulldozer Bait, *Guardian*, 2 November 1972
— (1973). A Roof over Every Head, *Guardian*, 2 May 1973
— (1974). Parliamentary Debates (Hansard) *House of Commons Official Report*, vol. 873, H.M.S.O., London
— (1975). Speech to Housing Centre Trust, June
Crossman, R. H. S. (1969). Speech to Association of Public Health Inspectors Conference, Eastbourne, June
Denington Report (1966). Central Housing Advisory Committee, *Our Older Homes: A Call for Action*, H.M.S.O., London
Department of Employment and Productivity (1966). *Family Expenditure Survey*, H.M.S.O., London
Department of the Environment (1971). *Report of the Committee on the Rent Acts* (Francis Report), Cmnd. 4609, H.M.S.O., London
— (1971). *Fair Deal for Housing*, Cmnd. 4728, H.M.S.O., London
— (1972). *National Movers Survey* (unpublished)
— (1973). *General Household Survey*, H.M.S.O., London
— (1973). *House Condition Survey, England and Wales, 1971,* H.M.S.O., London
— (1973). *Widening the Choice: The Next Steps in Housing*, Cmnd. 5280, H.M.S.O., London
— (1973). *Better Houses, The Next Priorities*, Cmnd. 5339, H.M.S.O., London
— (1974). *Land*, Cmnd. 5730, H.M.S.O., London
— (1975). *Some Social Implications of Improvement Policy in London* (unpublished)
— (1977). *Housing Policy: A Consultative Document*, H.M.S.O., London
— (1978). *House Condition Survey, England and Wales, 1976*, H.M.S.O., London
— (1978). *National Dwelling and Housing Survey Report*, H.M.S.O., London
— (1979). *The Financial Aspects of Council House Sales* (unpublished)
— (1980) *Appraisal of the Financial Effects of Council House Sales*, H.M.S.O., London
Dimson, G. (1978). Reported in Hencke, D., GLC facing £10 million loss on houses, *Guardian*, 14 November 1978
Donnison, D. V. (1967). *The Government of Housing*, Penguin Books, Harmondsworth
— (1979). The Empty Council Houses, *New Society*, 14 June 1979
Douglas Mann, B. (1972). A Time for a New Deal on Housing, *Labour Weekly*, 3 November 1972
— (1977). Letter to *Guardian*, 5 August 1977
Estates Gazette (1972). Improvement Grants, 9 December 1972
Fabian Society (1974). *One Nation? Housing and Conservative Policy*, T.432, Fabian Society, London
Foot, M. (1973). *Aneurin Bevan*, Davis-Poynton, London
Forester, T. (1976). Building for Whom?, *New Society*, 29 April 1976
Francis Report (1971). *Report of the Committee on the Rent Acts*, Cmnd. 4609, H.M.S.O., London
Gauldie, E. (1974). *Cruel Habitations*, Allen and Unwin, London
Greater London Council (1974). *Strategic Housing Plan*, G.L.C., London
Greenwood, A. (1969a). Parliamentary Debates (Hansard) *House of Commons Official Report*, vol. 777, H.M.S.O., London

— (1969b). Parliamentary Debates (Hansard) *House of Commons Standing Committee F, Housing Bill*, 1st through 20th Sitting, H.M.S.O., London

Greve, J. (1965). Private landlords in England. *Occasional Papers on Social Administration*, No 16, Bell, London

Greve, J. (1971). *Homelessness in London*, Scottish Academic Press, Edinburgh

Harrington, I. (1973). Reported in Hillman, J., Housing Groups Want More Help, *Guardian*, 13 August 1973

Harrington, R. (1972). Housing—Supply and Demand, *National Westminster Bank Review*, May

Hattersley, R. (1979). Parliamentary Debates (Hansard) *House of Commons Official Report*, vol. 974, H.M.S.O., London

Hencke, D. (1979). Tougher housing laws urged. *Guardian*, 28 February, 1979

Heseltine, M. (1979a). Parliamentary Debates (Hansard) *House of Commons Official Report*, vol. 974, H.M.S.O., London

— (1979b). reported in Young, J., Right to buy homes for five million, *The Times*, 21 December 1979

Hillman, J. (1969). New Houses for Old—when?, *Observer*, 2 February 1969

Holland, S. (1979). Budget that Sells Seed Grain for Next Decade, *Guardian*, 18 June 1979

Holmes, C. (1974). *A Strategy for London's Housing*, Town and Country Planning Association Conference, London

House of Commons (1979). *The Fifth Report of the Public Accounts Committee; session 1978/79,* H.M.S.O., London

Hunt, D. (1972). Speech in Leeds, 9 December 1972

Kaufmann, G. (1979). reported in Hencke, D., Tories face row over council house sales cost, *Guardian*, 21 December 1979

Kilroy, B. (1972). Improvement Grants Threaten North Kensington, *Housing Review*, vol. 21

— (1977). No Jackpot from Council House Sales, *Roof*, vol. 2

— (1978). *Housing Finance—Organic Reform?*, Labour Economic, Finance and Taxation Association, London

Labour Party (1956). *Homes for the Future*, Labour Party, London

— (1965). *Housing Programme 1965–70*, Labour Party, London

— (1972). *Programme for Britain*, Labour Party, London

— (1973). *Labour's Programme*, Labour Party, London

— (1973). *Economic Policy and the Cost of Living*, Labour Party—Trades Union Congress, London

— (1976). *Labour's Programme*, Labour Party, London

— (1977). *Building Britain's Future*, Labour Party, London

Lapping, B. (1970). *The Labour Government, 1964–70*, Penguin Books, Harmondsworth

Linton, M. (1973). Big Slump in Building, *Labour Weekly*, 4 May 1973

Lloyd, G. (1972). Price of Flats for Sale Rockets as New landlords Move into Big Blocks, *The Times*, 5 April 1972

London Docklands Joint Committee (1977). *Strategic Plan*, London Docklands Joint Committee, London

Marley Report (1931). *Report of the Committee on the Rent Restriction Acts*, Cmd. 3911, H.M.S.O., London

McIntosh, N., Augaton, H. and Kilroy, B. (1978). Letter to *Guardian*, 17 November 1978

McIntosh, N. (1979a). reported in *Labour Weekly*, 15 June 1979

— (1979b). reported in *Guardian*, 12 December 1979

Meacher, M. (1972). Winners and Losers, *Sunday Times*, 23 July 1972

Merrett, S. (1975). Council Rents and British Capitalism in *Political Economy and the Housing Question*, Political Economy of Housing Workshop, London

Miliband, R. (1972). *Parliamentary Socialism*, Merlin Press, London

Milner-Holland Report (1965). *Report of the Committee on Housing in Greater London*, Cmnd. 2605, H.M.S.O., London

Ministry of Housing and Local Government (1953). *Housing—The Next Step*, Cmd. 8996, H.M.S.O., London

— (1955). *Slum Clearance (England and Wales)*, Cmd. 9593, H.M.S.O., London

— (1965). *The Housing Programme, 1965–1969*, Cmnd. 2836, H.M.S.O., London

— (1968). *Old Houses into New Homes*, Cmnd. 3602, H.M.S.O., London

— (1969). *House Condition Survey, England and Wales, 1967*, H.M.S.O., London

Mooney, E. (1972). Parliamentary Debates (Hansard) *House of Commons Official Report*, vol. 853, H.M.S.O., London

Mullin, C. (1979). Secret GLC Reports Blames 'Failure' of Direct Labour Operations on Management Use of Private Contractors, *Tribune*, 29 June 1979

National Home Improvement Council (1979). *The Take-up of Private Sector Improvement Grants*

National and Local Government Officers Association (1973). *Report of Expert Working Group on Housing*, N.A.L.G.O., London

— (1974). *Housing—The Way Ahead* (Report of the N.A.L.G.O. Housing Working Party), N.A.L.G.O., London

Needleman, L. (1965). *The Economics of Housing*, Staples Press, London

Nevitt, A. A. (1966). *Housing Taxation and Subsidies*, Nelson, London

— (1978). Issues in Housing, in R. Davies and P. Hall (eds.), *Issues in Urban Society*, Penguin Books, Harmondsworth

Onslow Report (1923). *Report of the Departmental Committee on the Rent Acts*, Cmd. 1803, H.M.S.O., London

Page, G. (1971). Parliamentary Debates (Hansard) *House of Commons Official Report*, vol. 825, H.M.S.O., London

Pennance, F. G. (1974). Planning, Land Supply and Demand, in A. A. Walters, F. G. Pennance *et al.*, *Government and the Land*, Institute of Economic Affairs, London

Pickup, D. (1974). Housing Action Areas: The Provisions of the Housing Act, 1974, *Housing Review*, vol. 24

Powell, A. (1975). Homes: Bovis firm foundations. *Observer*, 17 August 1975

Rent Act Review Committee (1977). *Review of Rent Acts: A Consultative Paper* (unpublished)

Report of the Committee on Housing in Greater London (Milner-Holland Report), (1965). Cmnd. 2605, H.M.S.O., London

Ridley Report (1938). *Report of the Inter-Departmental Committee on the Working of the Rent Restriction Acts*, Cmd. 5261, H.M.S.O., London

Rippon, G. (1973). reported in McKie, D., Rippon Signals Retreat from Big Urban Planning, *Guardian*, 11 September 1973

Robinson, R. (1979). *Housing Economics and Public Policy*, Macmillan, London

Rogaly, J. (1971). Where Fair Rents Mean High Rents, *Financial Times*, 16 November 1971

Royal Town Planning Institute (1973). Memorandum M25, in *House of Commons Tenth Report of the Expenditure Committee, Environmental and Home Office Subcommittee, Session 1972/73*, H.M.S.O., London

Sampson, A. (1967). *Macmillan. A Study in Ambiguity*, Penguin, Harmondsworth

Shelter—National Campaign for the Homeless (1972). *Home Improvement—People or Profit*, Shelter, London

— (1974). reported in Hoggart, S. Housing Bill Gives Powers to Councils, *Guardian*, 19 April 1974

— (1979a). reported in Craig, T., Eviction fears by Shelter, *Observer*, 23 December 1979

— (1979b). *Facts on Council House Sales*, Shelter, London

— (1979c). *Roof*, November 1979

— (1979d). *Shelter's Election Manifesto*, Shelter, London

— (1979e). *Roof*, September 1979

— (1979f). *Home Truths in the Year of the Child*, Shelter, London

Stone, P. A. (1970). Housing Quality: The Seventies Problem, *Building Societies Gazette*, June

Taylor, A. J. P. (1965). *English History 1914–1945*, Oxford University Press, London

Thompson, E. P. (1968). *The Making of the English Working Class*, Penguin Books, Harmondsworth

Trades Union Congress (1972). *Economic Review 1972*, T.U.C., London

Treasury (1947). *Capital Investment in 1948*, Cmd. 7268, H.M.S.O., London

— (1975). *Public Expenditure to 1978/79*, Cmnd. 5879, H.M.S.O., London

— (1978). *The Government's Expenditure Plans, 1978/79 to 1981/82*, Cmnd. 7049, H.M.S.O., London

Walker, P. (1969). reported in The Housing Research Foundation (1970), *Home Ownership in England and Wales*, H.R.F., London

— (1970). *Press Notices No. 98*, Ministry of Housing and Local Government

— (1971). Parliamentary Debates (Hansard) *House of Commons Official Report*, vol. 826, H.M.S.O., London

— (1972). Parliamentary Debates (Hansard) *House of Commons Official Report*, vol. 845, H.M.S.O., London

— (1973). Parliamentary Debates (Hansard) *House of Commons Official Report*, vol. 853, H.M.S.O. London

— (1978). The Real Tenants' Charter, *Guardian*, 5 November 1978

Warner, P. (1975). reported in Powell, A., Bovis's firm foundations, *Observer*, 17 August 1975

Wicks, M. (1973). *Rented Housing and Social Ownership*, Fabian Tract 421, Fabian Society, London

Wilson, D. (1971). Landlord v Tenant, *Observer*, 7 February 1971

Wilson, H. (1964). Speech in Leeds, 8 February 1964

Wilson, P. and Braham, M. (1974). How to End the Mortgage Crisis, *Observer*, 17 March 1974

Wilson Report (1980). *Report of the Committee to Review the Functioning of Financial Institutions*, H.M.S.O., London

Young, M. and Willmott, P. (1957). *Family and Kinship in East London*, Routledge and Kegan Paul, London

Index